C000244551

THE FIRST LADY

THE FIRST LADY

I was a Vogue model and a national celebrity but I was
living with a secret that was to shake the world...

A P R I L   A S H L E Y

WITH DOUGLAS THOMPSON

JOHN BLAKE

Published by John Blake Publishing Ltd,
3 Bramber Court, 2 Bramber Road,
London W14 9PB, England

www.blake.co.uk

First published in hardback in 2006

ISBN 1 84454 231 9

British Library Cataloguing-in-Publication Data:

A catalogue record for this book is available from the British Library.

Design by www.envydesign.co.uk

Printed and bound in Great Britain by William Clowes Ltd, Beccles, Suffolk

1 3 5 7 9 10 8 6 4 2

Papers used by John Blake Publishing are natural, recyclable products made from
wood grown in sustainable forests. The manufacturing processes conform to the
environmental regulations of the country of origin.

Every attempt has been made to contact the relevant copyright-holders, but some
were unobtainable. We would be grateful if the appropriate people could contact us.

'What is a rebel? A man who says no, but whose refusal does not imply a renunciation.'

THE PLAGUE (1954), ALBERT CAMUS

'When I grow up I want to be a film star and live a lovely life.'

GEORGE JAMIESON (1946)

For Peter Maddock, against whom all other men pale.

ACKNOWLEDGEMENTS

This book would not be complete without thanking several people for their love and support over the years.

My honorary daughters Sigrid Hamerl (we are both 'Rainbow Warriors' having working for Greenpeace for many years) and her life partner Cindy Lapio; Miss Ingrid Ballard (Meow); Mrs Ann McNamara, who I love; Rita Wallace has died but she lives on with a new generation to spread her joy; the Maddock family whose very name equals love; my great friends Harvey and Polly Sambrook and their beautiful daughters Claire and Juno; Lee Williams, my friend with whom I worked in the art world for many years.

Miss Windy (yes, Windy) Farnsworth – words cannot express my gratitude for her constant help and support. And, of course, the incomparable Ulla.

Cesar Andreini for being so kind to me over the past year in the South of France, and for all the wonderful long lunches under the olive tree with friends from far and wide including Lesley

Thompson and her husband Douglas who was brave enough to take on this project.

Last but not least my cat Lily Ashley-Buttofuco-John Wayne Bobbit-Harding-Gululi. He has been with me now for sixteen years and brought me nothing but joy.

CONTENTS

INTRODUCTION
APRIL THE FIRST

'I never go out unless I look like Joan Crawford, the movie star.
If you want to see the girl next door, go next door.'
JOAN CRAWFORD, 1962

Greta Garbo wanted to be alone.
  I never did.

I love the Garbo turbans and the shady shenanigans, the emotions, but I never wanted to be alone. Yet, for so much of my life, I have been isolated. And I've survived.

But, don't go, this is not a rags-to-riches, tragedy-to-triumph, skip-over-the-difficult-hurdles, flickering biopic of my life. This is the truth, the whole truth and nothing but the truth, so help me God.

Which means I'm not keeping anything back for vanity or propriety. I'm at an age where you just tell it as it is – and was.

It involves incidents in my life that I've never been able to face or talk about properly. And you'd think that, with all that has happened with me, nothing would be taboo! But for years even my given name, George, was off-limits.

Just the thought that I'd ever been George would send me off like a rocket, at all sorts of emotional tangents. For most of my life, I denied that I ever was George Jamieson.

I *was* April Ashley.

April Ashley.

There have been some turbulent times so, yes, fasten your seatbelts, for at moments it will be a bumpy trip. But I retain no bitterness about the emotional and physical tortures; that's a complete waste of time. I have and have had so many good, good friends. Oh, yes, enemies and detractors too, but far outnumbered by my incredible variety of friends.

I grew up in far less enlightened times, and through my experiences, from my jangle of memories, I have been able to help so many that followed me. Sexual identity and confusion about it is far more open and debated today but that isolation, the heartache, the feelings and passions remain the same.

I hope my story helps and inspires everyone, no matter who they are or think they are, and what they must confront. It would be marvellous if this book of my life would take on a life of its own and be of help to others.

It is, almost always, not as bad as it appears.

I was a pioneer. Think stagecoaches. And wagon trains. At times, for me, it *was* like the Wild West.

So this is, I suppose, a mature reflection on, and a joyful celebration of, a busy, long life. Yet I still feel young and feisty. The calendar disagrees with me on part of that. But, believe me, I'm still feisty.

Just read on.

April Ashley
Tourettes-sur-Loup, France, March 2006

INTRODUCTION

'A scorpion, who could not swim, begged a frog to carry him to the other side of a river. The frog complained that the scorpion would sting him.

'This was impossible, said the scorpion, because he would drown with the frog.

'So the pair set forth.

'Halfway over, the scorpion stung the frog. "Is that logical?" asked the frog.

"No, it's not," answered the scorpion, as they both sank to the bottom. "But I can't help it.

"'It's in my nature.'"

Anonymous

PROLOGUE
THE POSTMAN CALLS

'Here's looking at you, kid.'
HUMPHREY BOGART TO INGRID BERGMAN,
CASABLANCA (1942)

It was the happiest day of my life.

Also, for me, the most rightful.

I'd been living in the South of France, high in the hills above Nice, for nearly a year.

I share a lovely little apartment with my cat Lily, who arrived here with me from California. Lily's getting on a bit and his eyesight is going but he is marvellous company. He doesn't interrupt, talk back or ever, ever disagree with me. I like that in companions.

My apartment is part of a beautiful estate owned by a long-time friend and there is a long curving driveway. The postman delivers at the gate and for weeks I had been listening out for him.

Day after day I would wander up the hill and there would be letters or postcards – and, of course, bills! Lots of them. I had no interest in any of it. I wanted a special letter. Then, on what was a cold and stormy day for September in the South of France, it arrived.

For a long time I couldn't bear to open the large brown envelope. The postmark was correct. It was from England. It was dated September 2005. Was this it? After all the years, was this what I had dreamed about forever?

I thought I might have a drink but wine or even a nice vodka didn't seem appropriate if this was what I'd hoped for. I gently opened the envelope, felt inside with my hand and pulled out the contents, like a rabbit out of hat.

Magic!

It was a champagne moment.

I live only a short drive from the medieval hill town of St Paul de Vence, and on the edge of this perfectly preserved place is the small hotel and restaurant, Colombe d'Or. The name means 'golden dove'. A young Provençal called Paul Roux began the business and in 1931 hung a sign outside reading: '*Ici on loge à cheval, à pied ou en peinture*' – Lodgings for men, horses and painters.

Matisse arrived first. And, just as artists had followed him to the Côte D'Azur for what he called 'the silver clarity' of the light, they stepped in his footsteps to St Paul de Vence. Léger, Braque, Chagall and Miró were regulars, paying for the meals and lodgings with paintings, some of which became priceless masterpieces. Picasso turned up in the 1940s, a barefoot Bardot after him. Jean-Paul Sartre, Simone de Beauvoir, James Baldwin, Charlie Chaplin, Cocteau, Truffaut, Orson Welles – all are names in one of the most eclectic visitors' books I've ever seen.

Matisse wrote that life, art, should be part of somewhere that offers 'a soothing calming influence on the mind, something which provides relaxation from fatigues and toils'. At Colombe d'Or, a portrait by Matisse looks down on you in the dining room. It's where I went to celebrate the arrival of my special letter. With champagne, of course.

I gazed around me and thought, with the silver clarity of hindsight, about what an extraordinary journey it had all been. I learned a long time ago to control myself, not to show too much, but there were some tears…

1

WHIPPING BOY

'I learned courage from Buddha, Jesus, Lincoln, Einstein and Cary Grant.'
PEGGY LEE

One of my mother's favourite tricks was to pick me up by my ankles and bang my head on the ground like a workman with a pneumatic drill.

It was unbelievably painful. I'd try to protect my head with my arms, yet sometimes she would be so violent that I'd have no chance and my head would just go *bang, bang, wallop, wallop, bang* on the concrete. I used to wish for one of those helmets the Nazi soldiers wore. Not that it would have been much protection against my mother. She was a powerful tyrant.

My mother was tiny, but, boy, was she strong. She could swing a sack of potatoes across the grocery shop where she worked like mad. I never learned anything from her – my mother would never speak to me. The only way I found out how I could punish her was to get the strength not to cry. I would look at her and she would hit me until I was black and blue. And I would not cry. I *would* not. It would drive her into a frenzy and make her hit me ten times more, but I would never cry in front of her. It used to drive her into a total frenzy. Then I'd wait until I was alone and have a good whinge. Even alone, though, I'd never cry.

Well, not very often.

As a child growing up during the Second World War, I was generally badly treated by everybody. When I was able to go to school, I was beaten up every day of the week. Thank God, they used to inspect the air-raid shelters every day, because the other kids would tie me up on the bunk there and jump up and down on me. The bunks were sheets of criss-crossed steel that you put a blanket or mattress on. Sometimes I would be tied up for hours (the marks from the steel would stay on my face for days) before the priest or teacher on inspection would find me. It was terrifying too, because sometimes I had to lie there, unable to move in the pitch black. To this day, I can't sleep in a room that is completely dark; I always have to have a light on somewhere.

My mother used to hit and beat me for no reason. I would be standing still or even talking to her and she would just smash me about. There was no logic to it. Maybe she was afraid of who, or *what*, I was.

From the very moment I could think for myself, I knew there was something wrong. It came very, very early. There was nothing obvious in my behaviour. I never played with dolls; my favourite character to read about was Edgar Rice Burroughs's Tarzan; another book I read again and again was *Huckleberry Finn*. It was the adventure of it all that I adored. And I loved history beyond words. I didn't like Beatrix Potter and all of that. Yet from the beginnings of my memory, I can remember people often saying to my mother, 'Is it a boy or a girl?'

It began when I was about three. I'd be standing there with her in the street when they said it. It would upset me terribly. I was very religious from a young age until I was about 15, and I always knelt down besides the bed at the end of the day and said, 'Pray for Mummy. Pray for Daddy. And let me wake up being a girl.'

It was very difficult too, because I didn't understand why! I *couldn't* understand why.

Life, even this young life, was so confusing – unbelievably confusing. I knew what I wanted to be, but there was nobody I could talk to and say, 'What is wrong with me? Why do I want this? Why aren't I like my brothers?'

My mother didn't treat me like them. She was tough on them too, but always, always tougher on me. Once, she was threatened with prison, for she had beaten me within an inch of my life. In those days, you never heard of anything about child abuse. But she had taken a belt to my back and hit me so many times that the doctors could put a thumb in the hole in my back and touch my spine. They told her if they found another mark on me the police would be called and she would go to court – and prison. My mother was furious, and she let me have it, a good couple of whacks across the face, once we got outside the hospital. That was the Alder Hey Children's Hospital in Liverpool, which I came to know well.

I was born with a severe calcium deficiency, which resulted in frequent accidents that left me unable to walk. There were weekly calcium injections at the Alder Hey. If I was out of action, my mother would have to carry me piggyback. She could rest on the tram, then pick me up again and carry me to the hospital. These journeys were made in complete silence, with her mouth set in an unnerving way. That's as close as it got to a smile. Or any display of affection. I certainly never felt loved.

I was conceived at the Fort Hotel on the Isle of Man, where my mother was a chambermaid. I was born a boy in the Smithdown Road Hospital, Liverpool, on 29 April 1935. This birthday I share with Emperor Hirohito of Japan, which makes us Taureans like Fred Astaire, Catherine the Great, Shirley Temple and Hitler. What a visitors' book that could make, but I suspect we all won't be in the same place in the afterlife. Well, I hope not.

My mother took me home to a dockland slum called Pitt Street and christened me George. You didn't get lower than Pitt Street. Even in those days, the police patrols there had back-up. If you moved at all, it could only be up. And we did, very slightly. When I was a couple of years old, the family was rehoused on a new council estate in Norris Green on the edge of town. Since the rest of Pitt Street moved with us, along with the equally notorious Scotland Road, the atmosphere continued to be full of fists.

At 51 Teynham Crescent, we had an outside lavatory and a bath full of coal. Families like ours stored coal in the bath to stop it being stolen. We had the luxury of three bedrooms. The smallest was reserved for me alone, because for the first 14 years of my life I nervously wet the bed. As a punishment, I would be locked in there without heat or light and told there were ghosts.

I was a true child of Liverpool. My parents were both Liverpudlians, but not the cuddly music-hall sort beloved by misguided novelists and playwrights. My mother Ada Brown was a Protestant. She married my father, Frederick Jamieson, when she was 16. He was a Roman Catholic and so she virtually dropped one child a year: Roddy, Theresa, Freddie, me, Ivor, Marjorie. Apart from us there were several who died at birth. I was told she was pregnant ten times altogether, but I think it was more.

I was the hand-me-downs child, stuck right there in the middle. I only once had new clothes, a pair of grey school socks. Everything else was grey hand-me-downs, patched, darned, frayed, ragged, faded, often torn, hanging off my scrawny frame.

Even my clogs – then *de rigueur* among poor Scouse kids – were second-hand. I thought I should never see the end of those clogs coming down to me, hard wooden shells with a steel rim nailed on to the undersides. These rims were always falling off and had to be hammered back on. I so often felt like a horse being re-shired.

My mother had fine brown hair and eyes and good teeth. As a youngster, she was pretty and flirtatious. She adored going out dancing, or 'jigging' as she called it, but such outings were rare as she was always pregnant.

What do they say about first impressions? My first impression of her was that she didn't like me. How prescient. But she was kindness itself to strangers. She was a very strange woman. Twisted.

My brother Roddy, all blue eyes and enthusiasm, went off to sea when I was toddling around. He would return home with friends, like wonderful-looking Reggie Endicott who was half-Indian and always laughing; he stayed with us for a long time and shook up the house by buying a gramophone and playing Frankie Laine records full blast. We had these wonderful sounds in the house that we'd never had before; the radio was just used for news and what was happening with the war. Suddenly, here was this very glamorous Indian man with the most beautiful smile you've ever seen in your life, and the most beautiful teeth, and he brought this marvellous music into our lives. It was quite extraordinary.

Also, there was lovely Phyllis. My mother had gone out to the lavatory one morning and found her in there asleep. In her arms was a baby covered with sores. She took them both in.

They were more welcome than my father, whom I adored. He was short, like my mother, and a cook in the Royal Navy. He wasn't often home but, when he was, there would be exotic — and I suspect, tall — tales of the world's seaports. He made it all sound so exciting — and like an escape.

My father was the first man I ever heard call another man 'darling'. Nobody took offence at the way he said it, because he wasn't being effeminate, he was just being jolly. He was the only one in my family who understood me. I saw him just before he died and he said to me, 'Darling, you're so beautiful. I always knew.'

He was an ordinary working man with extraordinary tastes. On his visits, he would soak up oysters and mushrooms, gently warmed in cream, and Guinness. He *was* tiny, though. I was the only one in my family who was tall – 5ft 10 1/2 inches. I inherited his strong, dark eyes. He had a heavenly, puckish smile and was a scoundrel; he spent every penny he could on booze. A total ne'er-do-well, I was mad about him.

But he wasn't often there. Childhood was raw and full of suffering. Looking back, I think I must have been so strong, inwardly, as a child. Physically, I was very weak; I was terribly thin. I was this really scrawny child. When I would take a bath, even my mother would say, 'Oh my God, look at those ribs.' You could see every single one.

I must have had this special strength, which I think I got from my father. He would take all the beatings my mother would give him. She used to abuse him. He never once hit her back; he would just turn away and walk out. She'd still be hitting him as he went off out the door to the pub. She was frustrated. I understood her. She hated the fact that we were all brought up as Catholics. She was Protestant. She hated the Catholic Church and she hated having so many children.

Roman Catholic Liverpool had 23 miles of docks, the largest dockland in the world at that time, and was bombed heavily during the war. When the siren blew at night, everyone was supposed to run into the Anderson shelter. These were made of corrugated iron and were to be buried in the garden and covered with earth. Ours wasn't. It was stuck out the back at a lopsided angle in a few inches of soil. There were three bunks on either side of it, full of fleas and bugs.

I detested going in there even more than into my single bedroom. If my father was at home, he would allow me to crouch close to him under the hedge while explosions shook the house and the sky over Liverpool turned red. But what I most remember is the smell of sea salt in his uniform.

In an omen of things to come, we weren't hung up on family relationships. My only living grandparent, my mother's mother, was so taken aback by the sound of the air-raid siren that she had a heart attack and died on the spot.

All I had were parents and siblings. But I soon discovered that the reality was that I was on my own.

2

A PRINCE AMONG MEN

'If you prick us, do we not bleed?'
THE MERCHANT OF VENICE, ACT III SCENE I,
WILLIAM SHAKESPEARE

My father, whom I loved, didn't really provide anything but
stories and stale chocolate. Ironically, my mother, who
beat me, worked very hard to keep all of us alive. She heaved
sacks of potatoes and boxes of oranges at the grocery shop and
during the war worked at the Fazakerley bomb factory.

She was around TNT every day and, because of it, she lost
much of her hair and all her teeth. Her best friend Doris Paper,
from across the road, worked with her. They would go off
together every day in their slacks and overalls, their hair knotted
up in turbans. One morning in the factory, Doris said, 'I feel all
queer.' She was burning up from the TNT. The two of them were
brought home in an ambulance. My mother made a pot of tea and
Doris started yelling, 'I've got to go to the lav! I've got to go to
the lav!' Ripping and tearing at her clothes, she ran out of the
back door. She was found dead on the toilet seat.

I was beginning, even then, to wonder if that was a solution to
my problems. My calcium deficiency was debilitating. One fall

9

left me unable to walk for three months. My brothers Roddy and Freddie made a go-cart from an orange-box and old pram wheels so that I could be pulled around the neighbouring streets. It was always breaking down, or smashing into walls when they raced it. People kept finding me lying in roads, which irritated them after a while. Well, how did they think I felt?

There was another snag in day-to-day life. I didn't like eating, didn't take to it at all. We lived on a basic diet of brown-sauce sandwiches. My mother would bribe me to eat these awful sandwiches with chip butties, which I did like. Sometimes I stole beetroots from allotments and ate them raw, or carrots that I would clean by scraping them on a wall and share with my mongrel pointer Prince.

Ah, Prince. Roddy didn't only bring back people from his travels. He brought back the first bottle of Heinz tomato ketchup I ever saw. And the first post-war banana. It was cut into six pieces, one each. Such a bizarre taste. I spat mine out and haven't touched one since. And, when I was seven years old, he brought back Prince. We adopted each other from the first moment together.

Prince would follow me to school and wait outside the gates until I reappeared. He followed me to the Saturday-morning pictures at the Broadway Regal, running along behind the tramcar, and while I was inside enjoying my favourite series, *The Perils of Pauline*, he would sit patiently outside.

No one else wanted to play with me. I was 'strange'. My brothers wouldn't play with me. My sisters wouldn't play with me. They wouldn't take me with them wherever they went and I used to get so angry. I would say to them, 'Well, you're taking Ivor with you' – and Ivor was younger than me – 'why won't you take me with you?'

They would shout back, 'We just don't want you with us.' It did create an incredibly lonely life and that's why I was glad for having Prince. Prince was always ready to play. Whenever I could, I would sneak off into the countryside and go poaching with him. I would go for hours and hours sitting in the fields with my head on my dog's tummy. As the one whom nobody wanted in their gang, I always felt safe with Prince.

I would sit there and daydream. I knew what I wanted to be, but I couldn't talk to anyone about it. Although I was brought up a strict Roman Catholic boy, I knew from the age dot that I was a girl. My only dreams were about growing up to be a woman. In those days, there was nothing you could do about that. In my sort-of belief in God, I simply believed that it would happen one day. Something extraordinary would happen.

Or I would just kill myself.

There is no doubt about it. I couldn't have lived on. It was almost as though it was clinical.

I was quite a happy child, in a funny way. When I was in the countryside with my dog, and I could escape, I was quite contented. But in the background there were all sorts of thoughts: 'Well, I'll give it until such and such a time and then I'll kill myself…' Then nothing happens and you don't know what to think. Later, I would give myself 'death deadlines'. I'm not being melodramatic. It was just the way I felt, just the way it was. I knew even then that I could not live my life as a man.

My childhood was difficult, painful, with no love from the usual sources – from my mother or brothers and sisters. My father loved me, but in a maudlin, drink-sodden way. He was not the person to give understanding counsel – he was the one that needed social services.

Loneliness is just one of those things you have to learn to live with. In the end, it rescues you. It prepared me for my life, enabled me to fight my corner on my own. I wasn't accustomed to help, so I never looked for it. I just fought on. People were recovering from the war and weren't interested in peculiarities like me. Even now,

I sometimes feel as though I'm from another planet. That I'm not a human being at all – just a space alien visiting!

I'd have these wonderful dreams where I would be a beautiful woman – Cinderella at the ball and midnight would never strike. I also dreamed that people would stop hurting and chasing me. There was nothing sexual about the dreams. I would dream and I would hate to wake up because I was having such a lovely, happy life in my sleep. Even as a schoolboy sitting in the English countryside, I knew that if I was to live it could only be as a woman.

That was the emotional and mental torture. In today's world of self-realisation, when all the closet doors are wide open, when there's sex-change on the National Health and gay weddings down the guildhall, it is hard to imagine the isolation.

It's still with me, too. I have failed throughout my life to be an ordinary person. Now, at my grand age, that is clearly beyond me.

The physical torture went on at home – and at school. I was supposed to be one thing and I was turning into another. My schooldays! Those nuns, those priests, those hopeless teachers, those disgusting children!

My father was in the pub, never the church, but nevertheless he insisted we were brought up as strict Catholics. I was sent to St Theresa's Primary School, a vicious and backward institution run by the clergy, where I was forced to my knees four times a day in prayer. It was very rough. We spent a great deal of time cleaning the floors with dusters tied to our clogs and if we were slow the nuns would rattle rulers between our knees. Knees were the big thing at St Theresa's.

The most important lesson I learned was how to run fast. I was a weed. My head looked far too large, something that was highlighted by my mother cutting my hair into a Henry V pudding bowl. That led the others to curse me as 'Sissy' or 'Chinky'.

Then, an eager young Canadian teacher, Miss Filben, tried to help. Oh my! She decided to make me class monitor with responsibility for distributing books. I pleaded with her, 'Please, Miss Filben, don't make me the monitor. I have enough trouble with the bullies as it is. If you make me the school monitor, it will look like I am a favourite.' She wouldn't listen to me, though, and of course that made life much more difficult. As I came by with the decomposing red textbooks, my classmates lashed out with their iron-clad clogs. Because of my privilege, my legs were as red as the books before turning into black-and-blue patterns, as though I'd been tattooed.

After a couple of weeks of my being kicked to bits, one morning Miss Filben, who had wonderfully even, white teeth, gently told me once more, 'OK, give out the books.'

It was an instruction too far.

I said, 'I will not do it.'

'*What?*'

'I will not do it, I am not the monitor. I will not be the monitor.'

You didn't talk to your teachers like that in those days. It's not like today, when the little kiddies bring knives and even guns into the classroom and often run riot in the schools. Back then, you addressed your teacher properly. You had to stand up when they came in, even if it was a junior teacher.

She looked horrified and the whole class went deadly silent. Looking back, it was quite a remarkable thing for me to do.

Miss Filben tried again, not so gently this time: 'Jamieson, will you *please hand out those goddam books.*'

By now, she was standing in front of me and sweating in a bright-yellow blouse.

I was paralysed. She tapped me in the face.

I slapped her back.

We were all flabbergasted. Her pretty eyes filled with tears — but thankfully I lost the monitor's job.

Something else in the academic line? An essay, entitled 'What do you want to be when you grow up?' I wrote, 'I want to be a film star and live a lovely life.' You were supposed to say you wanted to be a priest or a train driver. My answer brought on overwhelming derision from the others and found me sent off to the back of the classroom, out of the way.

It wasn't much fun in the other areas of the school curriculum either. Someone, somewhere, seemed to take a perverse delight in ridiculing me. The school put on a play, Shakespeare's *The Merchant of Venice*. I played Bassanio and I wore my sister's tights. It brought the house down – but not to my delight.

There were small triumphs, though not many.

'Can you swim, boy?'

I'd never tried, so I said, 'Yes, sir.'

'Dive in, then.'

I came up blue in the face and frantic, but from that moment I swam. Eventually, they awarded me a bronze medal for lifesaving. I have always been a strong swimmer, so at least I took something from my schooldays.

Then there was the only time my mother helped me, although I still have doubts about her motive. If I went home to my mother and complained I'd been beaten up, she would shout, 'You're a big sissy. Why didn't you hit them back?' She was in favour of positive action.

In class one day, the headmaster arrived to talk to our teacher. Suddenly, he turned around and bellowed, 'Who spoke?'

I hadn't heard anyone speak and I have marvellous hearing.

Suddenly, he pointed a long, bony finger at me and said, '*You*. You spoke.' He told me to stand up and repeated, 'You spoke, didn't you?'

I said, 'No, sir. I did not speak.'

He said, 'Yes, you did, and now you're lying on top of everything. Come here, you. How dare you whisper when I'm in the class?'

I said, 'I'm sorry, sir, it wasn't me. I didn't whisper.'

'Oh, yes it was.'

He hit me in the chest so hard it knocked me to the ground. I was a fragile little thing. So I ran home to my mother. She was angry. 'He hit you and knocked you to the ground? You come with me.'

No, Mother, please, please. No,' I pleaded. To no avail.

The headmaster was still in the classroom, lecturing about the evils of insubordination. Mother went in and confronted him: 'You hit my child for nothing?'

'Don't you dare speak to me like that, Madam.'

She was puce, clenching her fists so hard that the knuckles were white. She kicked him so hard she almost knocked him down.

'Don't you dare touch my children,' she told him.

He was speechless for a moment and then tried to patronise her.

'Don't you "My Good Woman" me!' she shot back. 'You bloody Roman Catholic, I'll kill you if you touch one of my kids again!'

'How dare you swear in my school!'

She decided to smack his face, but since it was about two feet above her she was forced to jump. 'Swear?' She was jumping up and down now, hitting him. 'I'll bloody well say what I damn well like, you silly bugger! I'm Protestant. I didn't want my kids brought up bloody Catholics anyway. I'm sick to death of them spendin' half their bloody life on their knees prayin'!' She slapped him again, grabbed my arm, and we left.

It was, as I said, the only time my mother ever helped me. When I got older, I realised that it hadn't been for me, but for herself. She wanted to give someone a good thump.

Thank God, it was him!

3

ANGUISH

'As for you my galvanised friend, you want a heart.
You don't know how lucky you are not to have one.
Hearts will never be practical until they
can make them unbreakable.'

THE WIZARD OF OZ TO THE TIN WOODMAN,
THE WIZARD OF OZ (1939)

Family life was hell, but my situation was made much, much worse. I became a victim of what today we call child abuse. The perpetrator – I presume he was a paedophile – was the husband in a couple my family were very close to. I adored them, for they were always very kind to me. It came as such a shock when I discovered George was like that.

It started when I was aged 11 and went on for more than a year. I have never told anyone before, never once mentioned it in more than half a century. George would make me masturbate him and try other sorts of things. I was so innocent. I'd never seen a man's willy. It was a shock. He wanted me to perform oral sex on him, but I never could. When he tried to force me, I'd be sick, truly sick as a dog. It never stopped him trying to make me do it, though. Masturbating him became the easier option for me, although I felt so terribly, terribly sordid.

17

When you're a child and somebody you love very much abuses you, it puts you in the worst position in the world – you don't want to rat on them because you love them so much, and yet you feel like a dirty little thing all the time. The conflict of my emotions, my needs, was overwhelming. I was already isolated from my own family; this made me become even more isolated. I was terrified of losing the friendship of George and his wife Helen.

I was just in the worst position. I trusted George. Yet I was abused and betrayed by him. It was so ugly. I was trapped. Something had to happen, because I went into the most incredible depression, though I didn't recognise it as such at the time. My life was a total turmoil. I was struggling with my own sexual identity and at the same time had this sick man preying on me. Yet I loved him. The sense of betrayal was horrendous.

Well, one day, George said he and Helen never wanted to see me again.

I said, 'What?'

He told me, 'Go home now to your parents and...'

'You can't do that,' I cut in. 'I love you and Helen.'

At that moment, Helen came into the room and it all came out. She already knew about what he had made me do to him, the constant abuse – he had told her. There was an almighty explosion. Then Helen pulled him aside and said to him, 'You have to be very careful; if he tells his mother, we're in serious trouble.'

So George decided that I wasn't to be banished from their lives after all. He was horrible. I was such an innocent child. And the disgraceful way he was going to treat me – how difficult for a little kid to handle an issue like that, particularly as I didn't have lots of friends like all the other boys and girls. I didn't know all about sex talk that went on. I was an isolated child to begin with. The sexual abuse made me even more isolated and devastated. All the magic had gone. Then to find that Helen took his side rather than mine... I was the one being used. I didn't think of it as abuse, because the word didn't exist in those days. But I was the one being wronged. When Helen took his side, it was the final straw, it was simply devastating. I loved these two people beyond words.

In fact, I felt more betrayed by Helen than by George. When the abuse was going on, I always said to myself, 'Well, at least Helen will stick up for me' – she would know that this was not right. I was an innocent lad but I knew instinctively that this was wrong. George would just say to me, 'Oh, don't worry... everyone does this.' Of course, I wouldn't believe him and then I closed all the walls and became a depressed child.

I became even more isolated than I was before. Nobody could get me to talk. There came a point when I couldn't speak for three days, and everyone said I had had some kind of trauma. Then, when I did speak, it was in a fractured voice. It remains with me to this day. It's not a natural voice. I had obviously done something to myself; it did have terrible effects.

I never think about it without guilt. I still feel guilty about it. Why is that? After all, I was the one being abused.

I never hated George. It's a funny thing. When it was all over, I never hated him – I just couldn't bring myself to do that. I suppose it's the Catholic thing that you've got to forgive everybody. Whenever I spoke about him in life – I've never spoken to anybody about this before, not to a single soul – my thoughts are always fond of him and his wife.

Yet, what torment I went through with him. How can kindness suddenly turn and break your heart? I will never know the answer. Probably there isn't one. I don't think victims of abuse ever get over it. It becomes part of your life, part of your personal history. It also makes you so much more aware of other people and more understanding of their problems. I can't see even a total stranger cry without imagining what had caused it and what might help. It's sad to contemplate.

It's a dreadful way to learn compassion for others. But learn it I did. The hard way.

4

GOLDEN NUGGET

'Nothing happens to any man that he
is not formed by Nature to bear.'
MEDITATIONS, MARCUS AURELIUS

I was lost in my lonely world. For so long I'd talked to God. Now, that wasn't an option. My faith had gone. It began with the death of my one friend and disappeared altogether when I started asking why would God create such a person as me, who was mentally one thing and another physically.

There were other, more blatant reasons. I saw that the priest got drunk and that used to upset me terribly because of my father being such a big drunkard – though a very nice one, thank goodness. My brothers would also get pretty drunk. The priest had been among a group I had seen drunk and cursing in their garden. That certainly did not boost my faith. One Sunday, I thought, 'I'm not going to go to Mass.' It was a big, big decision because I used to go to Mass practically every day. God was the only person I could talk to.

When I went next, the priest quizzed me: 'Why weren't you in church on Sunday?'

'I want to think about it, Father.'

'If you have to think about God, you're damned for ever! Get out of this church!' He threw me out.

I stood on the steps of St Theresa's and looked back and said to myself, 'I will never go in that church again.' I never did.

My doubts had begun with the death of my one school friend, Vincent Pattison, who was like a mentor to me. When I'd be beaten up, he'd come and help me. He was a big fat lad, incredibly nice. Liverpool is a very tough place to grow up, and was particularly so during the war, but I never once heard this boy swear or do anything untoward. I am convinced to this day that he was a saint because he was such a sweet person. He could beat the daylights out of anybody but he was as gentle as could be. He would only come to my aid if it was necessary.

One weekend he went off to Bromborough in Cheshire and drank from a polluted stream. Three days later, he was dead.

My only protector was gone. St Theresa's had more than 2,000 children in the school and the bullies were there and they would get me. I became the fastest runner in Liverpool! I'd be out of those gates like a shot... but if I didn't make it, and often I didn't, they would physically jump on me. I never got the feeling there was anything sexual in it. But they would jump up and down all over me.

When you're a kid and you're having the bloody daylights knocked out of you, all you can think of is: 'How can I get out of this? How can I get away from it?' The sheer torture. They jumped on my foot so badly once that I couldn't walk for three months. I did have brittle bones, after all. It was a hateful time for me because I loved being outdoors during the day. At night, you weren't allowed to move because everything was blacked out. We were off the streets at night, but all day long you spent the whole time outside.

Then it got tougher at home. My younger brother took to beating me up. I let him get away with it all the time, but I got him one day. He had just hit me so hard and for once I retaliated. I had my clogs on. He was going out the back door and I flew into an almighty rage. I kicked him so hard up the bum he couldn't sit down for three days. He never hit me again. A small triumph.

Yet my young life was to become more complicated, more distressing. My father, the only one who returned my family affection, had pushed my mother to her limit. She kicked him out of the house, which from that moment stopped being anything of a home to me. My father had got into the habit of returning from sea and then going on a bender, boosting the profits of distilleries (rum) and breweries (chasers of heavy beer) in a gargantuan manner.

The fights were never fair:

'But, Ada, love…'

Bash, *slap*, *slap*, *slap*, *slap*, she'd go at him.

Moment later, he would sit groggily in a corner.

My eldest sister always called her 'That Woman!' And she was wicked, evil.

An Australian, Bernie Cartmel, had followed Roddy back from sea and moved into the house. We kids used to call him a 'long streak of piss'. He was enormously tall and skinny and sloppy and had big floppy hands. None of us liked him at all; my mother did, though. After my father departed, she and Bernie lived as man and wife.

But it was another, altogether different couple who were to bring some light into my life at last. John and Edna Lundy ran a grocery shop in Liverpool's now-demolished old iron St John's Market. John's brother was briefly engaged to my sister Theresa, who enjoyed her regular and usually brief 'engagements'. I got a job as an errand boy for their shop, which was famous for its bacon. I hauled sides of it that were bigger than me. They called me 'Nugget'.

I earned half-a-crown (twelve and half pence) a day plus tips; it was a long day, 8am to 10pm, but meant astonishing wealth for me, who had never had anything. I worked holidays and weekends and regularly skipped school to put in more hours. I didn't care that I had to manage this huge cycle and take the groceries out into the countryside, though I'd have to rest in the fields so I could make it. Once, I had to take a big load and I said, 'John, I don't think I can carry six sides of bacon.'

'You'll be able to manage it,' he replied.

I got on the bike and went down the hill and suddenly the bike, because of the weight of the bacon, catapulted me right in front of a tramcar. I was almost killed. Happily, there was somebody who worked in the market close by — they took two sides and I was able to carry on. Yet all that was such a joy for me to do for half a crown a day because I loved John and Edna so much.

Edna was dark, with buck teeth and a rich Devonshire accent that fascinated me. I tried to imitate it and in doing so produced a hybrid sound. Over time, it became easy for me to speak with no accent at all.

John and Edna turned into surrogate parents and I lived for long periods in their warm flat. For the first time, I encountered wine and uncracked crockery and could sneak slugs of whisky from their cocktail cabinet with a musical cigarette-box on top. Yet I was still rooted in my very working-class upbringing.

Edna became pregnant, something I vaguely understood but in a strange, creepy way. At school, they had suggested something about it in readings from the Bible. Yet the nuns and priests, supposedly celibate themselves, circumnavigated the problem by filing it *en bloc* under the heading of 'Sin' and trying to pass their sense of revulsion on to us. At home, where we were frightened even to put our arms round each other, the entire subject was taboo. However, you can't live long in a town like Liverpool and remain ignorant of the facts of life.

The red-light district in the port was Sodom and Gomorrah with flick-knives. From my earliest days, the prostitutes were a city sight. It was said that if ever a virgin walked down Lime Street the lions outside St George's Hall would roar.

Each Friday evening, the girls would gather on Lime Street Station, wearing red lips and red shoes, to meet trains bringing in the GIs from Warrington for a dirty weekend. We would follow, making grabs at the handfuls of chewing gum that went flying across the platform as the carriage doors crashed open.

If any girlfriends were there to meet their boyfriends, the tarts would flay them with handbags – 'Piss off, ya lousy free fuck!'

When Edna became pregnant again and gave birth to a second daughter, I had to return to sleep at Teynham Crescent, obliged to run a gauntlet of catcalls and kicks from the tram stop to the front door; scarcely a day passed when I was not attacked or humiliated in some way by the neighbourhood toughs.

I knew I was unique in my environment, but it was drummed into me day after day after day. It was intolerable at times. Yet, through the hardship, a sense of my own uniqueness was forced upon me. Although I wanted to neither play with dolls nor dress up in my mother's clothes, I was constantly taunted for being like a girl – and, yes, I wanted to be one. Instinctively, without knowing why, we all knew me to be a misfit.

At age 15, I had no facial or pubic hair; my voice hadn't broken; I was not overwhelmed by sexual desire, and my size hadn't shot up. In comparison, many of my onetime classmates were hulking hairy brutes with attitudes to match.

I decided to face up to my situation. It was no longer any good wanting to be a girl. I wanted to be a man. I watched all the Robert Mitchum films and copied his swaggering walk. Now, there was a man who was all style. When nobody was around, I croaked away in the lower registers until my voice was forcibly broken. As a result, I couldn't speak for five days and the Indian doctor told my mother I had 'done something mental' to my voice.

Far more importantly, I privately determined to go to sea. All the other men in my family did, even little Ivor in the end. It seemed to be one of the things that made you a man. Of course, running away from anything is never the answer, but I didn't know that then.

I did have one advantage – I had money. My hard work paid off. It was still the time of rationing and John would give me a bonus in tea coupons. Everyone was desperate for more tea and I sold the quarter-pound packets for a shilling a time, a fledgling entrepreneur.

I bought presents for my mother, but she put them away in a drawer. My father had been invalided out of the Navy with shrapnel wounds in his stomach and legs that refused to heal. He worked briefly as a bus driver, then tramped round Liverpool on a tiny pension. He would wander about St John's Market and ask me for money. It should have been the other way around. I gave him what I had, and then watched him walk off to the nearest pub.

I learned the value of money, though. Prince was caught biting the head off a cat, and the outraged owners prosecuted me. I was able to pay the ten-shilling fine.

I hardly ever bought anything for myself. Except shoes. I have never been an Imelda Marcos, or had a fetish about Manolos – but the bliss of those first shoes! After a life in clogs, it was like walking in bed. Bliss, bliss, bliss.

I went to work for John and Edna full-time, one of the fortunate ones with a job to go to after school. My hair grew out of its embarrassing historical pudding bowl and, with all the bicycling, I developed slight roses in my cheeks.

I went to work one morning, put on my white coat and was about to nip under the counter to collect the orders, when Edna said to me, 'Why, Nugget, you're quite beautiful.'

A momentary dizziness. Physical references to myself always made me feel ill. I assumed I was ugly, a belief most others seemed happy to confirm. Later, I checked up on my appearance in the mirror. Thin and stunted for my age. Teeth crooked. Eyes dark, greenish brown, eyelashes very long and eyebrows finely arched. No spots – I never went through that ordeal. A bit of red in an otherwise gruesome pallor. Thick black hair.

The mirror didn't tell me anything I didn't know.

Not long after Edna's remark, I was returning from the Pierhead on the No. 14 tram with Jo, a neighbour from Norris Green. I dozed off. Unexpectedly, he knocked me in the ribs.

'Are we there?' I asked.

'No, but you fockin' wake up, you look like a fockin' woman when you're asleep.'

5

WALKING THE PLANK

*'A seaman's a seaman, a captain's a captain. And a shipman
is the lowest form of animal life in the British Navy.'*
CAPTAIN BLIGH (CHARLES LAUGHTON), MUTINY ON THE BOUNTY (1935)

'What are these, sir?'
'Knots!'

'What the bloody hell,' I thought. Knots. I never could do them. I did bows instead.

Happenstance had got me aboard the SS *Vindicatrix*, where I was training as a merchant seaman. It had been surprisingly easy to go to sea like my father and tough brothers — just a case of being in the right place at the right time. And that was the home of Mrs Rossiter.

She lived what I regarded as a fantasy life, a 'Desperate Housewife', if you like. She had wonderfully coiffed hair and these long red fingernails. The common folk went to her house and called at the tradesman's entrance. She had a sprinkler system on her lawn. Most people I knew didn't even have the lawn. She was a polite and pleasant woman to me when I delivered the groceries on my colossal cycle.

She asked me what I wanted to do.

'Oh, go to sea like my brothers,' I told her.

Her husband, it turned out, was an executive with Cunard. She arranged for me to have an interview with him at Cunard House, all very proper and above board, as it were.

'But you're much too young to go to sea,' was the opinion of Mr Rossiter.

I was 15 and looked about 11 years old. I was desperate and that made me answer, 'But I'm not too young to go to training school, am I?'

He gave me a magnificent letter of introduction on embossed Cunard paper. It cut through all the red tape, like medical tests and parental consent – which was just as well, for this was going to be my secret.

The night before departure, I came home and announced, 'Mum, I'm leaving tomorrow to join a cadet ship.'

She carried on frying Bernie's chips in lard and with her back to me said, 'Well, isn't that somethin'.'

Indeed, it was. For I was going to be a man.

On a damp November morning in 1951, I found myself at Liverpool's Lime Street Station with a small brown cardboard suitcase, waiting for the train to Bristol and the SS *Vindicatrix*. My only personal memento – rosary beads. How superstition sticks.

The course was a very intense six weeks. The first three were spent in Nissen huts. There were about two dozen of us. We were issued with blue serge trousers and a boiler jacket, thick woolly socks, square-bashing boots and a beret to be worn at a jaunty angle. There were no fittings. Everything simply came at you out of a big cupboard. All mine were far too large. I looked like a vaudeville act.

Up before dawn, ablutions, tidy the bed and locker, polish buttons and boots, clean the washroom, marching, breakfast, formal classes, lunch, potato-peeling and floor-scrubbing, physical jerks, dinner, lights out at 9pm. There was no time for conversation.

The second three weeks were more the romantic of life at sea

— and that's because we moved on to the SS *Vindicatrix* herself, a three-masted hulk slurping up and down alongside the River Severn. I was taught the practical skills of seamanship. I dashed up the rigging and out along the yard, and shouted 'Land ahoy!' with both lungs.

'Come *down*, Jamieson. We're putting you in charge of the yacht.'

The 'yacht' was an old cabin-cruiser used for navigation lessons. The captain shouted, 'Nor' Nor' East!' and I – straight as a matchstick behind the wheel – had to reply, 'Nor' Nor' East, sir!' and turn the 'yacht' in that direction. Every order on the Bridge had to be repeated to ensure there were no errors of communication. At night, we fell asleep exhausted, soothed by the creaking of the ship and the sound of water. I loved it all, especially this new experience of 'companionship', even when the others bragged about girls and I went peculiar inside. My only reservation was in having to occupy a bunk when most of the class were swinging glamorously in hammocks.

Shore leave came at Christmas, but those unable to afford the fare home were allowed to stay on board. It promised to be glum until an extravagant food parcel arrived from John and Edna. Included was a huge fruitcake. I cut myself a slice and passed the rest on. In return, back came a hunk of haggis, which I tasted for the first time and liked.

We shared everything, cracked jokes and in the evening ambled over to the Mission House where the tea ladies in flimsy paper hats made a sense of occasion out of lemonade and buns. On Boxing Day, three of us slipped away to the Bristol pubs and got tiddly – strictly against the rules and therefore essential to do. It was the most delightful Christmas I'd ever had.

My final report was creditable, apart from knots, which were disastrous. (Didn't even get 'v.g.' for the bows.) We signed each other's group photographs, pledged eternal friendship, vowed to meet up in Cairo or Rio or Tokyo, and all went home.

My mother was still cooking chips at Teynham Crescent. I wanted to escape more than ever. My sister Theresa was the unwitting partner in my getaway. Yet another of her fiancés was a young man called Colin Shipley, who was a ship's carpenter. He told me, 'There's a place going on my ship for a deck-boy, if you want it.' *Want it?* I would have killed for it. The next day, I picked up my cardboard suitcase, opened the front door, took a deep breath of air, coughed and set off on the road to Manchester to join the SS *Pacific Fortune*. That February night in 1952, I found myself with Colin at the entrance to the vast blackness of Manchester docks.

It was so dreadfully silent — apart from the squeaking of rats and the ominous ripple of unseen water. Black lines of cranes and sheds fell away into pools of ink. It started to sleet again, softening the smell of resin and old fibre. A policeman checked our papers from his little sentry box and let us pass. Colin walked ahead. I screwed up my eyes, stuck my head forward and stumbled after him into the murk, trying to avoid coils of rope and long cables mooring dead ships to the wharf side. Suddenly, the black hull of the *Pacific Fortune* hung over us. Except for half a dozen hurricane lamps, the ship was in darkness. The sailors were ashore.

I followed Colin up the gangplank. At the top, a man stepped out from the shadows. He was about 50 and cube-shaped. Swinging me into the lamplight, he looked me up and down, then said over his shoulder in a thick Glaswegian accent, 'Och, Colin, I thought we was gettin' a laddie!' Mr Macdonald, my new boss — the Bo's'n — chuckled at his own remark.

We crossed the deck, went down the gangway, flicked on a light, along passages, down again, along more passages, down, down, to the aft of the ship where the sea crew had their quarters. An iron door was opened and I was shown into a small cabin.

'You'll be all right here. Danny will be back soon — he'll

explain everything. Have you eaten? Good. Sign the list tomorrow at 9am. Welcome aboard, laddie.' And with that the Bo's'n took Colin off for a drink.

There were three bunks in the cabin. The two lower ones had already been taken. I clambered up into mine and sat there nervously swinging my legs. An hour later, the door opened and Danny came in. He was about 19, skinny with an unexpectedly studious air. Danny had a crisp tongue, which I later discovered enabled him to hold his own among the bigger, rougher sailors. Robby, a junior like me but a couple of years older, followed. Robby was amiable enough but overweight and afflicted with boils and indelicate odours. I was the youngest crewmember, the only one who had never been to sea before.

Danny showed me where to hang up my toothbrush, all that sort of thing, and then said, 'I'm bollocked so it's lights out.' (There was no doubt who wore the trousers in our cabin.) 'Besides, you should try and get a good night's sleep, you'll need it.'

I lay up in the bunk, heartbeat unnaturally loud in my ears, listening to the creaking of the decks, trying to decide whether I should have packed my rosary beads... but eventually I faded out.

Suddenly, there was a rumpus outside the door. Drunken sailors crashing back from the bars, a sound that was to panic me often in the future. The door sprang open and a light went on. Three young mariners were hooting round the cabin. They weaved across to my bunk and started to tug at the bedclothes.

The ringleader, a heavy leathery crewman about 25 years old, was bellowing in a Scots slum voice, 'C'mon, let's have a look! Ooh, 'e's wearing pyjamas!'

I held on tight and kicked.

Danny was shouting, 'Fuck off, Jock! We want our sleep if you want your breakfast! We've got to get up in the morning. Fuck off.'

A group of older crewmen turned up to investigate the noise and they restored order. Robby was giggling uneasily and playing with a boil on his neck.

'Are they always like that?' I wanted to say to Danny, but my mouth had gone so dry that the lips stuck to the teeth.

He saw the look on my face, though, and told me, 'They're OK really, they're just pissed.'

The next I heard there was an almighty clanging sound. The alarm shook me rigid at 5.30am. Robby was already pulling on his trousers and shouted, 'Get a move on, we've got to get the mess going before the sailors turn up. I'll show you the routine.'

I instantly realised that the lower your status on board, the earlier you had to get out of bed. We were the first up.

Robby led the way along brilliant-red decks and into the sailors' mess, which was spotless and had to be kept that way by us. He showed me how to make the tea, set the table for the crew, trot along – everything was done at a trot – to the Petty Officers' mess and set it up for the Bo's'n, Colin and the ship's electrician, 'Sparks', then along more corridors to meet Chief Ship's Cook Heywood, who resembled a barrel of lard. His face opened in a grin and he said, 'Well, I'll be blowed, whatever next!'

The stewards were now coming out of their cabins. They lived amidships with their own mess and waited on the officers and passengers. There was a sharp distinction between the sea crew, who actually moved the vessel, and the stewards, who provided service for the elect. The sailors dismissed them as a 'bunch of fairies'. Most of the stewards were English and all the sailors seemed to be Scotsmen called Jock. The passengers were even farther away; the *Pacific Fortune* was a 9,400-ton freighter carrying general cargo but with room for a dozen or so banana-boat travellers.

After the hot steaming galley, it was time to trot back to the sailors' mess to clear up the tea and ashtrays. The crew would work until about 8am, when we would serve them breakfast. Afterwards, Robby and I had to dash away to serve the Petty Officers. Colin said I had a choice – to call the Bo's'n 'Sir' or 'Bo's'n'. I chose 'Bo's'n' – much more nautical and *Treasure Island*.

I got to eat after all this was going – for about five minutes, before the clearing up had to be done. My duties were divided into one week in the mess, one week on deck, plus serving tea and breakfast daily. The money was £10 per week and a monthly allowance of £3. Mess duty was no joy. Waiting on the sailors, cleaning out their quarters, scrubbing floors, polishing brass, waxing teak, lunch, tea – after which many of the sailors would finish for the day – dinner, collapse.

Our part of the ship was usually silent by 9pm. I preferred deck work, especially when entering or leaving a port. My overseer on deck was a taciturn Scot. I can't remember his name, but presume it was Jock. I had to learn as I went along.

When I went to sea, I chose the hard side, because I wanted to prove that I was a man. All my brothers, my big tough brothers, went into the catering side, which is called the easy side of the Navy. I went on the deck. I was the one doing all the dangerous jobs. I was almost decapitated on the Manchester Ship Canal – and, if I hadn't been with an experienced sailor, I would have been. There are certain stops where they shoot steel cables; we were tied up and suddenly there was this enormous crack and this old seadog threw me to the deck. The wire came ripping right across the deck and, if I'd still been standing where I was, I would have been cut in half.

This was all because I was always trying to prove what I wasn't – a boy; to show how masculine I was. For me, that proved more than a challenge on the high seas. Especially as I had started to experience a spontaneous growth of breasts.

6

HOT FLUSHES

'Every time you hear a bell ring, it means
that some angel's just got his wings.'

CLARENCE THE ANGEL (HENRY TRAVERS),
IT'S A WONDERFUL LIFE (1946)

With my body developing in the way that it was, I wouldn't shower. The others kept asking me why I didn't take my vest off. They came in blind drunk and they wanted to have a bit of fun. I was a hapless, hopeless and truly innocent teenager. And I didn't know what I was.

Clearly, they were after sex. I think I might have gone to bed with a man had he asked me to. It probably would have been more like fiddling around. In truth, it would have been homosexual sex, but not in my mind.

In the first days of my voyage aboard the *Pacific Fortune*, while the crew were gambling or unwinding in their bunks, I climbed to a secret place on the poop deck and sat on a pile of ropes in my oilskin. Out in the Atlantic after dark, the world is eerily bright. I wondered about many things. It was all such a puzzle.

The weather became much warmer. The sailors began to take off their clothes, which was very disconcerting. I clung on to my jumper and black trousers. We worked without shoes or socks,

37

unless the steel decks became too hot, and put up a canvas swimming pool for the passengers.

About two weeks out, on the horizon a low green island wobbled between the blue water and the sky. Haiti. My first palm trees. I had never been anywhere in my entire life and now – whack! Palm trees! I kept rushing to the sides of the ship and shouting, 'Can't we get off now?' But we cruised on through the Windward Passage, for our port was Kingston, Jamaica.

The ship rode at anchor all day in the Bay of Kingston, waiting for a berth. I asked if we might swim ashore like the sailors did in *Mutiny on the Bounty*. 'Ever seen sharks, laddie?' asked Cook Heywood. I'd only seen the fin of one following the ship. An old salt had become very agitated. Apparently, the saying goes, '*Aarr*, if a shark do follow your ship for three days it do portend a death on board.' Ours disappeared on the second night and the old salt lived to sleep again.

Cook Heywood picked up a bucket of bones and offal and tipped it over the side. At once, and I mean *at once*, the water convulsed in paroxysms of pink foam and teeth. It was absolutely mesmerising. 'And be careful when you're ashore,' said Cook. 'It's a popular form of burial hereabouts.'

At about six in the evening, we upped anchor and sailed into harbour. The ship was overrun by hawkers in jazzy clothes, with whom the crew bartered furiously. Last to arrive was a black woman of enormous size. She wore a peppermint-green blouse that couldn't have been cut lower, a blue skirt daubed with flowers and a flamingo scarf tied round her head. She flapped on board in sandals. Actually, she sashayed. When she moved, *everything* moved, because she wore no undergarments.

'Hiya, boys,' she drawled on reaching the top of the gangplank. Indeed, she could have used a Wonderbra. This was Cynthia, the washerwoman, who had come to take the sailors' laundry ashore. Obviously, she was very popular and knew all the men by name. She boomed towards me, 'Oh! I's sure gonna take care ob dis lil baby!'

Two arms heavily laden with flesh cut out the light and I disappeared into a chest that sported the most tremendous pair of breasts I had seen in my life. They were phenomenal, and running down them was an unstoppable flood of sweat. I emerged damp and red with the promise that, 'One night, darlin', I's gonna show you der reeeel Kingston.'

Colin, whose uncle was the Chief of Police, had been invited to a starchy garden party in the grounds of Government House and he took me along. A group of young matelots moved towards me and I overheard, 'Look at that skin!' which is naval slang for 'That's a bit of all right!' They were flirting and asked me what I drank.

Only minutes before, to my huge and everlasting delight, I had discovered Coca-Cola. The Cokes started to arrive. 'This is the life!' I thought, until everything went around and I fell over. For the first but not the last time, I was horribly sozzled. They had fixed the Cokes with rum.

The next morning I made another discovery. My first hangover. Double agony, because our cabin was at the bottom of the ship, just over the screws, where the heat is at its most aggressive. There was a porthole, but this could not be opened in harbour because of rats. In fact, it couldn't be opened at sea either because we would have drowned.

But, when Cynthia, smoking a cigar, turned up to take me along the Kingston waterfront, I knew exactly what to order. In and out of the little wooden bars we went, where three-piece tin-can bands make the sound of 30, and smiles leer at you out of clouds of marijuana smoke. Eventually, I ordered so many rum and Cokes that I went quite off them.

I was feeling more like a sailor when we set off for Cristóbal, where South America begins. The older sailors were amused by the sight of me groping pathetically into the mysteries of alcohol and adult life. We went ashore across a solid red carpet of cockroaches the size of sparrows. With every footstep along the wharf, there was a ghastly crunch like the cracking of wood, followed by a sickening yellow ooze up around my feet.

We headed for the Panama Canal. The middle of it is a bayou, a steaming stretch of swampy water strung with liana and full of flying creatures straight out of Jules Verne. Here the issue of salt tablets was added to my chores. I hardly needed them myself, being a salt addict. Salt over everything, even anchovies.

Sailing out of the Canal into the boundless Pacific Ocean, we almost bumped into a whale; it rose out of the sea like a cathedral, waved and gracefully disappeared. This went on for 12 hours, because the animal had adopted our ship as a playmate. (If you ram a whale, you drive right into a mass of blubber and it sticks, forcing the ship to put into port to have the corpse removed.)

The first call on the Pacific Coast was San Pedro/Long Beach, just south of Los Angeles, where I stocked up on short-sleeved Californian shirts splashed with cacti, Red Indians and Hollywood film stars. Then, up the coast to San Francisco, where all the sailors had their special banging parlours to visit. I went into the city alone and gravitated towards Chinatown. We had one in Liverpool, but San Francisco's exploded all over me in a dazzle of Chinese neon. Too young to enter the bars, I walked around, agog, for hours and hours and formed a lifelong friendship with the American hamburger.

Then it went very quiet. It must have been the early hours of the morning. I had to return to ship and grew apprehensive between Fisherman's Wharf and dockland. No bright lights here. Out of the gloom, wailing and flashing, a cop car flew at me. Two uniformed cops jumped out, an entire hardware store hanging from their gunbelts. Hands up, against the wall, frisk; I knew the routine from James Cagney.

'How old are you, kid?'

'Sixteen, sir.'

'Well, at least the kid don't lie.'

It seemed to be an offence in California for anyone under 21 to be out so late. They clanked around for a few minutes, checking my papers, expressing surprise at my being at sea 'aweady', and told me to hop in. I was treated to a motor tour of the city before being dropped back at the ship.

We sailed out under the Golden Gate Bridge to Seattle and on to Canada, where I gave my first interview. Colin had something to do with it because the radio people were allowed to come on board. They introduced me to the listeners as 'the youngest person to go to sea since child labour was abolished'.

But I was ageing. I turned 17 as the voyage reversed itself. Whenever I could, I retreated to my secret place on the poop deck. While we were in and out of port, each man had plenty to occupy his attention, but now, back in the small claustrophobic world of a ship in mid-Atlantic, my dreads and dismays multiplied.

At mealtimes, the sailors flaunted their sexual conquests, while I sat in silence and became increasingly choked. With all the toil, I should have been developing male muscles, but I remained puppyish. Most of the men showered in the evening after work. Always secretive about bathing, I was now so ashamed of my body that I crept out to shower in the middle of the night so that no one would see me unclothed.

My behaviour, of course, only made them more curious. It was always a huge relief when the weather changed to wind and rain, so that everyone was covered in oilskins and there was no pressure for me to take off my top. I was phobic about anyone seeing my chest. Instead of the hard pectoral muscles that all the other sailors loved to display as one of the bonuses of physical labour, there was a pulpiness around my nipples – my rudimentary breasts. There was no disguising how effeminate I was. Sometimes the sailors would blow kisses and shout, 'Hello, ducks' or 'Hi, girlie!' They would wink, slap my bottom, slip an arm round my waist. What was one supposed to do back? All my wires were tangled up inside. And I was excited by it as well as afraid.

Had I been among the stewards, possibly it would have been easier. But I was at the men's end of the ship, in the throes of a profound identity crisis brought on by puberty (I never completed the proper physical cycle of male adolescence) but not explained by it. Why did I have this curvaceous body?

After three months of voyaging, the *Pacific Fortune* returned via Antwerp and London to Manchester, where I was asked, 'Will you be making another trip with us?' I had made the grade, earned my wings, as far as they were concerned, for the Bo's'n went on, 'And your monthly pay goes up to £4.'

There were a few weeks' leave, so, carrying scent, lace, American groceries, holiday shirts and strings of abalone shells, I went off to put my lightly weather-beaten face round the door in Teynham Crescent. 'Oh, thanks,' they said when I flung forth my treasures, and then withdrew back into themselves. I couldn't wait to return to the ship.

When I did, it was a comfort to see that the seamen were by and large the same as on the first voyage. At least I knew where I stood with them. And one – tall, too handsome, blonde – thrilled me strangely. I couldn't admit this even to myself. But I couldn't shrug it off either. I went groggy every time we met.

Life on board settled down to its jittery routine. One of the stewards I met in the galley presented himself as a suitor, but I didn't respond. Besides, the rejection of all advances had become automatic. Touching people is a very healthy activity. The absence of it made me morbidly sensitive. Nor could I accept my feeling for the Blonde Sailor who caused such an upheaval in me. I stared at him working on deck. He would look up and wink, and I'd turn away hot and confused.

I was convinced a monstrous mistake had been made and only my being a woman would correct it. There were no fantasies about dressing in such and such a way. I merely wanted to be whole. This was the start of it all, the moment of truth.

One night, the Blonde Sailor opened my cabin door, unbuttoned his shirt and started to kiss me. Two of his friends burst in to see how far he'd got. The Blonde Sailor laughed and went off with them. But I was engulfed by shame and driven closer still to paranoia.

In Kingston, Cynthia said to me, 'Why, honey, you sure is gettin' prettier every time I sees yooo.' She calmed me. Cynthia – all Earth Mother and soothing powers. Yet really she could do no more than she already did – which was my washing, free of charge.

Colin took me up into the Blue Mountains for a drink. The alcohol churned and threw up the conviction that not only should *I* never be normal but also that, instead of getting better, it was going to get worse – which, of course, it did.

I experienced an acute attack of panic, which suddenly began to break me up from within; the eruption of intolerable pressures, bringing with it a compulsion to jump. Reason played no part in it. The compulsion emanated directly from my body. It cleared, but I was debilitated and depressed.

As we sailed for the Panama Canal on a calm sea, I began to vomit from nerves and tried to pass it off as seasickness. The Blonde Sailor knew he had broken down my reserve. He appeared to swagger with extra self-assurance. The battle raged on inside me.

In the Pacific, the Bo's'n began to realise I was in a pretty bad way. He gave me work that meant I was either alone or with older men, but he couldn't isolate me.

Knots, always my torture. Now I had them in my chest, stomach and head, and they were getting tighter and tighter. Physically I had deteriorated; I was eating little, working feverishly in an attempt to block my thoughts – so much so that the Bo's'n took me aside and told me to take it easy. But I was under excessive emotional strain. It had all got too, too much for me.

We reached California. I was walking down the street in San Pedro when I saw a sign saying 'Doctor'. I went in and told him, 'I want to be a woman!'

Not for the first time, I was told, 'That's insane! You'll grow out of it.'

I didn't think so. What future did I have?

7

MISSION IMPOSSIBLE

'All men would be tyrants if they could.'

The History of the Kentish Petition (1701),
Daniel Defoe

It was California and it was pill time. I entered the 'Valley of the Dolls'.

The doctor was bemused but kind; he waived his fee, and gave me two sorts of pills, antidepressant amphetamines and barbiturate sleepers. He told me to visit a psychiatrist as soon as I arrived back in England. He might as well have said 'psychedelic'; back then, I didn't know my Freudian from my Jungian psychology. I'm not sure I do now. But I took his pills and wondered what a psychiatrist was. It was a new word, possibly appropriate for the new world that was opening up before me.

The amphetamines shrivelled up what remained of my appetite and shredded what remained of my nerves. The sleeping pills made me dizzier than I already was. By the time we reached Los Angeles, I was totally screwed up.

After clearing away the dinner, I stayed on board and when my two cabin mates returned I pretended to be asleep. At about 3am, there was a carry-on outside the door. It banged open. It was the regular panic. They were laughing and stank of drink.

I fought like a tiger. As usual, the older men broke it up and I was left on the floor with a nosebleed. The tension flowed out of me. I wept and wept.

I'd had enough. I decided to kill myself.

That resolved, I found I could sleep peacefully for the first time in as long as I could recall. The suffering and the torment would be over. I'd had the answer in my own hands for so long that when I decided to do away with myself I felt at peace.

The next morning I focused on my work. I didn't want anything or anyone to interrupt my mission. After all the chores were complete, I shut myself in the Petty Officers' mess, which would be empty until the next day. I knew from my reading that the easiest way to kill yourself was to overdose on pills. I knew, didn't I?

I poured a long, tall glass of water. Didn't spill a drop. I piled pills on the table in front of me. One pink pile. One yellow pile. Which pills would be the most effective? I decided to hedge my bets and to swallow both, first a pink, then a yellow, then a pink, then a yellow, until they had all gone.

I'd got halfway through the 'dolls' when I began to shake, tingle and sweat. My vision flashed on and off. It went into black and white. My final thought was: 'This is wrong but so is everything else...' The last thing I remember was falling off a chair.

It was like a rowdy New Year's Eve in my head. Rockets roared, sirens rang and my thoughts tumbled and tumbled down never-ending tunnels. There was no light at the end of these tunnels. I came to and passed out, over and over again.

And then, sod it, I was alive.

On the third day, I came to and managed to focus on the cheerful face of a middle-aged American nurse in a pale-blue and white uniform. I was furious! How stupid to have bungled it. I

46

wasn't even man enough to kill myself properly. Colin had found me, and the shipping line had moved me from the ship to Long Beach's Seaside Memorial Hospital. It was 8 August 1952.

'Oh, darling, you've got your whole life in front of you, how can you be so silly? It's a wonderful, *wonderful* life! It's a wonderful, *wonderful* world!'

Such rot, but I took to her immediately. She gave me something outlandish to eat called an avocado pear. It was divine. The pear was followed by a priest, a blue-eyed Irish-American with a chilling smile. He prefaced all his remarks with 'my child', which enraged me.

I finally said, 'Will you please leave me alone?'

When he'd gone, I picked up the other half of the avocado pear and munched it. It was as divine as the first bites.

Later, a somewhat embarrassed representative of Furness Withy visited with the news that the *Pacific Fortune* was back at sea. I would not, he said, be rejoining it. The company were marvellous in the circumstances, but even after all that had gone on I was sad not to have a ship, to have that home.

I was transferred to the Seamen's Mission, San Pedro, to convalesce and issued with meal vouchers to the value of $3 per day. These could be cashed in unofficially, so there was pocket money for bus rides out to the beach. The local Samaritans from the Norwegian Seamen's Church introduced me to teenage American voluntary workers who took me to Hollywood, to ball games, to the desert, to the Biggest Big Dipper in the World.

I'd returned to life so easily. I might have been dead, but that thought did not enter my mind very much. I was having a good time in a new world. I played around for weeks and weeks before being flown to New York, where I stayed in another seamen's mission.

I cashed in my vouchers, lived on hamburgers, hot dogs and French fries, and visited the Statue of Liberty. I was on standby for the SS *America*, which held the Blue Riband for the fastest Atlantic crossing. I was warned I would be forced to take only what accommodation was available. This turned out to be a luxury stateroom on 'U' deck with what appeared to me – more used to portholes – to be endless yards and yards of panoramic windows.

The menu was almost as big. And provided an astonishment. My love affair with caviar began – I've never thought it too lofty for mass appreciation. Or my mass consumption. I'm with Marie-Antoinette: if others don't like it, well '*Qu'ils mangent de la brioche*.' Or as we used to say in Wales, '*Gad I nhw byta cacen*.'

I could not bring myself to use the first-class dining room; my trousers were ragged and my thin Californian shirts frayed to rags. But this get-up was perfect for the fancy-dress ball on the last night at sea. I went as Robinson Crusoe. A man all but alone on an island.

The ship docked at Southampton. The man from Furness Withy met me with a train ticket to Liverpool plus the balance of my pay – £7 and half a dozen pennies.

I pulled back my shoulders, took two or three deep breaths and opened the front door of Teynham Crescent. The family were sitting round the wireless drinking tea. My mother looked up. 'What on earth was all that about?'

8

SHOCKING HEADLINES

'Fame is the sum total of all the misunderstandings
that can gather around one name.'

Rainer Maria Rilke

There was nothing to do in Liverpool in the early 1950s. The only nightlife was people being beaten up and murdered.

I had just about learned to live with the word 'freak', but I was not totally isolated. There were others on the fringes of society like Roxy. He was like a protector for me, a more progressive Vincent, but in an altogether different world.

On my return home, I'd tried to join another ship but was rejected; I was given a dishonourable discharge. To make some money I'd gone back to work for John and Edna at St John's Market. Yet I was in the Twilight Zone, existing in parallel universes. Roxy was a star in both. Slightly built, with a strikingly red face and a pot of green eye-shadow on each eye, he arrived to work on one of the stalls in the market. He was foul mouthed in the extreme, and a new type for me. At first, he frightened me, but the discovery of Roxy's throwaway attitude towards all that was considered reprehensible made me open my soul to him. The response, I was to learn, was typical Roxy: 'Now listen to me, you silly fucking cow. Stop all this shit about wanting to be a woman. You'll grow out of it. Man? Woman? Who cares? You've got it up here, that's what counts. If God had intended the genitals to be as important as the brain He'd have put a skull round them.'

Freudian? Jungian? I didn't care. I had a supporter, a friend. He invited me to meet his friends in the gay bars. There were two main haunts, one behind the Market, which I was reluctant to use for fear of being spotted, and another at the Stork Hotel.

The noise! The people! Many of the customers wore make-up and semi-drag. The more exaggerated ones had left home and gave parties. I went to one at the flat of two men who lived as women by night. Full of pink satin, white lace, gold tassels, doilies all over the place – it looked as though Liberace had thrown up in there. The atmosphere made me uncomfortable, for I was more formal in my appearance, a dark box jacket with padded shoulders to make me shapeless, black trousers, hair long on top but cut into a Tony Curtis at the back, and a white, untouched face.

Liverpool had – always has had – tremendous nervous energy, but, in those pre-Beatlemania Merseyside days, there was little to do after the pubs closed. Mostly, we just wandered around the Pierhead.

Our always grinning lodger, Reggie Endicott, took me to a boozing party at the house of a friend of his. It was a smart modern one, distinguished by an indoor lavatory. I stood behind a sofa feeling worse and worse and finally went off to this lavatory and locked myself in it. I looked in the medicine cabinet. Lots of 'dolls'.

I took down a bottle of aspirin and swallowed the lot. This second suicide attempt was even feebler than the first; it failed to connect at all. I crawled home with Reggie, slept for 18 hours, and awoke with a monumental headache. It was assumed

I had drunk too much — a permissible excess, denoting what a man I was!

Life wasn't getting any easier. A couple of evenings later, I was at the Pierhead. Roxy was bitching with another Liverpudlian queen called Little Gloria (as opposed to Big Gloria, who came from Leeds) over a piece of rough trade they both had their teeth into. As usual, I was outside of this debate. We had been to the pub behind the Market and had had a few.

I loved to drink. My manners had become even more reserved than before. Putting a psychological distance between myself and others was my method of self-protection. Only drink relaxed me, gave me a holiday from myself. But it took half a dozen gins before the lights started switching on.

Out there in the keyed-up atmosphere of the Pierhead, I overheard two young men discussing marriage plans, their future wives. I couldn't live that life. On the other side, the row between Roxy and Little Gloria grew intolerable. I couldn't live their life either.

Despair swept through me like a dry wind. Roxy, Little Gloria, me, everything was so sordid. At 18, I had no future, no chance for any kind of happiness, so I shot like a bullet towards the railings, jumped clear over them and fell 30 feet into the fast current of the River Mersey.

As I fell through the air, I registered the shocked silence of those I'd left behind. My fall was broken by an icy smack. I plunged in and the water carried me off at top speed.

My mind did somersaults, as my body did the same in the water: 'Thank God the tide wasn't out — it's going out now — I'm rushing towards the sea — I'm going like the clappers towards New Brighton — I'll float for a while until my clothes get waterlogged — then I'll be dragged under.' I settled into the current as if into an armchair.

On my way downriver, I passed beneath a line of pontoons. As

51

I sped out the other side, there was a frightful pull on my hair. For a moment, I assumed I had crashed into a post — until I found myself rising out of the water.

One of the young men contemplating marriage had seen me vanish under the pontoon, calculated the point at which I should emerge, ran about 300 yards, jumped down to it, and was now hauling me out of one of the most dangerous rivers in the world. Bastard!

I writhed and fought. Chunks of hair came out. But he was so strong I was saved. The *Liverpool Echo* headlined: 'YOUTH SAVED BY LONG HAIR'. My first press.

I ended up at the Ormskirk Mental Hospital. Think *One Flew Over the Cuckoo's Nest*. Now think of it without the Hollywood tinsel.

I came gagging out of the sedatives. I was in a soft white gown with no metal fittings on it. In the bed opposite, with jug ears and claw-like hands covered in black hair, a man was tied down and screaming. Patients were giggling, sobbing, releasing horrible howls from their throats; others shuffled up and down the ward with faces cancelled by drugs.

In the bed to my left was a young man with the loveliest pale features, with whom I struck up a conversation. We chatted normally until a fixed stare came into his eyes. He would start to shiver and to mutter. 'Arrgh... arrgh... I like them black, I like them big; they've got to be big and black; I've got to have them big and black.' Then the fit would pass and he'd continue the conversation as if nothing had happened. His obsession was the breasts of black women; he'd gone over the edge in that respect, and it had disfigured his whole outlook on life. It occurred to me that his best chance of a cure lay not in a madmen's ward but in a ticket on the first boat to Jamaica and Cynthia.

I wanted to go to the lavatory and was escorted there by two giants in white coats — and not allowed to shut the door. The inmates were not permitted to shave themselves either. There were no knives or forks with the food. I ate with a spoon, like a babe in rompers. The screamer opposite had to be fed by one of the giants, who wiped the slobbering mouth and chin after every spoonful. This filthy performance effectively put me off eating. The ward lacked all adornment and was painted a bleak white. The windows were barred and could open only an inch or two. The doors were bolted shut.

I had been imprisoned in a ward for violent maniacs.

When this dawned on me, I asked to see a doctor, and asked him, 'Why am I in a place like this?'

'Because if you do stupid things like you do, you *come* to places like this.'

'But I'm not mad. This is a place for raving loonies, this is not for me. I only tried to kill myself because I'm so unhappy.'

He was noncommittal, apart from informing me that I'd have to stay where I was, under observation, for at least three days. The two giants took me for a bath, which completed my humiliation. In the ward, the lights stayed on all night.

It was four days before my mother arrived, dragging Bernie along with her. It was agreed that I could leave, conditional on signing papers committing me to a year's psychiatric treatment as an outpatient at nearby Walton Hospital. It had one of the largest psychiatric units in the UK.

When I got home, my brother Freddie said, 'You silly git.' It was the nearest the family ever came to discussing what was happening with and to me. Lack of education? Fear? Or did they just not give a damn?

I went onwards to encounter the head-bangers led by Dr Vaillant. His dark eyes couldn't rest, least of all on anyone else's, and darted about in terror of everything. Small and twitchy, he reminded me of a rat in distress. After an interview with him, I was passed on to a much younger doctor who began the cure by putting a mask over my face and dropping ether on to it. The theory was that this would release my hidden depths by getting me as high as a kite.

'Why do you want to be a woman?'

Claustrophobia began to flow up my nose and oppress my chest. Through the stone walls, I could hear someone crying. 'We've got to go and help them! We've got to!' I was babbling and tore the sodden mask off my face.

There were four or five sessions with the ether mask and eventually I grew to like it. This was fatal for the therapeutic probes, however, because it meant I regained my composure.

The doctor asked me about homosexual activity.

'I'm approached nearly every day but I don't like it and I don't do it,' I told him.

After a physical examination, they put me on a course of male hormones. The dose was massive and might have encouraged a little growth in height but didn't give me facial hair or male muscle.

'No matter what you do, you'll never be able to change my mind,' I told the doctor, with a knowledge I didn't know I had.

Next on the menu was sodium pentothal, the truth drug. It was jabbed into my arm and injected slowly. I was quizzed – questions, questions, always the same ones, always the same answers, over and over again.

Eventually, they decided to go straight for the Main Nerve. Electro-Convulsive Therapy. For this, I was put in a public ward. Observing those who came out offered no encouragement. These blitzed souls returned from the convulsion chamber like zombies, their eyes blinking and heavily bloodshot, with an attendant supporting them on each side. A few hours later, they awoke in their beds with murderous headaches in comparison to which an aspirin overdose is like a day at the seaside. When it comes to medical matters, I'm usually very brave, but on these occasions I was not.

I was wheeled into the chamber and wires were attached to my wrists and ankles. A crown of wires was placed on my head. I was bound to the table by heavy canvas straps. Somewhere a finger was on the button. When they pressed it, I zonked out. I woke up with a head full of cannonballs and broken glass. What theory lies behind ECT, I could never grasp. And it was followed by more talk.

I endured six months of this. For no reason. At the end of it, the doctor told me there was nothing more they could do without wrecking me physically.

What had he found out? His reported noted, 'He presents a womanish appearance and has little bodily or facial hair.' Six months to discover this! Who was crazy? This was madness. I needed to meet a better class of scientist.

Not too long afterwards, I did.

9
MIND OVER MATTER

$$E=mc2$$

THE SPECIAL THEORY OF RELATIVITY (1905), ALBERT EINSTEIN

I was supposed to be a vulnerable member of society, today's untidy euphemism for those who don't like to work, but I felt the government could keep their sickness benefit. Work kept me sane, if that's not too much of a laugh in the context of this particular period in my life.

I was a pretty person. And the most mysterious at the Stork Hotel, where I went out of my way to look as straight as possible. Yet, constantly I was told, 'You've got a woman's eyes.'

I had my first clumsy affair with a man. Vic was tall and had an aesthetic aura about him. I met him at the Stork. The barman came across to me with a cheerful and by now not unusual message: 'Someone wants to buy you a drink'.

The sex was fumbling. I was always terribly drunk when we went to bed. I wouldn't let him touch me – I wouldn't let anyone touch me. I would handle him, masturbate him. But there was never any oral sex. I was to become a completely different person before indulging in that.

Occasionally, Vic would crash out on my mother's sofa. She quite liked him. But his insane fits of jealousy killed it before it had a chance to reach anything other than a fumbling friendship.

I had also met one of the directors of a local brewery, who offered to put me on a catering course. My first assignment was at the Commercial pub in Chester. An interesting spot with even more interesting customers. I felt some of them liked the look of me too much, though. I got cold feet about the extrovert clientele and asked for a transfer.

That request got me to the Westminster Hotel, Rhyl, where I was to learn how to work in dining rooms and kitchens. It was off-season, horribly boring for me and after some months I asked for another transfer. This time I went not too far away, to St Asaph in Denbighshire in northeast Wales, the site of the smallest ancient cathedral in Britain and the entry point for the Vale of Clwyd. Yes, it is as dull as it sounds.

I worked there with a skinny lad, two or three years younger than me, whom you wouldn't have recognised as a future Deputy Prime Minister of Britain. John Prescott had left home to work as a commis chef at the hotel. Commis, *not* Commie. He was a hard worker. He and I shared a room with another lad. I think with my androgynous look I was a little exotic for him at that time; nevertheless, we talked quite a bit. He found other digs quite quickly. I liked him, thankfully, for he would be very kind to me in the future. But I didn't get on with the family running the hotel; besides, there's only so much you can learn about a dining room. You set the table, put food on the table, it's eaten, you clear up. I was open to more interesting ideas.

It was Ronnie Cogan, a friend who'd gone to London, who presented one. When he returned from the capital, he would take on metropolitan airs, talk about Cuban heels, high fashion and high life. It all sounded so romantic and wonderful to me. I wanted to go to what Ronnie called 't' Smoke'. Immediately.

My mother regarded everybody to the south as 'freaks' and didn't want her own personal one joining them. She refused any financial help. I had a few pounds, though, which got me on the train south with Ronnie. At Euston Station, he announced, 'We can sleep on the floor of Big Gloria's room in Earl's Court.'

Which was fine. This was London: the West End, Buckingham Palace, Pall Mall, Trafalgar Square; I might see the Queen or the Queen Mother driving by. I was used to putting on the Ritz in Liverpool – now I was standing out in front of the Ritz Hotel. It was one of the most sensible things I've done in my life. London and I were not just compatible, we were *en rapport*. We were made for each other, the big city and I.

Certainly, in the beginning, life did not seem so complex and difficult. It's funny how these changes seem impossibly major while you contemplate them. But, when you *do* them, it's so easy – freedom and a floor like Big Gloria's had been waiting there for years.

But I had to live, make some money. Ronnie and I got work cleaning tables at Lyon's Corner House on Coventry Street. We worked upstairs at nights. With a salutation to Roxy, I smeared my eyelids with green paint, and ate Benzedrine inhalers – you took out the wad of inhaler, cut it up with scissors and swallowed the pieces with water. That had me buzzing and wiping tables and vice versa all night.

I started a drug craze. It caught on. In late 1953, if you wanted a cup of tea in central London at 4am, you went upstairs at the Lyon's Corner House. Customers were greeted by a chorus line of painted macaws screeching about on speed. I was the Queen Mum of the place.

Soon, my section was filled with fans, little old men and women to whom I gave free cups of tea from a gigantic metal teapot. They sat there all night drinking tea and going to the lavatory, before quietly and happily vanishing as dawn arrived. It was very George Romero.

Ronnie and I rented a small flat in Westgate Terrace in Chelsea. After sashaying around the Lyon's tables all night we'd rush home and scrub the flat in the hope of knocking ourselves out so we could sleep. My God, those Benzedrine inhalers had me flying. Three days later, I'd still going. Drink took the edge off the speed. Especially if I drank lots of it. A bottle of vodka before work was a pleasurable antidote.

The pubs we went to were the Fitzroy and the Marquis of Granby north of Soho, in a district hung over from Bloomsbury days and known to us as Fitzravia. The Fitzroy was the most outrageous pub in London and often raided. The police entered, the place fell silent, they bolted the doors, and anyone without identification was taken off in a Black Maria. As I still looked way under age, about 12, I always carried the passport I got for my sea travels, prepared for interrogations.

It was in the Fitzroy that I met Rock Hudson and Ava Gardner, who I would be friendly with for many years. After hours, a mixed bag, including Danny La Rue and Tommy Osborne, congregated in the Snake Pit, a Soho bombsite with railings round it and a tea caravan in the middle behind St Anne's Church. London was littered with bombsites. I used to shudder when I saw them, memories of the bombs over Liverpool but mostly of the bullying horrors inflicted on me in the air-raid shelters. Soho, as the Cockneys I met in London would say, was not my cuppa. But I did meet a famous scientist in a restaurant in Dean Street. No equation is anywhere near as recognisable as $E=mc2$. It seems so simple, three letters standing for energy, mass and the speed of light, brought together with the tightness of a soundbite. When I saw the elderly gentleman, I asked, 'Is it Mr Einstein?'

He turned and asked, 'Are you a boy or a girl?'

'I think I'm a girl.'

'Whatever you are, you should be Madame Butterfly with those long eyelashes.'

'Can I have your autograph?'

'But I don't like to do that, it embarrasses me so much.'

'Oh, go on…'

'Oh, all right…'

Albert Einstein gave me five autographs, one each for our table, some kind of record for him. Mine is in a trunk, somewhere.

That was huge fun. There were also traumas, though. Little Gloria came south too and brought the news that Vic had committed suicide on a camping holiday. At lunchtime, he'd walked into a Welsh reservoir. 'Don't be too long, food's almost ready,' his friends shouted.

He called out, 'That's OK. I'll not be back.'

The body was found a few days afterwards.

I was happy in London – working hard, playing hard. I had friends, companions. And it was a friend who raped me. I've never really confronted this before – like the child abuse, it was a betrayal of trust. I will be frank: the attack was so brutal that, even if I had one day wanted to have anal sex, it would be impossible.

My friend's name was Joe and he was very nice. He would always buy the drinks at the Fitzroy and we'd always chat together. Often he would say to me, as we would leave the pub quite late, 'Can I give you a lift home?' I usually agreed.

One night he said, 'Do you want to come to my house for a drink?' and I said, 'Yes.' I felt unafraid of him because I'd known him for at least a year by then. Well, he got drunk and violently raped me. I passed out and he did too.

In the morning, we both woke up and he said, 'My God, what's happened?

'*What's happened?*'

The bed was completely covered in blood.

'You've got a passport, haven't you?' he asked me. He flew me to Paris. I had to wear towels like a nappy as I was bleeding so badly. We got to Paris and he rang up this doctor friend of his who stitched me up.

The doctor turned around to him and said, 'Did you do this?'

He admitted he had.

The doctor told him, 'You should really be in prison for doing this.'

It had been a mad attack. To this day, I have problems caused by that terrible incident.

Later, when I saw Joe at the Fitzroy, he would always slink out of the other door. He was incredibly ashamed of what he had done. To be abused by somebody whom you really loved and trusted, and then to be raped by somebody you really liked, was a torment to me. It meant that sex was not to play a big part in my life for a long time – till I was someone else, in fact.

The first Christmas, I went home, laden with gifts, showing off in a royal-blue box jacket and slip-on shoes. Slip-ons had recently come into the London shops. Before it had always been lace-ups. I arrived on Christmas Eve.

My brother Ivor turned up – and not in need of communion wine. He was blind drunk, ready for Midnight Mass.

I was having none of that. 'No, Ivor, I'm not coming with you, I'm an atheist now.'

'I'll thump you if you don't come, you great sissy!'

'Not very spiritual talk for a Christmas Eve.'

The tyrant loomed. And my mother boomed: 'No fancy London stuff here, thank you very much. You *are* going with Ivor.'

'Well, what's happened to you all of a sudden? You're not even a Catholic. You're famous for encouraging people to defect! So leave me alone. I just want a quiet Christmas.'

My confidence astounded my mother. 'Get out of this house!' she bawled. And never *ever* come back!'

Luckily, I hadn't unpacked. Ivor sloshed along the hall walls behind me, attempting to get to the church across the way. He zigzagged all over the road. My mother was pushing him, abusing him, trying to stop him collapsing before he reached a pew. The two of them fell up the steps, he crashed into the door, and she shoved him inside.

I turned and called out, 'Are you sure you never want to see me again? Because if you say yes, you never will.'

My mother was out of breath at the head of the church steps, framed in the light of the doorway. 'I *never* want to see you again, d'you hear?' she shouted back. 'I've hated you from the second you were born!'

Well, Happy Christmas to you too.

10

STARS IN MY EYES

'It's better to be looked over than overlooked.'
Mae West

I was buzzing about, elbowing tea stains off the Formica at five in the morning at Lyon's Corner House, when a very pretty girl called Sylvia came in for a cup of tea. There was no one else around and we were chatting. I noticed that she kept looking me up and down.

She looked at me again and asked, 'Wouldn't you prefer office work to this?'

'This is OK. But I wouldn't mind a change.'

'I'm sure my boss would *love* you.'

I became the switchboard operator at J Rowland Sales Ltd, a theatrical agency in Charing Cross Road. For showbusiness, I gave up the Benzedrine and the eye-shadow and went legit. Maybe it should have been the other way around.

There had been inducements – I gave an inhaler to a fellow worker and he ran into a bus and was killed. Finally, when Ronnie metamorphosed into Humphrey Bogart in front of my very eyes, I knew I'd overdone the drink, drugs and sleeplessness.

It was at the agency that I met Duncan Melvin, a musical and ballet impresario whose wife owned Le Petit Club Franqais in St James's, a fashionable dining club for politicians and civil servants. Duncan looked like a little leprechaun, which is what I called him. Pink and chubby, always chuckling, he wanted to be my sugar daddy but I said no. I was too romantic to make it as a tart.

The agency was perfectly situated when the coffee-bar boom happened. Our favourites were nearby in Old Compton Street – the 2i's, where Tommy Steele used to sing before he became famous, and the Kaleidoscope round the corner. Here I first met my great friend, Rita Wallace. Like Big Gloria, she came from Leeds. Like Duncan, she looked like a leprechaun. Like me, she was a teenager, but half my height with wild red hair, ravishingly pretty and usually hysterical with manic laughter. Rita was doing the same thing that I'd done – waitressing all hours, Benzedrine inhalers, have another coffee on the house, have another Danish, have you met so and so?

When Ronnie moved on, I couldn't afford to keep the flat. A transvestite hooker friend, Tristram, who had a record of petty-mongering as long as your leg, said I could take a room in his basement in Victoria.

After a while, I had to put it to him: 'Tristram, I think somebody's been sleeping in my bed.'

'Oh yes, Eyelashes. This couple I know, she's a doll, he's a dish, so in love, so romantic, they had nowhere to go, sorry, I meant to tell you.'

'And, Tristram, you've given up going to work – how are you living?'

'Didn't you know, sweet? I have this private income.' He was a crashing snob, gave himself such airs.

A few weeks later, coming down the street after work a little earlier than usual, I spotted a young woman coming up the area steps. Nothing romantic about *her* and she was with a man a hundred years old at least.

And something else bothered me. I went up to Bill, one of the boys who lived upstairs, and told him, 'Do you know, I got the most shocking bill from our grocer. It's £43 and I hardly eat.'

'Haven't you any idea what's going on?'

'What do you mean?'

'You're in a very dangerous position. Tristram's letting your room to whores during the day. By the hour. By the half-hour when he can. They must be using your account at the grocer's too. And the house, you realise it's being watched?'

I went cold. Who would have believed I was innocent? Who *ever* believes it?

'I'm getting the night boat to Jersey,' said Bill. 'Why don't you come?'

He regularly went there to work the summer season. The night boat appealed to my sense of drama. We floated into St Helier at eight in the morning feeling gorgeous. The following day I was washing dishes. A few days afterwards, Tristram was arrested. He was described in one newspaper as appearing in court 'with heavy black beard poking through heavy white make-up'.

The day after that, the bush telegraph informed me of a more amusing job out at La Corbiere.

The hotel there was unfinished, plonked by itself on the edge of a cliff, with the lighthouse rising theatrically opposite. It was owned by Mr and Mrs Wormold, who lived in St Helier. He was a charming softie from the North of England. She had more zap, the double of Ginger Rogers, and was having a duet with his business partner who was no Fred Astaire but must have had something. Mr Wormold announced, 'We want someone who can do everything.'

'That's me.'

'So far only one bedroom's finished. You can have it as general manager and caretaker. Breakfasts, morning coffee, lunches, teas and the bar.'

'When do you want me to start?'

'How about now?'

It was busy in the day but at night I was alone, with only a black cat and a tortoise for company. I'd start the day with an early-morning swim, then open up, take in the milk, tidy the bar, put the chairs and tables out on the terrace, put on tea and coffee, cut bread for toasting, heat the fat in case anyone ordered a cooked breakfast, and sit there eating pieces of orange in summery bliss.

The first in would often not be until 11am – the new shift for the lighthouse wanting a drink. A few for lunch, mostly salads. Teatime was busiest, cream teas on the terrace, but the nights alone could get very gothic.

On my Sundays off, I'd sit in the Red Cabin Bar of the Royal Yacht Hotel and be sociable. I was overjoyed when Rita and the gang pranced in at the tops of their voices.

'Dwahling, it was such a good idea, we're going to slave here too.'

After work, they'd come out to La Corbiere to keep me company, turning up with the Sarah Vaughan records around midnight and ready for a party. The cuckolded Mr Wormold was normally off by 11pm. He knew about our get-togethers but didn't seem to mind. I was *such* a godsend during the day.

One night, Rita brought a new reveller. Yet it was me who made the entrance. The lighthouse men had been in and out and I was woozy from drinking with them. I'd gone upstairs to rest. Hearing a noise below, I went to the top of the staircase wound in a sheet. The party people were arriving.

Raising my hand like the Queen, I said, 'Welcome, darlings!' I tripped, and fell all the way to the bottom, where I rolled under the piano. Dazed momentarily, I grabbed one of the piano legs to raise myself up. It moved. I noticed it was covered in black cloth. My eyes travelled up this marvellous body to an equally enchanting face. For me the rest of the room had vanished into silence. All I could hear was: 'Let go of my leg, you bloody idiot.' He was young and sturdy. This was Rita's man.

A week later, while I was working late in the bar, he walked in. Rolling golden body, deep, deep tan. Taken unawares, I stuck my head in a glass of gin and scrutinised him out of the side of one eye.

'Remember me?' he said.

Knives switched under my ribs — I'd forgotten the tonic. 'Can I get you a drink?' I said.

He jumped up on a barstool and sat there grinning. 'Just a beer.'

I grabbed a bottle, snapped off the cap and sent it frothing across the bar. 'Oh here, you do it.'

I was pumping shots of gin into my glass with the other hand and failing to be blasé. I was tongue-tied. Whenever his own patter ground to a halt, which was quite often, he would look down and brush non-existent specks of dust from his thighs.

Once the gin began to soak in, I relaxed a little. I'm going to call him Joey. His real name can be a secret — for him, not me. In 2006, I was still in touch with him by remote control. He was living across the world from me, married again; he had a way with the ladies. Joey was a Cockney boy from the Isle of Dogs in the East End of London. Italian and Irish blood splashed together with the English inside him. He was so tremendously bright and alive and was working in St Helier in the office of a boatyard.

'They call me Eyelashes!' I blurted out.

'That's a funny sort of name. Can I have another beer?'

After closing, I walked with him to the bus stop. Before he climbed aboard, he kissed me. In front of all the passengers. I was completely floored.

When I fell into bed, I thought, 'What is going on?' He had walked into my mind and now squatted there. I didn't sleep.

When I met Rita in a coffee bar in St Helier, Joey was with her.

'Hi, Joey,' I said in my most nonchalant breeze.

'I don't want to know *you*,' he said. 'Eye-bloody-lashes!'

I was crushed. I returned to La Corbiere. But in a few days, much to my surprise, he called in again. After spinning a silver coin in the bar for half an hour, he said, 'I wanted to say sorry.'

'What for?'

'For being a prick in that coffee bar.'

'Oh that. Don't worry. I'd forgotten about it.'

'No, you hadn't. I thought you were a girl, then Rita told me…'

'Oh, it doesn't matter.'

At the time, I was dressing in a very noncommittal way, slacks and a sweater. The Tony Curtis hairdo had grown into an Audrey Hepburn. I let people decide for themselves what sex I was, behaving accordingly. On the beach, I hid under an all-over singlet.

Joey didn't catch the bus back that night. He stayed quite a few times from then on, despite plenty of girlfriends back in St Helier. Yes, he was sensationally handsome. With an unavoidable body. But in no sense was it easy. My penis was called a virginal penis. A very small one, like an elongated clitoris. Because of my loathing for my own flesh, for my genitals especially, I was a terribly uncertain lover – no lover at all, really. Joey didn't know what he was supposed to do, what I would allow him to do, or what he wanted to do either. What we did most that summer was talk about it. Hours and hours of talk going round in huge circles on the sand.

At the end of the season, we found ourselves on the beach. Joey came out of the water. I stared at him as he stood dripping in sky-blue briefs, covered in gooseflesh. I wanted to love him as a woman. At that moment, it was all I wanted from life. I told him, 'One day I'm going to be a woman. I promise you, because I love you.'

'Ha, you're *ridiculous*.'

I knew that only too well. And I wasn't prepared to live with it; I wasn't prepared to go on being ridiculous.

11
SEX, DRAGS AND JAFFA CAKES

'She has sex, but no particular gender; her masculinity
appeals to women, and her sexuality to men.'
KENNETH TYNAN ON MARLENE DIETRICH (1954)

They say you can get anything at Harrods. I was about to find that to be true. Yet, for the moment, I was in the business of bacon once again. The summer over, I was back in London and working in Gloucester Road at Waitrose the grocer's – a different world from today's supermarket chain – slicing bacon. But not bringing too much home.

And home could be anywhere. I and all the others lived like gypsies then, throwing things into a suitcase at the drop of a better address. For a long time I deliberately didn't acquire more than one suitcase of possessions. I was also at a loss for my own identity. George Jamieson had vanished without trace, like a snail with its shell.

I got around it in a small way by calling myself Toni. It could be taken either which way; it was noncommittal, unisexual. Little Gloria tipped me off about a room in Nevern Square, about a four-minute walk from Earl's Court Tube station, truly Muriel Sparks's far cry from Kensington. It was the land of crime and punishment.

71

The basement and the ground floor were inhabited by a family who acted as caretakers. They would have ignored an atomic bomb so long as it paid the rent – a blessing, because from the first floor upwards it was bedlam. Prostitutes, transvestites, drug addicts, petty crooks, and their guests, a non-stop party, doors banging, music blasting, lights on, 24 hours a day.

Little Gloria had come a long way since the Liverpool Pierhead. At night, he donned a shift, a stole and a wig and went out on the bash. He was tiny and I'm sure this helped; short people get away with drag more easily than tall people do. He was also a kleptomaniac and his room was an Aladdin's cave of glittering trash, interior decoration by Woolworths.

When Little Gloria invited you in for coffee, it was served out of one of your own cups. The form was, don't bother to say anything, just pick up your own bits and pieces on the way out. Shoplifting and spending sprees with stolen chequebooks were his speciality.

My room was towards the top of the house, and underneath it, 'making ends meet, darlink', was Sheherazade, a towering Titian redhead from the North, a lesbian and a harlot. Most of the women prostitutes were blatant men-haters. In fact, on reflection, she was not so much a lesbian as prodigiously kinky. Name it, Sheherazade loved it. Her predilection was for sadomasochism. With boots, leather and whips, she ran a prosperous business out of her severely furnished bedsitter. Apart from height, Sheherazade's most conspicuous asset was the bulk of her breasts, strapped up in a brassiere like a black-leather hammock to render them more victimising. They were magnificent.

On duty she added a pair of black leather briefs with apertures let into them front and back and decorated with curlicues of metal studs, Prince Charming boots, with seven-inch stiletto heels, reaching to her strong upper thighs, and round her wrists and neck coils of chain. They were cut to *precisely* the correct length by a man in the hardware department of Harrods, himself a suppliant of Sheherazade's peculiar brands of sexual delight.

A true exhibitionist, Sherry often patrolled the streets in full SM uniform with only a trench coat, at appropriate moments, casually draped over the top to prevent arrest. Once she called me in as I was walking downstairs. A client was with her. She urged me, 'Look at that! I mean, Toni. Go on, just look at it! What garbage we've got in today. Doesn't it make you want to spew all over it? Disgusting little worm! It's fit for nothing but the shit pit!'

The man's eyes were paralysed with fear. He was lying naked on his back on the bed. A leather thong had been tied fast round his flame-red testicles. This thong was looped over the old-fashioned light bracket in the centre of the ceiling and pulled tight by the weight of a heavy flat-iron hanging in mid-air from the other end.

Every so often, mouthing cruelties and curses, slapping her thigh with a riding crop, Sherry strode up to the flat-iron and gave it a yank. 'There! Serves it right for being such a pile of bile!' She turned to me, 'Go on, love, you give it a yank.'

'I don't like to, Sherry.'

'No? Do you want to whip him, then? Is that what you want to do? Go on, give him one. Give him several. Give him the bloody lot, the stinking heap of fishheads!'

Sherry was marching up and down with a bloodcurdling sneer on her face. I didn't know whether to laugh or run away. 'No? Well, watch.' She struck him smartly across the testicles with her crop and a charge of ecstasy rippled through his body.

'I was only on my way out to buy some Jaffa Cakes,' I mumbled inanely.

'Don't fret, darlink. He has to lie like that for an hour or more before he gets the inspiration. Then I give him one good tug, he comes and pays me 50 quid.'

To me, Sheherazade had passed on to the Higher Wisdom. She was so at home in strange waters. We always knew when she'd had a good day because that splendid red head appeared in the doorway, announcing in the vaguely Central European accent she affected, 'I've got an itsy-bitsy bottle of bevvy.' From behind her back she would produce a magnum of champagne. Nothing about Sherry was small.

I was not so much building my character as collecting characters. Eccentric was what it was – off centre. For me, the mainstream – reality – was on the bacon counter at Waitrose. Back home it was neighbours like Pussy and Ernestine, both waiters and, apart from myself, the only inhabitants in bona fide employment.

Next to them was Jicky, who named himself after the scent by Guerlain. He had a Garbo fixation and his room was improvised from packing cases in the Scandinavian style. Early Ikea, you might say. He would sit in it and say, 'Yes, sweetheart, today I'm suicidal; I think I must kill myself.' In the end he did, of course.

Our resident junkie was Dawn Roberts, much older than the rest of us, about 40. Dawn was a bony little blonde, actressy, with a slash of red lipstick for a mouth and blue skin. No one knew where her money came from but she was a close friend of the famous society drug addict Brenda Dean Paul. Brenda was always being arrested on charges of possession. She was the daughter of Sir Aubrey Dean Paul and his Polish wife, the pianist Lady Irene. Looking like Veronica Lake in dark glasses, Brenda flaunted her life like a total tragedy. (In 1959, she would be found dead in her flat, just before her 50th birthday.) Dawn was very far gone in the needle game, jabbing herself in the bottom several times a day; not bothering to lift up her skirt and slip down her panties, she simply jabbed it in through her worsted skirt.

Once a boy called Hilary stood to inherit quite a few thousand pounds if he married. For a fee, Sheherazade came to the rescue and we all filed off to the Kensington Register Office. Dawn was a witness. Halfway through the ceremony she took a syringe out of her black suede handbag and stuck it into her bottom. It was the middle of winter and she was in thick tweeds, so it took a bit of muscle. The Registrar looked up, blinked and carried on.

As a safeguard against incapacity, Dawn taught everyone in the house how to do it for her. Heat up the drug in a spoon over a burner, pull it up into the syringe, and so on. When drunk, in bits and pieces, or first thing most mornings, she was unable to supply enough willpower and co-ordination to her limbs to fix herself.

The most glamorous of the drag queens was Tallulah; he modelled his voice on Miss Bankhead's. He had big blue eyes, high cheekbones and a mouthful of white teeth; it was Tallulah's pleasure to flick his tongue in and out over scarlet lips and then slowly draw the lips back like stage curtains to expose those brilliant teeth. They would be held on view from ear to ear for as long as it took to get applause. In addition to the smile, there was the walk, an effortless glide that conveyed the impression that he was moving forward on ball-bearings. Tallulah's dilemma was that, in drag, he looked like a man and, out of it, like a woman.

He was especially fond of black men – 'goolies', as they were called. Oh, they *all* loved the goolies, whose constant presence in the house was indicated by the aroma of hashish on the staircase. Black women also came on occasions. One went by the name of Vernon. She had short curly hair dyed pink and always laughed instead of speaking.

Imagine returning from Waitrose to this! I never knew what I'd find. We didn't lock our doors, and were constantly rushing in and out of each other's rooms. Someone would say, 'We're all going to Jicky's for coffee, are you coming?' Jicky was only across the landing, but we'd make an outing of it. Anyone might be in there – Rita Hayworth, Marilyn Monroe, Judy Garland. They were extraordinarily gifted mimics.

Usually after work I went to Tallulah's room, which was the

most comfortable as well as *Hollywoochie* heaven. He'd draped tangerine and shocking-pink chiffon over the lights, covered the bed with leopardette scatter cushions, congeries of lace frothed at the windows picked out with velvet bows, hundreds of bottles of scent and cosmetics, a plastic Jesus that lit up from inside, musical movie posters on the wall, frilly frocks and wigs on the window sill.

Along with Roxy and Little Gloria, Tallulah indulged in a homosexual patois, which was very funny. Despite the laughs, however, I tried to stay away from the homosexual subculture. Occasionally I went moral on them and said they should take proper jobs.

'Hark at her! Proper jobs! What d'you think I'm doing every night bashing my feet to pulp? Window-shopping?'

It was the same with drag. Pussy in particular was always trying to get me into it, but I preferred to look androgynous. Sometimes I put the make-up on with them. 'Cor blimey, Gloria, go and get Sherry in for a varda. Oh, Tone, you should go all the way, you really should, you look like Lena Horne.' The foundation *was* much too dark.

All along, my mind was focused. Even in the circus of Nevern Square, I promised, as I always had, 'The day I dress as a woman is the day I discover I can become one.'

Visitors to Nevern Square included Ina and Audrey. Big Gloria brought them along. They were both in the RAF. Audrey had the largest feet you ever saw. He was from Leeds too and sometimes appeared in uniform. Ina, who was from Newcastle, would never do that. When going on leave, he always popped into the lavatory to change into something more *comfortable*. Audrey enjoyed his National Service because he had the pick of the men. Ina, however, was a true transsexual and very unhappy, as I had been in the Merchant Navy. He didn't want to be discharged for being a homosexual because he didn't consider himself one.

SEX, DRAGS AND JAFFA CAKES

All these men with female names were not doing it purely out of affectation. Like me calling myself Toni, it was a method of casting off the old identity – in my case, the person I didn't want to be. Cruelty was to call someone by their real name, Brian or Henry or whatever. I loathed people calling me George. We called each other 'she' and 'her'.

Bill Haley and the Comets must have recorded 'Rock Around the Clock' for us. It blasted out our message. Tallulah's only record, played over and over again on his gramophone. We rocked, we rolled and were generously lubricated on gin and 'poppers'. These are fine glass phials of amyl nitrate, which you crack and snort. The heart leaped out of my chest, my body glowed. For a few moments, you gibber inanely, then you go sky high. After a while, you have another one. We were all popped out of our heads. One o'clock – two o'clock – three o'clock... 'Rock Around the Clock' indeed.

How that house shook! Sherry, magnificent breasts heaving, was terrific at the jive. She loved to take the lead. Only Dawn couldn't make it to her feet – she clapped and chortled in the corner like something from my ward at Ormskirk Hospital.

One party night, I smelled burning. Little Gloria dismissed my concerns with: 'Have another popper, Daddy-O, and shut yer eke. Poppers, everybody!' The room went up in flames. There was a terrible scramble to escape. Chiffon and tulle flew in all directions. By the time the firemen arrived, most of the partygoers had gone to ground in the back streets of Earl's Court. The room was gutted.

I was still mooning over Joey, but Nevern Square saw me nicely through a winter without him. It was a happy house. In the spring of 1956, Tallulah began to get into deep water. His boyfriends deserted him and he owed three months' rent.

'Well, there's always the night boat to Jersey,' I said.

We looked at each other and took a taxi to Victoria Station.

77

12

A FAR CRY FROM KENSINGTON

'My girls are the crème de la crème.'
THE PRIME OF MISS JEAN BRODIE (1961), MURIEL SPARK

The Jersey policeman watched us carefully wander from the ferry. When he saw Tallulah, he seemed to go into a faint.

Tallulah was an astonishment. He had chrome-yellow hair, plucked eyebrows, wore a see-through plastic mac – known as French letters – the smile and the walk, and rather more than a touch of rouge. He couldn't bear to look pale. As we walked by, it appeared the island policeman would have benefited from a little rouge himself.

We washed dishes at a hotel managed by Mr Pomfret. He took a violent dislike to Tallulah, who was inclined to be over-careful with his hands.

'Can't you wash dishes like a man, you fucking freak!'

'Listen to this, Tone. Pomfret's gone all Hercules; he's been at the pills again.'

'Freak, freak, freak!'

'Don't you call my friend a freak,' I said. 'He's a very nice

79

person.' I hit Pomfret round the face with a wet teacloth. There was a scuffle and he locked us both in a cupboard.

'I'm calling the police,' he shouted through the wood.

'Fine. And hurry up about it because we want to get out of this cupboard.'

No police. Instead, the sack. I transferred to washing dishes at a small hotel at Greve de Lecq. I'd not been washing up long before their chef went sick. 'Who on earth is going to cook the 200 lobsters every day?' said Mrs Craven. Lobster teas were the house speciality.

'I'll do it,' I piped. I knew roughly from my brothers that it takes 12 minutes to boil a lobster, and that they have to be boiled alive. And I was the only person who didn't mind the screaming noise as the air forces itself out of the shells, although Rita told me I used to weep over the pans.

Later the manager took me aside and said, 'Would you like to run the dining room? And, with the season coming up, do you know anyone who could help you?'

By this time, Pussy and Ernestine had arrived on the island, also because of rent trouble. I met them with Tallulah at the Red Cabin Bar and asked them, 'Would you all like a job with me?'

A small staff cottage was set aside for us. What a bunch! Every morning I turned on the record player and woke them with 'The Farmer and the Cowhand Must Be Friends' at full blast. It wasn't popular, because they could drink distilleries dry and always awoke with ghastly hangovers, but by 10.30am they were blotto and happy again.

One of the things that fascinated me was that, although I received higher wages, they all seemed to be better off. 'Now listen, what's going on? How come you've all got this dough to throw around?'

Tallulah looked me straight in the eye, displayed the gorgeous teeth and admitted, 'We thieve £5 a day from the till. A fiver each.'

How could I have been so dim? 'OK,' I said, 'that's what you do, well, carry on, I suppose. But you're not to take so much or I'll sack you. And you're not to let me see how you do it or I'll sack you again. Now, back to work!'

As a troupe, we were a great hit in the dining room. The more flagrant we became, the more the tills rang. But poor Tallulah, he went up and down like a yo-yo. Either he was camping it up like crazy or in the deepest of blues. With the sea so adjacent, he found trying to drown himself an irresistible proposition. Twice I retrieved him from the waves and whispered thanks to my bronze medal.

One Saturday night, we built a bonfire on the beach for a barbecue. It was a great success – baked potatoes, sausages, chops – until Tallulah came out of the shadows, drunk, wearing a white sheet.

'This is the end,' he announced and, delicately lifting the hem of the sheet, walked straight into the bonfire. It must have roused him from his sorrows because he came out the other side like an express train, but he couldn't walk on his feet for weeks and served the customers standing in enormous blocks of bandage.

From nowhere, Joey appeared. And presented me to his fiancée. I swallowed hard. He looked ill and was cold. We walked along the beach, drawing in deep breaths of air and letting them out again without speaking. For a long time he didn't realise how completely I had fallen for him. Brooding about him made me even more exhausted by the end of the season.

I needed a holiday. I could see France from Jersey, and decided to go to Cannes.

Being a freak has its compensations on the Côte d'Azur. In singlet and Audrey Hepburn hair, I walked out of the *pension*, down to the Eden Plage, and into a crowd of faces from London. Eric Lindsay and Ray Jackson, who ran the Heaven and Hell Coffee Bar next to the 2i's, were among them.

'Why don't you go to Le Carrousel?'

'Le Carrousel?'

'The most famous nightclub in the world for female and male impersonators. They'd love you. We're driving to Paris; we'll give you a lift.'

They waited while I got my things and cashed in my air ticket. I jumped in the car. Paris! The Eiffel Tower looked fabulous, unutterably foreign. Little did I know it at the time, but I had found another home.

The boys took me to the club's 9pm floorshow. We walked through the foyer, through the Long Bar, to the tables and chairs, seating for about a hundred. The interior was Parisian red plush and gilt, with a small stage and band at one end. The curtains opened and I was transfixed.

It was more than I'd ever imagined. Not the bewigged and painted dames of Nevern Square, but beautiful girls. Two of them, 'Coccinelle' and 'Bambi' according to the programme, held my attention throughout.

'They can't be men,' I said to Eric.

'Of course they are. That's the whole point.' He then confused me even more: 'Except that one there, Micky Mercer. He's a woman. Let's come back tomorrow and see if we can get you backstage.'

'But I can't dance, I can't sing, I can't do that stuff.' The whole idea petrified me. I could not – could not – stop myself returning, though.

The Artistic Director, Monsieur Lasquin, agreed to see me. He called in a Canadian, Les Lee, to act as translator and to check the credentials on my passport.

Les, turning towards me, half-in, half-out of drag, said, 'Brother, you'll knock 'em dead.'

Bambi came in, pursed his/her mouth at me and started speaking huffily to Monsieur Lasquin. '*Il faut attendre le patron – Monsieur Marcel*,' replied Lasquin.

The boss took hours to show. I was a dither of nerves. A tough French Algerian, he barged in scowling. He looked me over as if I were a piece of furniture, went out, came back and said in broken English, 'So what you do?'

'Nothing, monsieur.'

'Nothing. I see. Nothing...'

Monsieur Marcel frowned, walked behind his desk and scratched his square blue chin, muttering, 'Nothing... nothing...'

Then he looked up and burst out laughing, 'OK, we teach you.'

And they did. Very well indeed.

13

VIVE LA DIFFÉRENCE

'Thank heaven for little girls.'
HONORE LACHAILLE (MAURICE CHEVALIER), GIGI (1958)

What a world I had parachuted into. I'd lived through the craziness of London and the madcap adventures in Jersey, but nothing had prepared me for 1950s Paris.

Or Le Carrousel.

I took my hard-won 'sophistication' and much naivety with me to Le Carrousel. The first day, I walked into the dressing room and was confronted by a parade of beauty. The startling thing was all the 'girls' looked the same. I said to Les Lee, 'Are these people related?'

'No, darling, they've all got the same nose because they've all been to the same plastic surgeon.'

They all did have the same nose. It was a silly thing. They couldn't believe that I had had nothing done.

As a beginner, I was paid about £12 per week by Le Carrousel. My room was a couple of miles from the club and in order to save the Métro fare I'd walk to rehearsals each morning along the Boulevard St Germain, across the Seine to the Place de la

Concorde (where the most famous guillotine of the Reign of Terror chopped off 1,343 heads), up the Avenue des Champs-Elysées to the club at 40 rue du Colisée.

Even by Parisian standards, I was an odd-looking creature, yet I always felt safe. Only once was there trouble. I was walking to work at night and took a shortcut down a side street; a man emerged from nowhere and put a gun in my back. It was the time of the White Slave Trade scandal. I saw myself caged in an Oriental harem with a potentate who would beat his gong and demand my favours. It was a tiresome prospect and I screamed, 'Damn! Damn! Damn!' very fast, very loud. The gunman was so startled he ran off and I dived into the nearest *boîte* for a cognac.

The dressing room was divided in half by a row of back-to-back dressing tables. On one side were the stars like Coccinelle and Bambi and on the other the would-be stars. Luckily, I was seated with the stars, who were to instruct me in the techniques of make-up and presentation. On stage, I was to be a woman.

With my penis being what it was, concealing it would not be a problem. For someone like Les Lee, there was much more to organise. Les was a real sort of man. He was a female impersonator, but did not want to be a woman at all. To him it was a job. He had the most enormous whanger you have ever seen. He'd chase us all around the dressing room waving it at us and, if he meant to impress, he did. His huge thing had to be tucked between the legs and they had special straps made for him.

All I had to do was wear a tight girdle. They said I looked a dream in a backless dress; what I did was use ordinary plaster and just tape myself down. In a skintight dress, you couldn't wear underwear or it would show and the tape did the necessary.

I was, again, marvellously lucky to get to work there because it showed you all the different shades of the drag queens, the female impersonators and the would-be transsexuals. The most extraordinary one was an American called Sammy. He had no desire to be a woman at all; like Les, it was a job to him. But he had these enormous implants. Enormous boobs, like Jordan 50 years later. And he didn't want to be a woman. It was a complex world.

For Les Lee, once the show was over, off came the wig, off came the make-up and you had a very nice-looking man. Kiki Moustique was one of the most glamorous performers – incredibly elegant and beautiful – and was married with a little boy. At the end of the show, Kiki took off the wig and make-up and was back to being a man. He was quite short and the audience didn't have the faintest idea that this incredibly glamorous person they had been watching a short time ago was this little man in a suit with a briefcase who appeared to be going home from the office. In his way, of course, he was.

I already had fledgling breasts. Bambi took me along to Dr Four once a week for expensive shots of the female hormone oestrogen. These assist feminisation, but not fundamentally. The most important effect is the promotion of breast development. As the breasts enlarge, they redden and become sore. The nipples become particularly touchy.

Oestrogen must affect people differently, because my breasts never amounted to much, whereas Ruby, another of the female impersonators, had enormous bosoms. She'd take off her brassiere and wail, 'My God, the floor's cold!'

Coccinelle's were quite a bagful too, the consistency of India rubber because she'd had them pumped up with silicone. You could knock them and they wouldn't budge. Eventually, of course, they would begin to sag and Coxy had to return for boosters.

Monsieur Marcel was pleased to see me become friendly with Bambi who, unlike most of them, was halfway respectable, didn't go in for harlotry after hours and didn't have a team of sugar daddies in train. Bambi lived quietly with his mother, both of them refugees from Algeria. He was the most beautiful of the troupe.

The most striking was Everest, six feet five inches without heels. He was sheer pantomime. He performed a brilliant strip with clouds of talcum powder puffing out from all the naughty places in his body stocking.

I asked to do it on those days when Everest was absent but the management said it would undermine the image of my routine, which was to be, God help us, 'M'Lady'. Les Lee had a lot of raucous comedy in him too, although his expression was often that disquieting mixture of toughness and melancholy that one saw often on the faces of the transvestites.

Indisputably, the star was the Parisian Coccinelle, known to us as Monique or Coxy, and christened Jacques. While constantly in pursuit of the rich, he kept a whole string of lovers for his own pleasure. They frequently came to the club full of grievance because it was Coxy's fancy to coerce them into women's clothes from time to time. Being so full of machismo, they fretted terribly in frillies. But of course they needed their keep. Coxy was nuts about drag. He thought the whole world should be in it.

He had a sensational collection of minks, all dyed different colours, which could have been why he owed Monsieur Marcel so much money. Marcel didn't mind because it guaranteed Coxy's permanence in the show. He was a great performer in the vaudeville tradition, ostentatiously vulgar. He liked to blow raspberries in the middle of his lilting rendition of 'Love Is a Many Splendoured Thing'.

At premières it was the same – a rubbery breast would topple out in front of the cameras, which he would thereby hog. All his frocks were cut low enough to reveal nipples when he exhaled. Lips were Coxy's obsession, because he had virtually none of his own and therefore spent hours with a scarlet lipstick, smearing it on, layer upon layer, spreading it up to his nose and down to his chin like strawberry jam on toast, glossing it over, then applying yet more layers of lipstick, until in the end he'd achieved his objective: a mouth like a baboon's bottom.

Later in life, Coxy had a sex-change and married her favourite boy, François. Being a faithful child of the Church, she booked Notre Dame Cathedral for the ceremony (which she attended in another off-the-nipple gown). When the newlyweds appeared on the cathedral steps for photographs, the crowd gave them a terrific send-off – apart from those who pelted them with tomatoes.

Le Carrousel was the most expensive club in a wildly expensive city and the regime was very strict. If you missed a rehearsal or a performance without notification, you would be suspended without pay. For fighting, the suspension was ten days.

As most of us were living hand-to-mouth in hotels, suspension could be a disaster. No drink backstage and no visitors except by permission of Monsieur Marcel, and absolutely no fraternising in the *salle* (where the public sat) – again, except with his permission.

He was quite the autocrat. His wife owned Madame Arthur's, Le Carrousel's poor relation in Pigalle specialising in grotesques. They could be a fierce couple.

Only Bambi and Coccinelle addressed him without the title Monsieur, until one night he popped into the dressing room and I said to him, 'I'd really like a new frock, Marcel, I'm fully bored with this one.'

Coxy's lipstick stopped dead in mid-air for the first time in history. He didn't take his face out of the mirror, but I knew what he was thinking: 'That cow's got a bloody nerve!'

'Yes, you crazy English,' said Marcel. 'I think you look tacky too. Get off to the fitters tomorrow. Will you stop grumbling now? Can I have some damn peace?'

I went off to the dressmaker's in Montmartre and called him Marcel from then on.

I was learning to love Paris. I smelled it in the streets, saw it in the faces in the cafés, a feeling that to be elsewhere was to be in

Siberia. I'd read about the beatniks and existentialism in the newspapers (I read newspapers cover to cover, plus Georgette Heyer historical romances) and knew that 'Left Bank' meant dressing in a black sweater and black slacks and regarding the world as your oyster.

Already I had the wardrobe. Now I wanted to try out the behaviour. So I took a room in the heart of it, in the Hotel Jacob, rue Jacob, off the Place St Germain. It was winter and the cafés were glassed in, but this didn't discourage the human traffic up and down the wide pavements of the Boulevard St Germain, existentialism's main trawl.

The first place I went into was the Café Flore – and there was Françoise Sagan sipping an aperitif with Simone de Beauvoir. Expatriate Americans and English, many of whom had deserted from the Korean War, tended to gather at the Café Odéon. Hemingway materialised there, still the great literary lion but increasingly over-served with alcohol. When we drank with him, the form was very debonair. You didn't make a song and dance, you sat down, became part of it. A tab accompanied each drink and in due course they would all find their way across to Hemingway's area of the table. By the end of a drinking stint, he'd often have 50 or 60 under his chin. Before his eyes finally glazed over, he would pay them all and stumble out. Around him, there would be tourists with Métro tickets marking their places in Hemingway novels. It was sad and it was ironic. Heroes shouldn't have clay feet, but so often they do.

Then, I'd be off to the Club Tabou or to L'Ange Bleu, or the Club St Germain, where Stephane Grappelli swung his violin, or uptown to Le Boeuf sur le Toit, where Juliette Greco sang her *chansons réalistes* as if she were hacking her way through a jungle.

After Hemingway, the other great figure was Jean-Paul Sartre. On the tourist map, he was taken in between the Louvre and the Hotel des Invalides, by way of the Brasserie Lipp where he lunched in his dingy overcoat. I never saw Sartre wear anything other than this overcoat, whatever the weather, whatever the time of year. And there was no question of small talk. Like the others, I collected a cup of coffee and sat down at his feet. At this time, he was being watched because of his opposition to French policy in Algeria, so his eminence was tinged with insurrection, which further excited us, his disciples.

What was strange was that these famous men and women of whom I was in awe regarded me as a surreal object, as I was on stage at Le Carrousel, known as the Mecca of every female impersonator in the world.

With a new name.

14

MY FAIR LADY

'Nobody's perfect.'

OSGOOD FIELDING III (JOE E BROWN) –
LAST LINE OF SOME LIKE IT HOT (1959)

With the New Year, we put on a new show. We all had solo parts and I was determined to put on a performance. I wanted applause for the new me, Toni April. My spot, Monsieur Lasquin decided, would consist of me dancing a mambo in printed leopardskin trews and a tied-shirt top, followed by singing, 'Venus, if you will, please send a little boy for me to love', in a long white Grecian dress.

'It's a nice contrast, don't you think?' said Monsieur Lasquin, 'the animal and the cerebral, the concupiscent and the virginal, the...'

'The dirty and the clean?'

'That's so English of you. Now run through it again with Monsieur Tarquin.'

Monsieur Tarquin was the choreographer who felt he was the new Leonid Massine and that it was only a matter of time before he too found the fame that had been bestowed on the Russian choreographer of the Ballets Russes. Meanwhile, he fluttered with zeal.

Opening night – and was I on hot bricks. I danced that mambo so fast that the band were still playing it long after I'd fled the stage asking everybody, 'How d'I do, how d'I do?' But they were speechless with laughter, all except Tarquin who was hissing at me, 'Merde, merde!' There was no ovation, not a twinkle, twinkle, from my rival stars.

I had to ignore Tarquin and I quickly changed into the white gown. I slapped my thigh, did a mental giddy-up and reared back on to the stage to slaughter the song. Again, I dispatched it so quickly that the band were in the middle of the last verse when I was back in the wings.

Tarquin was jabbering from a corner with tufts of hair in his hands. 'Bow-wow, bow-wow, you forgot to take a bow-wow, you, you...' I thought he'd flipped and I'd be given the sack.

I never overcame stage fright, but Toni April (the name inspired by the month of my birth) did become more professional. Yet, if ever anyone got by on looks alone, it was I. It would pass through my mind while I was up there on the shiny wooden stage, rasping and twirling in silks, that, 'I'm getting paid for this rubbish – it can't be true!'

Monsieur Tarquin wasn't overflowing with the gifts either. He was happy for the show to be a string of solos plus finale. I said to Marcel, 'I'm frightful at this mambo and Venus thing.'

'Of course you are.'

'Can't I do something more interesting? A sketch with some of the others?'

'Have you tried working with them? They're monsters. Underneath they're all trying to slit each other's throats. They all want to be big solo stars; they refuse to share the spotlight with anyone.'

'But I don't mind working with someone else. I'd love it.'

'You find someone and maybe we try it out. Talk to Monsieur Lasquin about it, I haven't time for this. Where's my taxi?'

Audrey came over to Paris. He'd been training at the Royal Ballet in London and I grabbed him. Monsieur Lasquin worked out a routine based on *My Fair Lady*. I was to be Eliza Doolittle. It involved fast, dramatic costume changes for me and was a great success with the audience because it provided a change of pace from all the drag queens trying to be Marlene Dietrich taking her clothes off.

After this, if ever the cast thought I was getting above myself, they'd address me as 'M'Lady' in scornful tones: 'Look at M'Lady, she's just off to Heaven to have lunch with God.' But there was perhaps a genuine resentment because I was now dressing full-time as a woman and looked authentic. George Jamieson had gone. Even the hybrid Toni was no longer. I was Toni April and – in every way except the most important way – a woman.

Most of the others were a sad sight offstage. They murdered their features with paint, wore dreadful dresses and forced their boobs up and out. I was never a great one for cleavage. Among them, only Bambi could also get away with it off-duty, although he cultivated a fringe because he had a receding hairline. I didn't, and wore my blue-black hair scraped back in a bun or chignon to prove it.

I was exquisite, with slim shoulders and wonderful legs and incredible skin. My bosom was the perfect size considering how tall I am – just a mouthful, I would say. I could be on the booze all night and go out the next day and be a sensation.

Bambi and I were ladies. We never tarted ourselves for anybody, although there were all these stage-door johnnies and sugar daddies with peculiar interests. Lots of the 'girls' made money that way, and most evenings there was a rush for the stage door. It was never something I ever considered. For others, it was a two-way turn-on. For some, the unusual is all that matters.

Coccinelle had real talent but the others had only their talent for disguise, for turning their dreams into illusions.

But the public was fascinated by it. The stars who visited thought they were being very existentialist and avant-garde. We always knew when they were out there because the buzz from the *salle* would flow backstage.

They timed their entrances considerately, coming in about 10.45pm for the 11 o'clock show, so as not to steal the spotlight from us. Some of the names were legendary – Ginger Rogers, Claudette Colbert, Marlene Dietrich; what surprised me was that all these stars were so tiny yet their personality, their aura, was overwhelming. They had that Holy Grail, that 'it' that graduates a person to stardom.

Marlene certainly gave me the once-over hot-eyed appraisal before she told me she thought there should be a 'lesbian cabaret' club too. Well, she would, wouldn't she? But then she actually did something about it. She put up some of the money for a place called Freddy's, which was all about women pretending to be men. I'm sure that delightful Blake Edwards film *Victor/Victoria* had some of its genesis from that. At the time, it was all as confusing for many people as it was for Julie Andrews and James Garner in that movie. Me? I just wanted to be a proper girl.

Les Lee introduced me to Rex Harrison, who was wonderfully suave and polite but had sadness in his eyes. 'It's all too intriguing,' he told me. He was with his wife Kay Kendall but the cancer that would kill her had stolen her sparkle.

When the grand pioneer fashionista Elsa Schiaparelli came to the show, she was wearing a rose in her hair. But being 'Skap', it had to be sticking straight up on a stalk so that it looked as if it were growing out of the top of her head. Coccinelle noticed it, grabbed a bunch of roses from the bar, and distributed them backstage. We went on in the finale, a row of roses nodding on the tops of our heads. Schiaparelli ripped the rose from her hair and noisily stamped out – she adored being given the opportunity to do this sort of thing.

Before the new show began, I had made a fast trip to London to collect all my belongings. Home was now Paris. I caught up with Joey, who was no longer engaged. He was still friendly with Rita. He was disdainful about me working in what he called 'a drag club'. As patiently as I could, I explained it was simply another step towards the promise I had made to him on the beach in Jersey – where I'd still be if I'd listened to him.

Rita had been very friendly, promising not to lose touch. I returned to Paris with thoughts of Joey crowding my mind. When I walked around Paris dressed as a woman, men would come on to me like mad. I'd always say to them, '*Nous avons une petite inconvenance.*' Not once did any man say 'Goodbye'. They all said, 'It doesn't matter.' But I was still in love with Joey. I wouldn't be unfaithful to him.

One afternoon I was sitting outside the Café Flore having coffee. What happened next was straight out of a 'Paris Holiday' sort of movie. Rita and Joey walked by carrying luggage. 'It was pouring with rain in London so we've come to live with you. Do you mind?' My room at the Hotel Jacob was strictly single, so we moved next door to the Hotel d'Isly where they had rooms for three.

Rita – or Gigi, as we began to call her – was determined to make Paris a success. We went to the Café Odéon. While Rita was rolling her green eyes and being enchanted by Marcel, a big Jewish American with a gap in his front teeth, I said to Joey, like Scarlett O'Hara, 'You'll never be free of me as long as you live. I'll always be there. I'm the only person you'll ever really love.'

I don't know how we survived. But we were young, of course, and over the moon, which makes things much easier. They always met me at the club afterwards and we'd walk home together, stealing milk from the crates to go with our bread and cheese.

Rita became adept at sneaking tomatoes and apples from the stalls, but there was never enough to eat.

One morning, after a long night, Les Lee decided to take us all for *le petit déjeuner* at the Flea Market. When we came out, the sun was up. Joey said, 'You look as though you've got a suntan.'

'Take off your glasses,' said Les. (I always wore dark glasses in the early mornings when I still had full stage make-up on.) 'Oh shit, your eyeballs are bright yellow – you're ill!'

I'd been feeling lethargic and losing weight. Hepatitis was confirmed when the results of the blood tests came through. I was told to go on a special diet – no fats, no chocolate, no alcohol. But imagining hepatitis was akin to seasickness – that is, something that went away by itself – I ignored the doctor's orders.

Rita had more or less left us for her Marcel Wallace, who between classes in French Literature at the Sorbonne was taking her everywhere. She gossiped, 'Do you know what he told me in the bar of the Ritz? That a woman should be able to make a man come just by trembling. He's teaching me so much. He introduced me to Sartre the other day.'

'Dingy overcoat in the Brasserie Lipp?'

'That's right. How did you know?'

Joey and I moved to a cheaper hotel, where we were robbed of everything. They even stole Joey's soiled underpants. It was all getting rather desperate.

Les Lee pulled me up sharply: 'Unless you're prepared to be very ill indeed, that boy must fend for himself. You've got to eat properly.'

Les was always enormously kind to me. He had all the old-fashioned vices, but all the old-fashioned virtues too. He sent money home to his parents every month. He saved, had a budget for everything, made all his own dresses, sewed every sequin on himself.

I crashed out in Les's bed one night. He'd just had his eyes lifted by a plastic surgeon. When I awoke, I thought he was dead on his back. His eyes were open and rolled back into his head showing only the whites. After such an operation, you cannot close the eyes for a few days because the lids won't stretch, so you must sleep with them open.

Joey had returned to London, and Les found me a room in the Hotel de la Paix in the rue Roquepine, next door to his hotel so that he could keep an eye on me. I was put on a course of vitamins and plain boiled foods. If I went for a glass of wine, Les would snatch it away, warning, 'You look ugly with yellow eyes – remember that!'

I soon got the idea. It took me nearly six months to recover but at the end of that time I was rewarded by being chosen to play Le Carrousel's summer season at Juan-les-Pins on the Côte d'Azur, which meant promotion – and more money. I was off to the Riviera. Imagine! The Pierhead in Liverpool was a fading memory of a different world. I still had not achieved my only purpose in life – to be a *real* woman. Yet I did look all woman.

While Coxy remained with the show in Paris, Bambi and I stopped the traffic along the Côte d'Azur. Quite literally. We would appear on the boulevard and the brakes would squeal in applause. Part of our job was to be seen in the best places to intrigue people:

'*It can't be true – surely they're girls.*'

Their curiosity brought them to the show. Often we'd drive half an hour along the coast in Bambi's Simca and sit drinking cocktails on the terrace of the Carlton Hotel in Cannes like a couple of neon lights. Everywhere, we were importuned. Our strategy was to say, 'OK – for £1,000.' Even then, we had takers and so resorted to our second line of defence: '*Mais, monsieur, nous avons une petite inconvenance.*'

'Oh, I see, you're two lesbians?'

'No!'

We would crook our little fingers, wiggle them a little and hope the penny would drop.

15

ARE YOU LONESOME TONIGHT?

*'Hey big spender, hey big spender, hey big spender
spend a little time with me...'*

'BIG SPENDER' (1964), MUSIC BY CY COLEMAN,
LYRICS BY DOROTHY FIELDS

Heaven: the Côte D'Azur, where you can lie on the sand and look at the stars. And vice versa.

Juan-les-Pins is a crowded carnival of a place in today's summers, but back then it was relatively undeveloped, the nicest of the resorts. Le Carrousel's premises there were not as opulent as those in Paris but attracted a similar mix of the straight, the bent, the curious, the young and old, plus a quota of celebrities.

Bob Hope and his wife Dolores came and took me out for breakfast. He didn't crack one joke. Les Lee explained that his wit was thin without cue cards. Margaret Lockwood – a great star of the British cinema, especially since putting her cleavage (censored for American audiences) on display in *The Wicked Lady* in 1945 – was a great fan. She brought her daughter Julia or 'Toots' as she was known. Julia was to become, and stay, a very dear friend.

As I squeezed past her, Margaret Lockwood said, 'I've been dying to ask you, I hope you don't mind, but what –' she put her nose in the air and swooned like one of the Bisto kids '– is that divine scent you're wearing?'

'Ma Griffe by Carven,' I answered bashfully, as I was so aware of her star status. I shouldn't have been. We all became wonderful friends. While Margaret sat in a deckchair doing endless crossword puzzles, Bambi and I joined Toots and her boyfriend Simon Gough on the beach near the Lockwoods' summer villa at Cap d'Antibes.

It was very private, unlike the beaches in Juan, where we were mobbed by trippers and photographers, especially when we wore bikinis. They would point meaningfully at our knickers: 'Where is it?'

Sadly, in my case, it was still there.

I was to find that most people had secrets – some, in their own way, as delicate as mine. A German woman called Ariane came to the club. She had a brandy-coloured suntan that showed off her platinum hair. We took to one another immediately and met for lunches and drinks. After a while, she said to me, 'You're English and I'm German – the war was a terrible thing.'

'But it's over now.'

'Yes. And I've an awful secret to tell you. My sister was married to Goebbels. I'm his sister-in-law!'

I wondered how she was even alive. Hadn't the lot of them killed themselves along with Hitler in the Berlin Bunker?

'I was in the Bunker at the end. Goebbels and my sister, they murdered their six children and then poisoned themselves. But I was only 12. They said, "You are not immediate family, you leave." They sent me away in a car.'

Ariane inherited the family fortune and would spend it in the most intriguing and controversial circumstances, as I was to find out. I seemed to be a magnet even then for those who would play a part in history. However, I was still waiting to establish my own future.

When work was over at two or three in the morning, we'd drive off again to Cannes, to Le Whisky A-Go-Go on Palm Beach. If the others in the show came with us, they usually changed into men's clothes. At the Whisky, it was all fizz and cha-cha-cha. And men.

The whole atmosphere along that coast was so clamorous. I could have been a great courtesan if only I'd known how to cope in bed. But I had no interest. I only wanted one thing to happen. All the stories were that it was possible. And then sex would be something I could concentrate on, learn about.

Les Lee was quite different. I shared a big apartment with him and had hardly any sleep. There were troops of men through the flat all night long while I snuggled up to Frou-Frou, his dog, christened after the underskirt of a cancan dancer.

In the club next to ours, Edith Piaf was singing. She was a wonderful talent but could be an absolute monster. Apart from opiates, her favourite enjoyment was vigorous young men from underprivileged backgrounds. She flaunted them on the beach. When she'd had a few drinks, you could hear her ranting at them, 'Yes, go and brag to your friends how you've had the great Edith Piaf! I don't care. You can't break me. I'm broken already. But try! Try!'

She had her problems. I had mine.

Bambi and I searched for the miraculous surgeon who would, we dreamed, make us 'normal'. The sex-change of Christine Jorgensen carried out in Denmark was front-page news in 1952. Also christened George, she was not the first surgically altered transsexual woman, but she did change in some positive ways what being transsexual meant in public perception. George was fortunate to find sympathetic surgeons and endocrinologists in Copenhagen. When George wanted to become a woman, sex-change surgery was illegal in most countries and it was still a great secret in Britain at that time.

Now the details of the Christine Jorgensen story were familiar and strengthened our resolve.

We were told of a prospective doctor in Nice and visited him. He gave us hormone implants. A small cut is made along the pubic bone and pellets are inserted, which operate on a slow-release principle. They last much longer than the shots.

'Not only can I perform surgery on your genitals,' he added, 'but also I want to transplant wombs.'

'How wonderful,' said Bambi.

'Wonderful? You're crazy! Bambi, if you want to give birth to monsters and maybe die on the slab, you go ahead. But count me out. He's mad!'

I returned to Paris with my body as it had been. My pay should have dropped but it didn't, which was tantamount to a rise. Off the breadline at last! It's a glorious moment in anyone's life when this happens. And I could begin to save. I knew I'd need the money if I was to have my operation.

After work, Audrey and I began to frequent Le Bantu, a late-late nightclub behind the Lido where artistes unwound when their shows were over. I first went with Harry Laubscher, a London friend in the throes of depression. As we left, the manager called me over and gave me a wedge of francs.

If you were in the business yourself and introduced business to another club, you received your cut. The cut was a lot of money. A third of the bill. Le Bantu became my regular move-on after work and I was soon earning as much money there as at Le Carrousel. If Audrey came too, we'd treat them to a few wild rumbas – the management used to ply us with champagne to get us going.

They did the same with the strippers who came on from the Crazy Horse Saloon – Dodo Hamburg, whose angle was to strip off widow's weeds out of a coffin; Rita Renoir, wearing dark body make-up and whooping around as if she had live fish in her

knickers; and Rita Cadillac, a tall, pouting blonde. I became quite friendly with Miss Cadillac. We went to Joffo's Salon together, where Robert did our hair, and we once spent a weekend at Joffo's chateau near Tours. She turned out to be a superb shot, bagging six rabbits to my one.

The Alaria Ballet, an exotic South American macambo troupe, came to Le Bantu when they were performing at the Lido. Jean Marais kissed my feet there. Genevieve Fath gave me her earrings to dance in, two pearls the size of ping-pong balls, one white, the other black. Genevieve was said to have the largest single-piece marble dining table in Paris.

The Bluebell Girls who worked at the Lido were regulars and should have been nicely tucked up in bed by this time. And many of them were – with Elvis Presley. Their boss, Margaret Kelly, a Liverpudlian, was very tough with them, desperate that none should go astray. But Elvis managed to tempt them. He liked virgins, and went through lots of the Bluebell dancers.

Elvis was stationed in Germany and flew to Paris with an entourage for dirty weekends. His military crew-cut made him strikingly boyish and it stunned you to realise what a looker he was. The most remarkable thing about his looks was the colouring – blue-black hair, golden skin, lips so cherry-red they looked artificial and brilliant-green eyes.

One night, one of his aides took me aside and asked if I were prepared to 'go with Elvis'. He had taken a fancy to me. Elvis wanted to go to bed with *me*! Now, given the hysteria around this rock icon, '*going with Elvis*' wasn't something even I had to think about for very long. I could see Elvis looking over at me and grinning. He gave some sort of a wink. To bed with Elvis? Sadly, he was a little too premature in my life. I wasn't altogether prepared, as it were, to properly entertain his intentions. I felt obliged to point out, '*Mais, monsieur, nous avons une petite inconvenance.*'

There was panic in the Elvis camp. Old Colonel Tom Parker, his manager, nearly choked on his cigar. Presley, puritan as hell but a polite Southern boy nonetheless, came across and said, 'I hope my friend didn't embarrass you, Ma'am. Do have a drink, Ma'am. It was really good seein' you.'

There were no more personal approaches, but he always sent champagne across when we coincided. He was always sober, looked slightly uncomfortable, but loaded with charisma even in that dark, glittering den. So, I was lonesome that night.

But not on many others. Les Lee introduced me to many people including Judy Garland and Anton Dolin, who looked like my father and whom I called 'Daddy' Pat Dolin until his death in 1983. He was a wonderful friend to me, a legend. He joined Serge Diaghilev's Ballets Russes in 1921, was a principal there from 1924, and was a principal with the Vic-Wells Ballet in the 1930s. There he danced with Alicia Markova, with whom he founded the Markova-Dolin Ballet and the London Festival Ballet.

It doesn't get much classier. I also adored Josephine Baker. Before the war she *was* Paris, the most celebrated of the black dancers who bewitched Europe in the 1920s. She had been nicknamed the Black Pearl and compared to a figurine from Tanagra. In my Paris time, she contrived a comeback show, *Paris, Mes Amours*, and took it to the Folies Bergère, the scene of her original triumphs, but they rejected her. She booked the Olympia herself and smashed all records. I asked her why she'd gone back into showbusiness and she explained, 'Because I was broke.' The reason she was desperate was that she'd taken on masses of orphans and refugee children. I was right to like her.

At that time, I became friends with a 17-year-old newcomer to the troupe, Franco-Oriental Peki d'Oslo, otherwise Alain Tapp, later the super-successful entertainer Amanda Lear. He was a talented painter – which made him even more excited than the rest of us when Salvador Dalí visited the club.

Dalí came to see me at Le Carrousel every night for six weeks.

He specifically wanted to see me; he was excited by me. Put simply, Dalí, the Great Masturbator, liked chicks with dicks. (And the masturbation of and by them.) There's got to be a name for it – she-males? – for it's so terribly popular. There are thousands of internet sites about it.

Dalí gave me lots of presents and wanted to paint me naked as Hermaphroditos, the son of Hermes and Aphrodite. In mythology, he was joined in body with Salmacis the nymph. It was before my operation and the whole idea was anathema to me. I said absolutely not. I said no, never, never, never. And he begged me and begged me. I was appalled at the thought of being immortalised as neither one thing nor the other – the thought of being seen like that on the walls of the Tate Gallery was too horrible to contemplate. Besides, I didn't know if I was one or not. Hermaphrodites have both sets of organs; they're incredibly rare, but do exist. As far as I was concerned, in my mind, I was a woman. My penis did not exist – the purpose of a sex-change was to make that fact, as well as my psychological certainty.

In fact, Dalí's cousin was more exotic even than him. But I didn't want to involve myself directly in his peccadilloes. He invited me for dinner at his flat and served spaghetti. Instead of Parmesan cheese, he took out a box and sprinkled tintacks all over his and walloped the lot down while giving a monologue on horseracing. I had the cheese.

Dalí persisted with me, turning up all the time with chocolates and champagne. I introduced him to Peki aka Alain Tapp (though she claims she met him later). Peki was always with me. I couldn't get rid of her. She was very amusing and funny; she was my protégé and, when someone looks up to you like a big sister, you do want to help them. She wasn't ready at that time – she wasn't pretty enough. But after two nose operations, and after the hormones kicked in, she was marvellous.

It was Peki whom Dalí came to know really well. She was his

muse. I don't know what went on between them sexually – probably more mutual marketing than mutual masturbation, I think – but they were close for 15 years. In her 1985 book *My Life With Dalí*, she wrote, 'Dalí is a genius who likes ambiguity and he tends to talk to women as if they were men.' More than interesting, given our circumstances. Of course, the men who came to Le Carrousel knew we were men dressed as women – it was the most famous drag club in the world.

Later, I heard, Dalí would show cohorts photographs of Peki/Amanda or point to her swimming naked in his phallic swimming pool and take great joy in revealing, 'She's a man.' Ian Gibson, in his fabulous book *The Shameful Life of Salvador Dalí* (1997), quotes Nanita Kalaschnikoff who knew them both: 'Amanda's transsexuality was part of her attraction for Dalí. He loved collecting oddities.'

Peki, as I still knew her then, told me hair-raising stories of Dalí's artistic orgies staged outside Paris and attended by Pompidou and other prominent figures. One was an exercise in symmetry. The maestro masturbator arranged two beds in the centre of the room, co-opted two pairs of twins, one male, the other female, and urged them to make love with their opposites.

I still wasn't one or the other. But soon, soon.

Le Carrousel organised tours to Germany, Scandinavia, Italy and South America. In the autumn of 1959, after the regular season at Juan, the promoters of the Italian tour specified in the contract that both Coxy and I had to be part of the package. The tour opened and closed with long runs in Milan at La Porta del Ora, a lavish club with plaster scrollwork on the walls, mock Louis Seize furniture, and a barman who seduced me with a stream of dry martinis.

In Milan, I shared a room with Audrey. He had a maddening habit of jumping out of his bed at 4am shouting, 'I've got to have a man, I've got to!' and charging out of the door.

So when Peki said to me, 'I want to be a lady just like you,' I started sharing with her and for the rest of the tour Peki was under my wing.

The manager of La Porta del Ora indicated that it was part of our job to sit with the customers, encourage them to order champagne, sleep with them if possible, and drag them back in again the following day. I agreed to eat there, but just with Peki.

We danced on.

Bologna was freezing. The club was snowed in, so practically no one saw us. In Naples, the club was run by a countess who always had a dead rose in her hair and a dead cigar in her mouth. After Milan, Naples had the best audience in Italy. Florence was chaos. Then back to Milan, where Shirley Bassey followed our act. Shirley didn't understand the Italian audience and, thinking the incessant talk was down to disrespect for her voice, hit one of them round the head with a stick.

It was in Milan that I announced I was leaving the show to have a sex-change operation. They gasped, but not at the thought of the surgeon's knife. They believed if I left the show the tour would be cancelled. I told them quite adamantly, 'I made a pact with myself a long time ago to be a woman by my 25th birthday. Or kill myself. The moment I knew it was possible, the promise to kill myself by the time I was 25 became the promise to have that operation by the time I was 25. I've saved enough money and I'm 25 at the end of this month, 29 April 1960.'

I was desperate to proceed. But all the kids in the troupe got me and said, 'You know we only earn so much more money on tour. If you leave, the tour is finished.' They pleaded with me to wait just a little longer. I had already written to the doctor I wanted. But they pleaded with me.

Une petite inconvenance.

16

THE VAGINA DIALOGUE

'Oh, no, it wasn't the airplanes. It was beauty killed the beast.'
KING KONG (1933), SCREENWRITERS RUTH ROSE AND JAMES A CREELMAN

It was the moment of truth. For me, it wasn't a matter of 'Wouldn't it be fun to have a vagina?' That was essential for my life to continue. Without such an irrevocable change, I could not live on.

Reflecting back, more than 40 years on, it seems so obvious. I was lucky I was able to do what I did. I would have died if I had waited for medical opinion and science to catch up with emotional turmoil. It was be a woman, or be nothing – evaporate from the torment.

Church and state demand that we be either male or female. But there is also something known as a 'sexual rainbow', 17 physical states ranging from the normal female to the normal male. Most people fall comfortably at one end or the other, but a small number fall into the intervening states known as 'intersex'. Simply, it's to do with what hormones get to the brain just before the birth, a question of the right hormones not getting to the brain or the wrong hormones going to the brain.

Later, one expert believed I was among this small number and entitled to surgery to eliminate my physical limbo and allow my psychological orientation, which was female, to flourish. But in 1960, I went on in my own – unknowingly pioneering – way, losing any chance to ever verify if I was in the intersex category. I don't know if I was born a male or a female.

I feel that, despite my great social confusion in the early years, the question was settled in the subconscious long before doctors entered my life, perhaps even before I was born. I started out life as a boy. As I grew up, I turned into a feminine-looking boy. Perhaps I should have accepted my androgynous nature; most feminine-looking boys do, both heterosexual and homosexual ones. I couldn't accept it because I felt myself to be essentially female. Why, I don't know. But I did. And the feeling went as deep as feelings can go. Doctors could argue among themselves forever. I came to realise what I had to do to sort myself out. The taking of oestrogen satisfied the transvestites but not the transsexuals. I've seen men who've been taking hormones for 25 years and they still look like men with breasts stuck on to them. But my mind had made an internal choice of sex to which the external did not conform.

My male genitals were quite alien to me. To think that I had them still gives me goosepimples – it was so wrong. As I explained, I would never let anyone touch them, not even when we slept together, not even Joey. And I never once went to bed with a man without being blind drunk. As I grew older, this physical secretiveness grew worse. The elimination of these organs became essential to my finding life tolerable. A vagina wasn't just a fancy, it was a *need*. My early life had been such agony that now there was a great sense of purpose to make things right, make everything correct.

I was wandering around Europe, to all eyes a woman. It was horrid, a life of ambiguity and disguise, the constant fear of being exposed. I could not live with it and remain sane. I would attract men to whom I was attracted, but, when the moment came to go beyond kissing, the illusion would fall apart and I would be utterly lost. Even when they said it didn't matter that I was a boy, it did to me. I regarded myself as neither transvestite nor homosexual, although aspects of my life inescapably overlapped with these.

I found comfort in the terms 'transsexual' and 'intersex'. It meant that, instead of being a freak, the condition I had was identified and, as importantly, could be dealt with; the joy I had was in knowing that I was *something*, and not merely monstrous. I was a rarity, which made learning to cope a very hard lesson, but I was not outside the discernible laws of nature.

Sexual trauma was paralleled by social trauma when I had to identify myself formally. 'George Jamieson' was on my passport, though I had long ago stopped resembling the picture inside it. So, as my life as a woman became more convincing, the fear of exposure became more acute. I'd given myself a deadline. It was time, very much about time.

A few months before the Italian tour, Coccinelle had vanished. When she reappeared, she was smirking her head off. What had changed? Coccinelle was in no mood to keep it a secret. She had thrown off her clothes, fallen theatrically backwards on to a sofa with her legs in the air and wide apart, and pointed between them: 'Now, M'Lady, what do you think of THAT!'

She had a very pretty body and now there was no doubting the brilliance of the work between her legs. She had, as far as one could see without getting too close, a five-star vagina.

'Where did you get it?'

'Aha, that would be telling. I've been sworn to secrecy!' She could be such a tiresome beast. Coxy donned a blue chiffon confection trimmed with ostrich feathers. It was totally see-through and she posed about in it so that everyone could see that there was nothing dangling.

I knew then that I had found my doctor.

Coxy had undergone countless cosmetic operations and now had practically no nose; it had been whittled away in five operations. The mink coats dyed pink, the most beautiful feet in the world and an outsized artistic temperament. As I explained, to upstage was second nature to Coxy. She would infuriate all the big movie stars of France by arriving at a première and letting one of her boobs fall out of her dress. Boobs weren't so often displayed in those days. Well, after that flash, who cared about the movie's stars? Or the movie, come to that.

In our priggish way, Bambi and I disapproved of Coccinelle. We'd sit in the Calvados Bar opposite the George V Hotel, listening to Salena Jones at the microphone, and pose there, me as Audrey Hepburn, Bambi as Grace Kelly, and talk about it all.

We did what we did in Paris, Milan and Juan because we had to earn a living. But at heart we felt we were true ladies. Nevertheless, it had been Coxy who had the operation. I was driven out of my wits by her refusal to name the surgeon who had operated on her *zee-zee*. All she'd tell me was: 'It cost £1,500, so that rather cuts you out, doesn't it?' It didn't, but I wasn't going to tell her I'd saved more than £2,000. I pestered and pestered but it was Kiki Moustique, not Coxy, who gave me the information: Dr Burou, Clinique du Parc, 13 rue Lapebie, Casablanca, Morocco.

My eyes dilated in wonder. That evening I wrote a letter: *Dear Dr Burou, I got your address from Coccinelle. I am 24 years old. I want a sex-change operation. Would you accept me for an interview? It's very important.*

A secretary replied. It was brief and to the point. I was to present myself at the clinic on 11 April. I postponed for a month to stay with the troupe.

In Paris, the whole club tried to dissuade me. Les Lee said, 'Honey, when you see that knife, you'll be back.' It was different for Les. He had adjusted to being what he was. But for

me the idea of flouncing round Le Carrousel in drag for the rest
of my life was totally unacceptable. There was a big daylight
world outside and I had to face it; I wanted to explore it, it
fascinated me.

I said, 'Well, Bambi, aren't you coming too?'

She looked at me with her big blue eyes. I thought she was
going to burst into tears but she said, 'No, it's becoming too
fashionable.'

I couldn't believe what I was hearing. 'Fashion? What's fashion
got to do with it? This is our future, our destiny; you've got to see
it through. This is what we've talked about for years.'

But Bambi didn't want to talk about it any more. Then the
Bluebell Girls heard. Sandra Lebroque and Gloria Paul came at
me like a delegation: 'You're not going, and that's that!'

All this opposition had a consolidating effect. I'd never before
felt so calm, so centred. Toots Lockwood was sweet and girlish
on the phone: 'If it's what your heart tells you, Toni, then follow
your heart.'

And Coccinelle was downright positive: 'Yes! Go!'

Mine was the courage of desperation.

I bought a Casablanca street map and studied it at night, trying
to imagine myself there. A French-Moroccan boy working at the
club supplied the address of a clean, cheap hotel.

On the morning of 10 May 1960, I went to Orly Airport. I
thought it appropriate to go alone but Les, Peki and Skippy, an
American dancer from the Lido, insisted on coming and really I
was grateful.

Les kept up a patter: 'But Africa, dear! And all by yourself! It's
a disgusting thought. You'll be murdered at least twice. I know it's
not *darkest* Africa, but there are no smart bits, you know, to hide
in. Have you thought about dirt? There will be heaps of it
everywhere. And you'll catch something incurable from a camel
– people always do in Morocco…'

'Stop it, Les! I'm petrified as it is.'

Then they all broke down in tears.

We all kissed and hugged. I was about to go through the departure lounge. Skippy was the only one who was holding my hand. Just as I was saying goodbye, he said to me, 'I'm going to be the first, aren't I? When you get back?'

My whole body heaved with emotion. I was still in tears when the jet engines of the Caravelle airliner thundered into life. I shut my eyes tight. A cold sweat dampened my forehead; my heart began to pound violently. My stomach was a fist and would admit no food. A glass of gin and tonic fizzed and went flat in front of me. I couldn't even drink.

I was departing my twilight life as a man who body had gradually, steadily, become more and more womanly. The fear and adrenaline brought me so alive.

This was my flight into the unknown world as a woman.

17

AU REVOIR, MONSIEUR

'The world will always welcome lovers As time goes by'
'As Time Goes Boy' (1942), words and music by Herman Hupfeld

I arrived in Casablanca in time for tea.

The heat slapped me in the face. At the hotel, all I wanted was rest, to lock myself in this room in a strange city where I knew no one and doze until the following morning. I'd been doing this for about an hour when my eyelids slid open and I thought, 'You lazy, miserable sod! This is Casablanca, this is Bogart and Bergman, the Atlantic coast of Africa! It's time to stop flopping on the bed, time to stop hiding. Celebrate.'

In an hour, I appeared at the top of the staircase groomed to kill. A black cocktail dress with a cute bosom, six rows of artificial pearls cooling the lower throat, a chignon so sleek it might have been painted on with a brush, my most regal maquillage, and a tiny evening bag filled with crisp banknotes. Perfection.

Slowly making my way down the stairs, I saw the jaw of the desk-boy drop lower with every step I took. At the bottom, I realised with sudden pleasure that I was starving. I asked him for directions to the very best Moroccan restaurant where a lady might be seen dining on couscous alone; it was delightful.

The cab returned, by chance, alongside Dr Burou's Clinique du Parc. I got out and gazed at it under an African moon; back in the hotel I did not sleep at all. I arrived at the clinic early. A blonde receptionist asked me to wait, but I couldn't sit down. The Clinique du Parc was a maternity clinic for Moroccans on whom fortune had smiled and the place was filled with the bawling of the rich newborn. Eventually, a nurse beckoned.

Dr Burou's consulting room was reassuring. Calf-bound reference books and old French furniture whispered quality. Two things struck me when the nurse closed the door behind her. Firstly, the silence; the room was soundproofed. Secondly, Dr Burou. He was facing the window, then he turned round dramatically. I'd been told that he was handsome but hadn't expected the classic French features, dark-brown, aquamarine eyes and dazzling smile. I was awed.

Dr Burou greeted me with a simple handshake, and with his hands slung in his pockets started to walk round me as if I were an exhibit in an art gallery. Or a zoo. His hands were muscular, expensively manicured, and every so often he'd pull one of them out and make a slight gesture with it as if to emphasise a point to himself. '*Vous êtes le spécimen parfait.*' He went on in English: 'My God, you are so perfect.

'Please take your clothes off and lie down over there,' he said, indicating a couch covered with a starched linen cloth.

Everything he said was in a sardonic, slightly flirtatious tone. It was immensely attractive, not in the least off-putting, and he soon had me giggling. He examined me from top to toe to make sure I was all real and expressed pleasure in the fact that I'd had no cosmetic surgery.

He asked my age and about my family. I lied and said I hadn't seen my family since I was 15. 'Are you prepared to sign a paper absolving myself and the clinic from all responsibility should anything go wrong?'

'Yes.'

'Are you absolutely sure you want this operation?'

'Yes.'

'How?'

'Because I'll kill myself if I don't.'

'Don't talk nonsense. What illnesses have you had?'

'Hepatitis three years ago.'

'Any serious maladies, allergies, heart trouble?'

'No.'

'Are you afraid?'

'Yes, I am.'

'Do you realise you might die?' (Apparently, there is a huge loss of blood during the operation.)

'I accept the risks.'

'Do you realise that I haven't done many of these operations, that you are a guinea pig?'

(I believe I was Dr Burou's ninth sex-conversion.)

'Are you prepared for a shock?' he continued. 'Right now?'

'Yes – what?'

He went to a desk and took out a file of photographs, then handed them to me one by one. They were pictures of the operation, cut by cut, in vehement technicolour. The gore, the knives... The photographs looked horrendous and it showed you each stage of the operation. All the time, he gave me a detailed running commentary in terms I could understand all too well. Nothing was left to my imagination about how he was going to intricately rearrange my body. The blood was everywhere. If you had any doubts about yourself, if you were not a true, true transsexual, you would have run screaming out of that office.

You wouldn't have been able to look at the second photograph, let alone the first. The first one he showed me, you would have turned around and run. To see a whole book of it, from beginning to end, was mind-bogglingly horrific. Yet nervously, all I said was: 'Are these pictures of Coccinelle? Because if they were she'd had the most enormous zee-zee.'

Dr Burou laughed and ignored my question. He promised not to photograph me during the operation – something that was usually done – and said, 'You know, I think you're quite special. When would you like this operation?'

'As soon as possible.'

He stunned me with his reply. It simply overwhelmed me. After all the years, all the torment, the wonder and the unknowing, he said, 'Move into the clinic this evening. We operate tomorrow at 7am.'

I left and walked for such a long time. I had expected weeks of psychiatric tests and a clinical run-up. There were a thousand questions suddenly. Money, for example. He hadn't mentioned it. I thought of my family, happy I did not have to try and explain to them.

At the clinic, Dr Burou introduced me to his wife. She was a compact middle-aged Frenchwoman with short, mousy hair beautifully set, a Dior suit and small pieces of high-grade jewellery. She pottered around being 'Madame Burou', organising the administration of the clinic, helping me to fill in forms. I met Marie, the matron, six feet tall with heavy shoulders, and a young nurse, Jeanne, who was to look after me during the night. Jeanne took me up to my room past the Arab cleaners shuffling about with buckets and mops.

The rooms were not numbered on my floor, but identified by a panel of flowers on the door; otherwise, the place was plain and functional. I was in 'African Violets', decorated in mauve, with French windows on to a balcony with a view straight into an apartment block opposite. The room had a radio and a private bathroom, hospital luxury after my previous experiences with the electric-shock merchants.

With two nurses as witnesses, Marie came with papers for me to sign. Dr Burou returned, intent and serious, and again went through the reasons why I should not have the operation. At the end of his lecture, I asked for something to eat. 'Not before an operation,' he replied, 'the anaesthetic would make you vomit into your lungs and you'd suffocate to death.'

At about 10pm, a nurse appeared with a syringe in a metal dish. 'I expect you didn't get much sleep last night – this will help.'

It didn't seem to. I lay there pondering on the decision I had made, the woman I wanted to be. But I must have slept.

On 12 May 1960, at 6am, two nurses woke me. 'We must shave you. Down there.'

'Could I shave myself? Do you mind?'

A pre-med injection followed and I was in a dream world. I hazily asked if I could walk to the operating theatre. Two girls in blue coats wheeled me along on a trolley. I counted off the corridor lights as they flicked overhead. Into a lift – but whether it went up or down was impossible to tell. Then more corridors, more claustrophobic now.

It was rather like being swept pleasantly out to sea, and by the time I rolled into the theatre I was grinning from ear to ear. The anaesthetist, the only other man I ever saw in the clinic, said 'Bonjour, monsieur.' It struck me as hilarious, a game of charades.

With a mask across his face, Dr Burou said, 'I must ask you again, any doubts…?'

'Do your finest work, Doctor.'

Then they gave me the final jab.

Dr Burou bent over and breathed, 'Au revoir, monsieur.'

He smelled of gardens. Of lavender.

18

BONJOUR, MADEMOISELLE

'Hang on to your turban, kid. We're going to make you a star.'
THE GENIE TO ALADDIN, ALADDIN (1992)

When I awakened from my drugged sleep, I saw the tanned face of Dr Burou, who said quietly to me, 'Bonjour, mademoiselle.'

I asked him in French if all was well.

'Indeed it was. I'm very proud of you. All is well, but you must prepare yourself for some rough days.'

Then I passed out with relief. I kept coming to and passing out, realising what had happened, unable to believe it. Whenever I attained consciousness, I experienced overwhelming rushes of deep peace and these would phase me out again.

'Rough' was not the word I would have chosen. The pain I was to suffer is one of the most acute a human can experience. Post-operational shock caused all my hair to fall out. For days, I was almost blind. I faded into a skeleton of skin and bone. When I was bathed, I almost fainted at the sight of my body. Yet not once – not once – did I wish I had not gone ahead with the operation. I was a total woman. The operation had lasted seven hours and involved removal of the testes, surgery on the outer genitalia and the construction of a vagina. There were no ovaries and no womb, of course.

I think there are very few people in the world who can have felt such joy and happiness as I felt that morning after the operation. To know that at last my mind was in line with my body and my body was in line with my mind. It was something unbelievably precious and wonderful and magical.

Every single word you can think of, that's the way I felt. I felt *whole*. It must be like somebody who is blind and then suddenly they can see. It's just unbelievable the happiness that I felt and that has lasted right up until today. It's never gone away.

The happiness will be here tomorrow too.

The brilliance of Dr Burou's technique was that he did this retaining the maximum nerve tissue and inverting it into a vaginal lining so that erogenous sensitivity was not destroyed. The adrenal glands continued to produce sufficient androgen for orgasm to be possible by stimulation of these nerve endings. And afterwards the taking of oestrogen is no longer necessary. Some sex-changes claim that the operation makes them more sensitive than ordinary women.

I did ask Dr Burou if it would be possible for me to make love and achieve orgasm and he said, 'Theoretically there's nothing to stop you. Whether you do, and how often, is entirely up to you.'

The day after the operation, I sent telegrams to Les Lee, Sandra and Gloria, Julia Lockwood. I wanted to send one to Joey, because I knew that I could now make him happy. But for him I felt too much emotion for a telegram.

As the anaesthetic wore off, I became aware of a most hideous pain. It was as if branding irons were being vigorously applied to the middle part of my body. I screamed and a nurse came quickly with a painkilling injection.

'You are going to have to be *very* brave,' said Dr Burou, 'because we can give you these painkilling shots for three days only. Otherwise you'll develop an addiction to them.'

Dr Burou was very strict about the pain and getting used to it as quickly as possible. No heavyweight painkillers. I had some morphine a little bit for the first few days only because the pain was unbelievable.

It's more than 45 years now since my surgery. Nowadays, when the operation is carried out, it's done quite painlessly. And it can be got on the National Health. I was a guinea pig. Dr Burou was perfecting his skills so each new patient that came benefited from what I endured.

The injections stilled the pain but put everything else at a distance too, as if the world were taking place in slow motion on a screen. However, they did allow me to give myself a superficial examination. My middle was grotesquely swollen and bound inches deep with bandages into which blood continuously spilled and congealed. A rubber tube for peeing came out of it. Pints of sweat poured off me and this was exacerbated by the oppressive heat of the day.

The noise of carts, donkeys and motorcars came through the balcony windows and the crying of babies through the walls from the maternity wards. I wanted my exit visa from Casablanca.

Feverishly, I ran my fingers through my hair. It came out in handfuls. My lovely thick black hair, it covered the pillow. 'Nurse! Nurse! I must have a hand mirror!' My hair was in patches from the shock of the surgery. She assured me it would grow back again. It did, but was never afterwards thick and healthy and soon went grey. My face was puffy with drugs and sleeplessness. The skin looked bruised and drained, as if I'd been in a car crash.

Les Lee and Julia phoned. I couldn't make much sense of what I was saying or hearing but it was a comfort to know they were out there.

I listened to the newborn babies. *I* had been reborn. I was a woman in Casablanca and in agony but my spirit was soaring. When I recovered, I thought, 'World, I'm going to knock you for six!' But the world would have to wait a moment or two. I had to deal with torture first.

On the fourth day, as the branding irons descended and sizzled across my body, I screamed as usual for the nurse. Instead of a jab, she gave me tablets. The pain mounted and closed in on me. She held my hand and said, 'Scream, yes, scream, it helps.' It rang throughout the building, a terrible roar of pain, and the poor women waiting for the onset of labour must have shuddered with anxiety. The nurse tried to mop my brow as I threw my head from side to side, clenched in spasms, and gave issue to long gurgling groans.

The pain, which came in waves like everything else in life, was aggravated by movement of the hips. The slightest shift would set it off. Night-times were the worst and Jeanne helped me through them. She kept going above my dreadful moans, chatting about her son who loved mathematics, who wanted to be a racing driver, who wanted to go to college in England, and how wonderful it would be if he could, and would I teach her some English?

I looked at her as if she were mad and then the pain hit me again. Occasionally, my eyes lost focus, ceased to convey coherent information to my brain, and I would go into a semi-blind hysterical state, which was usually followed by unconsciousness. I was soggy the whole time. It was delightful when they came to wash me, even though the refreshment was brief. Lightweight meals appeared and were taken away barely touched.

Then came the first of what I called 'the horrors'. At the end of the operation, a speculum was inserted into my brand-new vagina. It's like a big steel beak that can be screwed open and closed, to ensure the elasticity of the vagina; it's also done to guarantee smooth healing of the vaginal walls, which are heavily clotted with blood while the blood vessels realign themselves. If you don't do that then, when the vagina started to heal, it would close and then you wouldn't be able to have intercourse. I cannot tell you how painful that was. They had to keep reinserting it. I'd always wanted to win an Academy Award, so I called it 'Oscar'. Later, when my body was more settled, I nicknamed it 'Donald Duck'. You do the math.

But in the days after the operation there was nothing amusing about 'Oscar'. It had to be removed every morning to allow for examination, ventilation and mopping up. This was Marie's job. She put a hankie into my mouth and told me to grip the bed rails by my head. Marie was built like a bull and her movements had a physical assurance that was a comfort.

She unbandaged me, removed the speculum, and then the nurses swabbed me. Tablets cannot touch pain at this level. Worse followed in the evening when she came to replace it. Marie told me, 'There are two ways of doing it. Slow – which takes a long time and is very painful. Or fast – which is much more painful but soon done. Whichever way you choose, you must get accustomed to it.'

'Fast,' I gurgled through the hankie.

She didn't wait a second! My head hit the rails behind the bed so hard that I almost knocked myself out. Then I was rebound tightly and she wished me a good night's sleep. We took more care in future over the arrangement of the pillows.

The nights were harrowing. I lay there hot and soaking, screaming, moaning, smelling foul with clogged blood, bruised and swollen. Yet I was so grateful – elated, completed at last, a relief so marvellous and life enhancing I imagined nothing would ever hurt again. Then, I would remember that Marie would be along with 'Oscar'. I used to quake at the thought.

In two weeks, I was allowed up to bathe and, with a nurse in each armpit, take a few disorientated steps across the floor. It was suggested that I might like to take the air. Since there was no garden, this meant hobbling into the street. Making myself as presentable as possible, but slandering a Balmain suit all the same, I began an epic voyage through the clinic to the outside world.

My legs were ropes of jelly and pains shot upwards from my thighs to my chest. I got outside and I fell right away into the gutter. When I came to, I started screaming with laughter and the nurse was terribly worried because she was screaming for help, for the others to come. I was just sitting there, chuckling in the road like a drunkard.

Yet each day they encouraged me to walk farther. Dr Burou visited me with pep talks and, as life seeped back slowly into my system, he christened me 'Mademoiselle Glamour Girl'.

Julia Lockwood was a fabulously successful actress on television and in films; she'd been working since she was five years old. So the fact that she came out for the last two weeks that I was in the clinic was amazing. They let her sleep in the same room as me. Dr Burou was a little bit in love with her; she was quite beautiful and only 16 years old.

When Julia arrived, she was full of schoolgirl gush. Nothing in her manner betrayed shock or disgust at what she found. Although still a teenager, she capably took over from Jeanne as comforter and friend. I'll never forget it. Even the 'Oscar' performances didn't throw her out of gear. It was quite remarkable for one so young. Dr Burou suggested she take me out for dinner and he made all the arrangements. I felt emotionally strong and Julia didn't stop talking.

'You must meet my great friend Sarah Churchill, the daughter of Him, as she puts it, Winston that is. She's my A.M. [adopted mother] and I'm her A.D. [adopted daughter]. You could be Sarah's A.D. if you liked. And you are my A.B.S. [adopted big sister].'

She could go on for hours with these games. Julia was an only child and had been brought up by a nanny. It must have been a lonely childhood. Margaret was a tough career woman and, though she was never unkind to Julia, I never thought of her as an especially warm mother. Toots was not starved of love but she'd been short of affectionate companionship.

'And,' she went on, 'I think you should leave Le Carrousel. I mean, I adore Les Lee and all that, and I *adore* Everest, but I think, now, really, I don't think it's the life for you any more.'

'Toots, you don't have to tell me that. I want to marry Joey, adopt children, be the housewife.'

'No, I didn't mean that either.'

Dr Burou followed up dinner-therapy by suggesting that sunshine would be good for me. Julia and I scrambled into a cab and drove to one of the many swimming pools along Casablanca's coast. I looked like a ghoul in a bikini but was not ashamed – except perhaps of my kneecaps, which looked abnormally large. Julia dived in. Like her mother, she was a fish. I craved the crisp water in that heat, but I was frightened to go in.

After ten minutes of watching her sport about, I said, 'Hey, I'll sit on the edge and let my poor little ankles sort of dawdle.'

A waiter turned up with two Singapore Slings on a silver tray. I drank eagerly.

'Yes, you're right, Toots, I've got to take the plunge sometime. Get ready in case I sink straight to the bottom.'

'Oh, well, no, perhaps it would be better to wait until you've asked the doctor.'

The 'no' was all I needed. Carefully I lowered myself into the pool and managed a few paddles. I smiled at Toots and announced, 'Well, at least it's watertight...'

At the end of the week, Julia had to go back to London but offered to travel via Paris if I'd like to be escorted there. Dr Burou said I should stay an extra two weeks but I was running out of money and told him so. He waved the subject aside but I didn't want to enter my new life shackled to debts. When the bill came, it was a surprise to read that the operation itself cost only £70.

But Coccinelle was right, the subsequent treatment boosted the total to more than £1,500.

As I left, Dr Burou, as godlike as ever, kissed me on both cheeks and said, 'I hope you find your happiness now. Remember, remember, it's all up to you.' He presented me with my 'Oscar' and told me I had to carry on with it for at least the first six months, three times a week. I've still got that 'Oscar'. There are some things you don't give up.

19

DEFLOWERED

'La grande ambition des femmes est d'inspirer l'amour.'
MOLIÈRE (1654)

O ften I had wondered, 'Why me? I had four brothers and
two sisters and why me?' Yet I was incredibly lucky that I
had the right looks. When I see some of my fellow transsexuals,
it's very obvious that something has happened.

I got on a flight to Paris looking like a stunner. My, oh my, how
the heads turned. I loved it. Yet there's something about pride
coming before the fall. The flight was terrible. Air France were
having a strike of ground staff and we circled Orly for an
eternity while they improvised below. The delay meant that Julia
had to board her connection directly and so I went into Paris
proper alone.

At the Hotel de la Paix, there was a letter waiting for me, from
Joey. I recognised his writing at once, like a lot of baby
matchsticks falling over. Our letters must have crossed in the
post. A thrill ran through me. The past month had been so
extraordinary, I needed to feel him close and I couldn't wait. I

131

opened the letter on the spot: *'Darling Toni — I hope you are well, I'm sure you are. I am, thank God. I wanted to write before but plans got in the way.Well, I've got to tell you, last week I got married to...'*

I collapsed in the hallway. For four days, I stayed in bed, refusing visitors. The letter — I read it again and again and cried and cried. It was so awful, the timing of it, everything. On the fifth day, Les Lee forced his way in. 'What's happened?' he said.

I told him.

'No, no — I mean Casablanca, the operation.'

'Les, I'm so mixed up now, Joey's gone, and — yes, Casablanca, it's done, it's wonderful, but...' And I started crying again.

'What are we going to do with you, eh? You've just gone through the most amazing experience in the world and all you can think about is some bum who's married some slag!'

This was the treatment I needed. Les brought the gang to see me for reports. Besides, reality wouldn't let me wail for long — I was almost out of money. Joey's marriage was the greatest shock of all but I returned to working at Le Carrousel.

It was topsy-turvy, I went back to work at the club to earn the money that would enable me to leave it. But I had a relapse and Marcel loaned me some money to have a holiday. Robert Bodin drove me south and along the coast to St Tropez, but the Brigitte Bardot set were screeching into the early hours and I couldn't get any English tea in the place. Instead, we did all the tourist spots as well. Villefranche when the French fleet was in, St Raphael, Cagnes, Antibes. At Vence, we joined the queue of trippers to see Picasso making ceramics in his studio — he looked like a Gila monster in shorts. He remembered me. In fact, Picasso had wanted to work with me but I was too young and too afraid of him — he had a lecherous look and I thought he would not be kind — in bed or at the easel.

At Menton, the harbour was dominated by the *Creole*, Stavros Niarchos's three-masted black yacht, then the world's most beautiful ship. In Juan-les-Pins, I had a platonic liaison with Tom, who came from north Paris. He tried to seduce me but I wasn't ready and explained my history. Tom was sweet and told me that he was separated from his wife, who lived on the other side of Juan. Later, I read that he'd stabbed his wife's lover to death outside La Vieille Colombieuse.

On Bastille Night, 4 July 1960, the club was booked solid. This is the night when France goes wild. *Wild*. Audrey and I caught the atmosphere and went straight to Le Bantu at 3am, my first night out in Paris since Casablanca. The Bluebell Girls, the Alaria Ballet, everyone was there, wound in streamers, high on champagne. But I still tired easily.

As I was leaving, Skippy tapped me on the shoulder. He was as skinny and speedy as ever, with a little golden moustache, and said, 'OK, tonight's the night. You're coming home with me.'

I said, 'Oh, Skippy, don't be ridiculous.'

'No, no, no. You're coming.'

'Skippy, I know what I promised but please, not yet.'

'Don't be chicken, honey, it doesn't suit you. You've got to find out sooner or later.'

'Well, bring a bottle…'

'There's plenty at my flat.'

I was a basket of nerves. Very gently, he undressed me. Despite the wine, I was tense.

'Come on, relax. I'm not going to hurt you. If I do, I won't insist.'

He made love to me so tenderly and afterwards asked, 'Was it OK?'

OK? I was sobbing and laughing. I couldn't stop. 'It's the happiest moment of my life!' I howled.

As we lay side by side, stroking each other, he said, 'Listen, honey.' The window was open. Cars hooting, fire crackers, shouting and singing in the streets. He led me to the window. The bars were buzzing and everywhere flags flew, rockets shot into the sky. 'Well, I'll be damned, they're celebrating the loss of your virginity.'

It was the most normal thing in the world. It was the magical moment. It was the most magical person. A wonderful friend. Very good-looking man and so funny and amusing. I couldn't stop crying.

He said, 'What are you crying for? This is absolutely marvellous.'

I said, 'I'm crying because I'm so happy. It's marvellous and I can't thank you enough for making it so easy for me.'

We never went to bed together again after that, but it was just a magical, magical moment. I still think of Skippy very fondly.

I was to make another dear friend through Toots Lockwood. True to her word, she told me Sarah Churchill was coming to meet me. As children, we had been brought up with two gods, God and Winston Churchill. Now I was to meet his daughter. I knew her story. The whole world did.

Towards the end of 1935, Sarah, then 21, the third of Winston Churchill's five children, persuaded her parents to allow her to go on the stage in the revue *Follow The Sun*. The star of the show was Vic Oliver, one of Britain's highest-paid entertainers, and a man with a liking for younger women, whom he was constantly taking under his wing.

He did not always have the best of intentions. Sarah, 16 years younger than him, caught his eye. In one scene, wearing a very short skirt and frilly knickers, she was part of a chorus line who presented their befrilled bottoms to the audience while singing, 'How low can a chorus girl go, before she is called a so-and-so?'

When Sarah told her parents that she wished to marry Oliver, they were appalled. And when Sarah took Oliver to meet her parents at Chartwell, the Churchills' magnificent home in Kent, Churchill refused to shake his hand. But Sarah was stubbornly set on marriage. While Churchill was on holiday in the South of

France, she fled to New York on board the *Bremen* hotly pursued on the *Queen Mary* by her brother Randolph, who said she was too young to know her own mind. He failed to persuade her of that, though. Vic Oliver married Sarah at New York City Hall on Christmas Day 1936. To Churchill's fury, the dissolute entertainer became his son-in-law. Vic Oliver only had $60 to his name when they were married – it was the kind of thing that impressed me.

With Toots, I met Sarah at the Hotel Bristol where the Churchill family usually stayed. Now aged about 45, she was a natural aristocrat with Titian hair and brilliant-green eyes emphasised by a green silk dress. 'How wonderful to meet you,' she said. 'Julia's told me so much I had to fly over and see for myself.'

I went all silly and said, 'I never thought a Churchill would ever travel ten feet to meet me.'

Sarah cured my shyness with that uniquely English charm, a combination of elegance and sauciness, innocence and worldliness. She had a light, fruity voice and used it to great effect without overdoing the theatricality. There was in her a streak of melancholy that all the Churchills had except Mary. Sarah's sister, Diana, committed suicide, and poor Randolph's life was no advert. Of Marigold, the one who died young, there was little mention.

It must have been oppressive to the point of despair, having so illustrious a parent. Perhaps that was why Winston detached himself from them, gave them total rope. Sarah and Julia were very luvvie, discussing the theatre, who was in what, who was getting good or bad notices. Sarah told me that in Hollywood she'd danced in a film with Fred Astaire, and was terribly proud of being a quarter American (through her grandmother Jenny Jerome, Lady Randolph Churchill).

Lunch was in a modest bistro in St Germain where Sarah was

known and treated like a significant deity. 'Whatever you're eating,' she said, 'we must have red wine – it's so full of goodness.' Sarah enjoyed goodness in her life. We lunched. Her plane was at 5pm and she was gone.

'Flying to Paris just for lunch – that's so stylish,' I said to Julia, for Sarah had made an enormous impression on me. With time, she was to teach me much about how to conduct myself in pubic. And how not to.

The sex, the wonderful new sensations to which Skippy had introduced me, I explored with a young Italian called Giancarlo. He was very vain in a simple-minded way, always smartly dressed; he was hopeless at conversation but tireless in love. I never discovered what he did for a living. He said he was kept by a woman. I was keeping myself, but within a few months I'd saved several hundred pounds. It was time to face England. Paris had been marvellous to me; I could never have earned the money that I did in any other city. And Le Carrousel had taught me much about the world, about celebrity, about how to – and how not to – treat other people. Everyone is different in some way. The thing is to understand, to make time for compassion.

As a new woman, in every sense, I was determined to go on to a different life. Marcel offered to double my wages, but money was no longer the important thing to me. What finally persuaded me to cut loose was Julia's offer to put me up temporarily at her flat in Dolphin Square in London. She came over to accompany me on the journey. We took sleeper berths on the *Fleche d'Argent*.

At Dover, I struck the customs desk as questionable – all in black, wearing dark glasses. The immigration officer looked at my passport. 'I'm sorry but I can't accept this as your picture.'

I started to panic.

'Take your glasses off,' he said.

Julia was behind me, blocking the view of the others in the queue, who were beginning to stare.

'This is *not* you – please take your hat off.' He was getting aggressive.

My long dark hair escaped like a waterfall and cascaded to my shoulders.

'I knew it,' he said in triumph.

The picture was six years old. I felt my legs going and held on to his desk, saying almost under my breath, 'A great deal has changed since that picture was taken.'

He looked at me long and hard, then suddenly his whole expression altered. 'Oh, oh, oh... I apologise, I'm so sorry, forgive me if I embarrassed you.' He took me by the arm and rushed Julia and I through.

I was in England, shaking from head to toe, but deliriously happy. I was a woman for the first time in the land of my birth.

Whatever next?

20
MODEL BEHAVIOUR

'Miss Caswell is an actress, a graduate of the
Copacabana School of Dramatic Arts.'
GEORGE SANDERS INTRODUCING MARILYN MONROE
IN ALL ABOUT EVE, 1950

Before the operation, the only people I knew were my family. I didn't have any good friends that I had to cope with, to explain what had happened to me. I didn't really have anybody other than Julia Lockwood – and she more than anyone knew what had happened. It was up to me, as a woman, to make a load of new friends. And I would have to introduce myself. But who as? I decided to change my name by deed poll. Legally, it had to be my full name.

Whenever I was out and about, people would always say, 'Oh, you're so bloody English.' I love maps. I read them like other people read a novel. I noted that there was an Ashley in practically every county in the British Isles, whether it be a village or a town or whatever, so I thought, 'What could be more English that that?' So that's why I chose it. I did want it to be as simple as possible. Always go that route. I could do nothing about my birth certificate. In the 20th century, although people could have their condition biologically explained, medically diagnosed and successfully treated, their transition from one sex to another had not taken place in the eyes of the law.

For £13, I became April Ashley. I still think it a good name, distinctive; the two 'A's place me at the top of invitation lists alphabetically arranged. And it's very easy to remember and pronounce: April Ashley.

Julia had a small flat, but she was away much of the time rehearsing *Peter Pan* at the Scala Theatre. She'd played Wendy twice – once to her mother's Peter, once to Sarah Churchill's. Now she was Peter himself and looked it, with her thin boyish body, and honey hair sliced in to the neck.

Sarah had a flat on the riverside of Dolphin Square. When the porter discovered that she and I were friends, he started to ring me up. 'Miss Churchill's gone out again – could you help?'

I'd go in search because she could get up to tricks after a drink or six. Once I found her directing traffic on the Embankment in her nightie.

Everyone found me interesting; I was the new girl on the block. But how could I make 'interesting' profitable? At night, Julia often returned with members of the cast. One evening I was asked, 'What are you? An actress or a model?'

I didn't know what to say. 'She's a model,' said Julia, with a nod towards me.

Why not? Modelling was quicker than acting – and I'd always liked things to happen fast. A photographer printed up a box of test shots, I asked which was the best agency in London, was told Cherry Marshall's and went along. Miss Marshall asked me to twirl.

'You're a natural,' she said and took me on the spot. This was a surprise, because modelling was far more formal then than it is now; training was considered essential, but I'd learn to pepper my conversation with the magic word – 'Paris'.

'Paris, yes, I've been working in Paris for the past four years,

Miss Marshall, that's why you don't know me – Paris and Milan – appearing for Schiaparelli, that sort of thing…'

Two days later, the agency rang and asked me to go in the following morning. My first booking. I was up at dawn, painting a masterpiece. When I walked into Miss Marshall's office, she was sitting upright and immobile. 'Is it true, April, that you worked at Le Carrousel?'

It was as if a statue had spoken! I felt sick. Yes, it was true.

'Then I must tell you, I can't have you on my books.' She wouldn't reveal the source of her intelligence.

I had no time to nurture hurt feelings. I'd taken on a small top-floor flat of my own at 14 Harrington Gardens, a house in South Kensington filled with Persian students. I needed to pay the rent. And to eat. I scooted around to Fashion Models, which was run by Signon, a Eurasian who had been the Queen Mother's favourite mannequin. Despite her penchant for cursing, Signon was graciousness itself, jet hair sleeked into a chignon and always pinned with an orchid, fine pearls at the neck. I was put on the books.

Fashion in 1960 was only just coming out of the rigorous Barbara Golan look, dresses with 20 yards of material in the skirt, stiff underskirts, dozens of matching accessories. Signon warned me of the risks of the modelling business, amphetamine slimming pills followed by too much to drink in order to relax, the perils of the casting couch. I could cope with all that, but what I liked least were the auditions. A mass of girls would clog a hallway until a harridan came along and shouted, 'Throw up the bars, let them through one by one.'

The big models – Sandra Paul, Bronwen Pugh, Grace Coddington, Sue Lloyd – were only the crest of a neurotic, hard-working groundswell, every one of whom had to be up early and perfectly groomed in case a call came through.

Our heroine was Fiona Campbell-Walter, who in 1956 had married Baron Heinrich von Thyssen, a magnate whose family fortune had survived the war more or less intact. Marriage was the way up and out of the fantasy of fashion. With marriage, Maggie Simmonds turned into the Countess of Kimberley. Sandra Paul became Mrs Robin Douglas-Home, and later married Michael Howard, one-time Home Secretary and Tory Party leader. Bronwen Pugh became Viscountess Astor and endured the Profumo Affair – her estate being where the War Minister first encountered Christine Keeler; in the aftermath, her husband Bill Astor took a liking to Mandy Rice-Davies. I rather liked Mandy. It was in response to Bill's denial of sex with her that she uttered the fabulous line: 'He would, wouldn't he?'

I, too, was to be dragged into the generally absurd antics that were to help bring down the last, arguably, aristocratic British government. Maybe David Cameron will preside over another one. I have a special interest in that. Also, I understood perfectly what poor Harold Macmillan meant when asked what you can't control in life: 'Events, dear boy, events.'

In tandem with my fledgling modelling career, I was carrying on a love affair. With Joey. I had contacted him through his parents. He was living in Wapping and invited me to a party there to meet his wife. She was small and sweet. To Joey, I said, 'You're looking well.'

We began seeing each other again and made love to Renata Tebaldi records, arias from *La Bohème* and *Manon Lescaut*. It was divine. Mother Nature had equipped Joey magnificently for love, and I felt it fully for the first time. The way I'd always wanted to feel it.

I had Joey to sort out. The more I loved being with Joey, the more heartbreaking it was when he left. I wanted to do things with him. He was quite unlike anybody else I knew. But Joey belonged to no one but himself; it was one of the most attractive things about him, that wilfulness.

Joey could do anything with me, so I knew I had to be extra strong, make a decision and act on it, or else we should drift in

Top left: A face in the crowd at St Theresa's Primary School, Liverpool: George Jamieson on V.E. Day, 1945.

Top right: Aged thirteen with my brother Ivor, nine, and sister Marjorie, seven, outside our house.

Bottom left: To be or not to be? Playing Bassanio, aged fourteen, in 'The Merchant of Venice'.

Bottom right: My expression says it all – a very confused fifteen-year-old schoolboy.

Les-Lee

Coccinelle

Audrey

It's astonishing what a little make-up can do! The two faces of Le Carrousel – and a rare programme for the show. Coccinelle was the undisputed star of the show.

Amanda Lear

A Mamma et Martin
en leur souhaitant un
joyeux Nöel
Peki

Kiki M

TONI APRIL

Exclusive never-before seen pictures of Kiki Moustique (*above left*),
Amanda Lear/Peki and me in my days as Toni April, during the 'pache dance'
with Novak. I'd forgotten all about these photographs and only found them in
an old trunk towards the end of 2005.

I did like to be by the seaside. Pre-op at Juan-le-Pains on the Cote d'Azur with a friend and (*below*) Bambi.

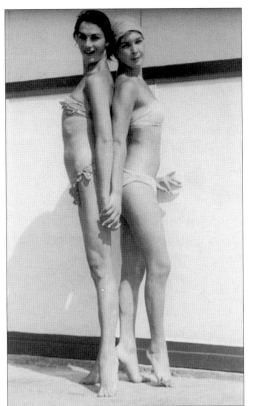

The summer of 1959, a time of confusion as well as sunshine. I do adore the South of France and these pre-op photographs bring back so many memories. The bottom picture is of me with Martine Zacher.

A model life. On the town (*top left*), in Paris with Les-Lee (*top right*) and early days in the fashion business.

Top: With Bambi (*middle*) and Martine (*right*) on a night out with the boys. Wide-eyed at the glamour of it all, with Kiki Moustique at La Poerta del Ora, Milan, in 1959 (*below left*). Still in Italy, with Peki/Amanda Lear, on the left, attacking pasta in Milan (*below right*).

Peek-a-boo!
Thank heaven for
little girls: this is me
at Le Carrousel in
Paris in 1958.

no-man's-land forever. I decided to finish it, to see him no more. I deliberately took another lover. He could not compete with Joey deep down, of course, which is exactly what I wanted:

I was introduced to him by an Australian model and knew at once that he was the one to refresh and simplify the air. Apart from being very good-looking, he was uncomplicated company. I took him along to Signon, who said, 'What a corker!' He didn't have a work-permit but she still found him plenty to do. He became so successful that he gave up modelling, married an English girl and bought a hotel in Austria.

My very first job was a three-day fashion show in the Stratford Court Hotel in Oxford Street for a manufacturer from the north of England. Oh my. It was brown twin-sets, grey trews, plaid skirts and pleated shirt-waisters – country-bumpkin couture in the first flush of manmade fibres.

Signon trained me in how to show off a hat, how to throw off a coat or jacket – it was essential to look down at the lapel and feel it compulsively with your fingers, apprising the audience of its fetishistic sumptuousness before slipping it off your shoulders, catching it by the tab, standing immobile for a moment with one foot pointing out, before turning and walking off.

Photo sessions I had least flair for, because I was used to an audience and didn't know how to play to a machine. I tended to freeze. The wonderful Terence Donovan once photographed me in a poncho for a cigar advertisement, and in order to give me a surprised expression he had two cowboys fire blanks across my face with six-shooters. Terry was already very successful by then; roly-poly belly, a Rolls-Royce and a studio in Yeoman's Row, the first of the new breed of self-made photographers along with David Bailey and Terry O'Neill.

Sometimes I froze. Literally. I became one of *Vogue* magazine's favourite girls for underwear, photographed by Duffy or Honeywell. Bronwen Pugh had announced to me,

143

'Darling, don't do underwear. You'll never get back into clothes.'

It didn't bother me. I mentioned this to Signon, who said, 'I'm inclined to agree with you, April. Who gives a fuck when you're being paid eight guineas an hour? And they've booked you for the whole day.'

That led to a soap advertisement with nothing on at all, except a towel strategically draped. They stood me in a bath that was so slippery I kept falling over. Instead of running to help, they all gasped and turned away every time I went flying. They were only trying to preserve my modesty, but I was black and blue by the end of the session.

Television commercials were more prestigious, because you moved. This form of advertising was still new to England and they were hopelessly amateurish. Arrid Underarm Spray Deodorant; the rulebook did not allow me to be filmed in the fully frontal act of spraying my armpits. They shot my underarm, then cut to my hand going 'psh! psh!' with the canister against a blank background. Armpit and hand could not figure in the same shot because it was considered obscene; I feel that the way they did it was far more salacious, because of the prurience it implied. What a strange time it was all these worlds ago, worlds that knew nothing of my secret.

I'd never earned more for a day's work. More than £160 – with a free carton of underarm deodorant thrown in. Stardom at last. I daydreamed then of using the TV commercials as a step towards the movies. I have always loved films; from my early days, they were an escape.

When the word went out that United Artists were looking for six beautiful women for *The Road to Hong Kong*, filming at Shepperton Studios, every girl in London with a portfolio put on her best sling-backs and marched towards Mayfair.

A *Road* picture. With Dorothy Lamour. And Bing Crosby. And Bob Hope.

Would he remember me from Paris?

21

THE THREE AMIGOS

'The average Hollywood film star's ambition is to be admired by an American, courted by an Italian, married to an Englishman and have a French boyfriend.'

KATHARINE HEPBURN (1954)

I was early for the audition and went for a cup of coffee. The steam went up my nose, I sneezed violently; one of my eyelashes flew off and landed in the breakfast of a man opposite. Happily, I followed the Boy Scout Movement motto – Be Prepared. I always carried spare eyelashes.

There must have been more than 200 models and would-be actresses – even proper actresses – frantically retouching themselves from compacts and with lipsticks. The noise was awful and I almost turned back but I couldn't afford to waste the taxi fare.

The six beauties were supposedly Chinese, but fidelity was not the prime consideration. A scout was scrutinising from the gallery and I was one of those summoned upstairs, past a line of put-out noses, to the drawing room. This was first base.

A short dark-haired girl stood beside me, suckling on cigarette after cigarette. 'Are you an actress, then?' she said in a madly affected voice.

'No, I'm a model.'

'I'm an actress and actresses need work. I've been trained to be an actress,' said Sarah Miles, for it was she. This, of course, was before her international acclaim a couple of years later in *The Servant*.

'We're all here for the same reason.'

'This is actress territory.'

I told her to drop dead, and went in.

'She's very tall,' I heard someone say.

'Lovely face, nice figure,' said another.

'And divine legs,' I added, to help them along.

'Say that again!'

'Say what?'

'Is that voice real?'

'What do you mean?'

'We've got to give her a speaking part. Let's see those legs, then.'

Damn the legs. A speaking part. What I had to do was ask an imaginary Bob Hope to 'Follow me, sir, please'. I said it half a dozen times.

'We'd love you to have a speaking part, but we must see your walk first. Pretend that clock's Bob Hope and approach it.'

'Follow... me, sir, please.'

'She hasn't got a very sexy walk.'

'Would you do it again – and make it sexier.'

'Follow me... sir – please.'

'I think she's got a sexy walk. Kinda snooty sexy.'

'No, I don't think she has.'

'What do you think, Lorna?'

'Follow me, sir... please.'

The hooker's roll didn't come naturally to me, and even in

make-up I didn't look remotely Chinese, so this helluva speaking part went to an Oriental girl. But I was in the movies. Well, the movie. I was cast as one of the six beauties. We had to geisha around Bing Crosby and Bob Hope in a futuristic hideaway and my special task was to feed Bing marshmallows with a pair of tongs.

We were collected at five in the morning for make-up. There was a fabulous hairpiece sitting in the dressing room. It was huge and matched my hair perfectly.

'That's a super hairpiece,' I said. 'Can I wear it? It would be fantastic down my back.'

'I'm sorry, Miss Ashley,' said the hairdresser, 'that's Miss Collins's fringe.'

Joan Collins was, in effect, the star because Dorothy Lamour was making only a guest appearance in this picture. My greatest fear was that Bob Hope would remember me from Paris and make something of it. He did remember me, but said nothing publicly. Maybe he was recalling his time in the French capital making 1958's *Paris Holiday*. The idea was that an American comedian met a French one in Paris. The great French comic Fernandel co-starred with Hope. At one point, they posed for a publicity photograph with one of the 'girls' from Le Carrousel. They all had their arms around each other. All three of them had erections.

Certainly, Hope never even hinted to me about our having had breakfast together in Paris. But he must have told Bing Crosby about it. The lecherous crooner was always coming over to me and singing 'April in Paris'. I would sing back to him 'Bing in Shepperton'.

It was fun, but there was always the anxiety of being exposed and ridiculed. And I'm sure that happened with *The Road to Hong Kong*, but I suspect it was a jealous performer rather than Hope or Crosby who gave me away. For, after all the raving about me, the small part I'd been given was handed to another girl. I was

147

still in the film but I had my back to the camera all the time. You see me for one second. I had a tiny bit of revenge – more like a bit of triumph than revenge. There is one point where we girls have to carry Bob Hope out of the room on our shoulders. I was at the back and I did the unforgivable. I looked straight into the camera, threw my head back and laughed. If you blink, you miss it. That was my tiny little triumph there. I was determined they were going to see my face.

Hollywood was one thing, but live fashion shows were my bread-and-butter and the best of these were for Roter Models, owned by Mr and Mrs Schroter, a Jewish couple from Vienna. Their top designer was very highly strung, so it all came pouring out in those crazy frocks. He had every design book in Europe and he'd take features from Chanel, Givenchy, Cardin, Courrèges, push them together and then EXPLODE them. Today they'd be selling them in the streets or off stalls in Hong Kong. Yet, like most clothes designed by men, they were wonderful for wearing on marble staircases, impossible to shop in.

The atmosphere at Roter Models was unusually good natured. Conversation was very open in the dressing rooms. Women, when they forgather, can be quite as filthy as men. A German model, Hildegard, complained, 'My husband, he fuck me every morning before work, every night after work. I'm so sore, so fed up with it; he have such big dick.'

'How big?' I asked, filing a nail, one exaggerated eyebrow raised.

'I don't know. Eeenormous!'

'Get a tape-measure out tonight,' said another.

The other girls must have overheard because the next morning all of them had measured their husbands and lovers. Hildegard got more sympathy after this. Her English husband was just too *eenormous*...

My most important show was a charity at the Dorchester Hotel in front of Alice, Duchess of Gloucester. I was dressed like a Christmas trees in Kuchinksy jewels and draped in Deanfield furs. I was accompanied by two detectives to and from the ballroom. I asked how much I was worth. 'At the moment you're wearing over £150,000 worth of swag,' he said, sounding like a *Carry On* movie.

As I was the only dark model, they gave me the only white mink. 'How stupid,' I said, 'I haven't got a black skirt to show it off.' I borrowed a pencil one, which was far too tight. When you do a royal show, you ignore everyone else, walk right up to the Royals, do a deep curtsey and trail round the riffraff afterwards. With my legs in bondage, it was bad enough trying to walk, but when I curtseyed there was a long ripping noise muffled by mink. My first thought was: 'Oh my God, I bet the Duchess thinks I've broken wind.' My second thought was: 'I can't get up.'

I seemed to be stuck there. While I made rapid calculations, the Duchess must have thought I was seeking some kind of acknowledgement, because she finally muttered, 'Yes, it's very nice, dear.' It broke the ice. I pushed hard, shot upwards, drew my legs smartly together, and made a controlled exit.

Charity balls were very common. Signon would be given a bunch of passes and there we'd be, looking ravishing scattered around the newspaper columns. At the Bubbly Ball for Cancer Research, Lance Callingham, Lady Docker's son, trod on my foot. It didn't matter because the organisers had laid on 'foot revivers' – electric plates that warmed your feet back to life so that the dancing need never end. But the reason I recall this occasion was that it was when the scales dropped from my eyes about the press. I had assumed, halfwit that I was, that whatever appeared in the newspapers was more or less true. At the ball, a gossip columnist asked me for my name. 'Agatha Christie,' I said. My picture appeared in *Tatler* and, under it, Miss A Christie.

I was growing in confidence. With each job, I made further advances in my campaign against shyness, learned more and found myself entering a brand-new social world. A world of actors and aristocrats. All of whom desired the company, and possibly more, of the extraordinary model April Ashley. The attention only made me more fearful of discovery, yet determined to flourish as a woman.

22

ANOTHER OSCAR

'It's show time, folks!'

ROY SCHEIDER, ALL THAT JAZZ (1979)

L ondon was beginning to swing in the first couple of years of
the 1960s, but there were still formalities that people
observed. Peter Finch wasn't keen on them.

I'd become great pals with the award-winning actor. He was
born in England but had spent years in Australia before returning
to become a sought-after film star. When I met him, he had
recently completed *The Trials of Oscar Wilde*. None of the
mannerisms of the movie had stayed with him. His come on was:
'You don't beat about the bush in the Bush.'

Despite this, he was charming. 'Doing anything tonight?' he'd
said over the phone. 'Come on then, let's go to Winston's and
push the boat out, Danny La Rue's appearing there.' Back then,
nightclubs always wound up at 4 or 5am, so it was late when
Finchie dropped me back again at Harrington Gardens. He
decided he was coming in and paid off the cab.

My landlady was Turkish and specialised in Moslem
gentlewomen studying English; she had a house rule: no men

after 11pm. But Finchie, boozed to Brisbane and back, was making such a hullabaloo on the steps I thought I'd better smuggle him in before there was a scene.

Once in my room he threw off his clothes and said, 'Right, take yours off now and get down on the bed so I can screw you.'

'No, you won't, Finchie.'

He nodded.

'Stop nodding!'

He bulged his eyes instead and his tongue fell out like a furry animal. I did my usual trick and pointed between his legs. 'You couldn't, even if you wanted to. Get out before you get me evicted.'

We started laughing and he crawled round the floor, pulling on his jacket, trousers and shoes. Everything else was stuffed into pockets and he said goodnight, blowing kisses and bowing from the waist like a cartoon admiral.

His exit was followed by a sequence of wince-inducing crashes. I rushed on to the landing. Finchie was sprawling at the bottom of the stairs with a nosebleed. 'Shh, shh, shh,' he whispered at the top of his voice and I heard the door close.

At 9am precisely the next morning, there was a knock on the door. The landlady, a spinster and religious maniac, stood in the doorway, an expression of utmost disquiet on her face. 'Do you know anything about these?' She held between finger and thumb a pair of blue knickers as perhaps she had once held a dead rat in Istanbul. Finchie's Y-fronts.

I was persuaded to seek other accommodation. I moved to an airy flat near Gloucester Road Tube in Emperor's Gate with another model, Della Young. My social life was buzzing, just like the switchboard in my talent-agency days. And once again Duncan Melvin was in my life. I was walking down Walton Street in Chelsea, when I fell over Duncan. He clapped his pink hands, wrote down my telephone number and invited me to a buffet Sunday lunch in his house in St Leonard's Terrace.

The lunch was in honour of Vittorio De Sica, who had won an Oscar the previous year for directing Sophia Loren in *Two Women*. Buffets were very much the vogue at the time. They'd just been discovered. London was suddenly full of people walking about rooms with plates of food in their hands, whereas before they would have been bolted to tables. The informality of the Sixties had begun.

Duncan gave so many parties. At one, a young man kept me supplied with drinks. He was very stylish, and wore a flowing neck scarf. I asked him if he was an actor. 'No, I'm not,' he replied, 'but come out to dinner anyway. My name's Tim.'

He wished first to change, so we went to his house in Wilton Row, off Belgrave Square. A manservant opened the door and said, 'Good evening, m'Lord.'

'Good evening, George. We'll have a bottle of champagne in the garden, please.'

Lord Who? It was as if I had strayed into the pages of a Georgette Heyer.

'Wander around and have a look while I take a shower.'

I stepped into a music room with a grand piano in the centre and blooming daffodils visible through the windows. Some writing paper lay open on a desk and I tiptoed over. It was embossed in copperplate: Lord Timothy Willoughby de Eresby. All those exotic twirls of letters, those hanging 'y's like licking tongues. He returned and I asked who he was.

'You saw the writing paper on the escritoire. My father is Lord Ancaster of Drummond Castle and Grimsthorpe, quondam Lord Great Chamberlain of England. It'll all be mine one day. Let's go to the Stork Club. I'll get your coat.'

He was fun to be with. Al Burnett's Stork Club was a popular retreat yet, because of the childish licensing laws, champagne was served illegally and, they hoped, anonymously in plain-glass water jugs to people like Tim whom it would have been counterproductive to refuse. There wasn't a better escort in London.

The next morning, my landlady brought me a bouquet of yellow rosebuds bearing an inscription 'From Big Tim' – the conceited ox. It was the beginning of a close and very dear friendship that endured until his final, mysterious disappearance.

Sudden disappearances were one of Tim's hobbies, and he would as abruptly rematerialise with tales of the South China Sea or Chichen Itza at sunrise or a fancy-dress ball on the Grand Canal in Venice. His skin seemed permanently tanned. He loved to take liberties with his wardrobe; sometimes he affected odd socks – one green, one black – or would arrive in full evening dress with fresh dandelions in his buttonhole.

He was one of three investors – the others were Bernard van Custsem and Simon Fraser – who guaranteed the rent of 44 Berkeley Square so that John Aspinall and his gentleman business partner John 'Burkie' Burke could establish the Clermont Club, for a time one of the most famous gambling clubs in the world. I met Aspinall, who I didn't much care for, and also Lord Lucan – who, like Tim, was also to vanish off the face of the earth. Lucan was very formal and polite. He made me uneasy. Often, Tim took me to the Clermont and to Annabel's, the basement nightclub run by Mark Birley and named after his wife who eventually became involved with that loveable rascal, the financier Jimmy Goldsmith. They were quite a bunch. It was there that I once again saw Françoise Sagan and also met Ian Fleming, who certainly gave me the once- or twice-over.

I was to meet so many people with and through Tim. He had fallen madly in love with me. We always did such grand things. He was wildly liked and sought after, a real gentleman. Duncan Melvin told Tim all about me and afterwards Tim called me his Bettina, a reference to the Aly Khan's mistress who, by staying in the background, outlasted all the wives.

Debutantes were forever at Tim's heels. They approached me for advice: 'How can I catch him?'

'By just being yourself,' I always replied, but that presupposed that you know what you are, and none of them did.

Tim was a bedroom nomad and stuck nowhere. He was always saying he would have married me if I could have had children.

Tim used to screw everybody. It never bothered me. I was still at the stage where I didn't have the confidence. I'd only just become a woman. I didn't feel I had the right to be jealous. He and I slept together often, but we lunched at the Mirabelle more frequently than we made love; Beluga caviar, an iced bucket of it left in the middle of the table with a scoop, and champagne – perfectly simple, never anything else. In the evenings, he took me greyhound racing at the White City Stadium with Alan Clark's brother Colin.

It was his style often not to say where we were going. One night, we turned up at a grand porch in Hyde Park Gardens. I was appalled to see the other guests arriving in tiaras and tails, because I too had stunning things to parade in. Luckily, I'd thrown on a little black cocktail number that you could take anywhere.

At the top of the staircase, Tim said, 'April, may I present you to the Earl and Countess of Perth.'

Butlers, footmen, dinner, cabaret, a small orchestra for waltzes and fox-trots.

'Just having a few friends in,' said Lady Perth. 'So glad you could join us.'

After dinner, a group of men collected to smoke and drink in the library and I found myself among them. Lady Perth, Nancy Fincke from New York City as was, popped her head round the door and said, 'April, wouldn't you like to powder your nose?'

'Oh no, Lady Perth, I'd much rather stay with the men.'

I was quite taken aback when they all burst out laughing. Only

Tim realised that I hadn't intentionally cracked a joke. What did I know of women withdrawing?

And I was a woman. But I'd been born male. In all these social circumstances, there was always the fear of discovery. And though I moved unsuspected through the saloons of wealth and rank, my voice was always noticed. At one party, I tripped over a girl and the two of us went bumping down the stairs until we reached the bottom.

'Sorry,' I said, when we regained consciousness.

'By Jove,' she growled, 'you can't possibly have a voice deeper than mine.'

'Oh yes, I can,' I replied, getting as low as possible in an attempt to out-husk her. But I don't think I could. Her voice was like a steamroller driving down an unmade road.

She turned out to be Pauline Tennant, Hermione Baddeley's daughter by David Tennant, and we slung champagne down each other's throat for the rest of the night. Hermione Gingold, of course, has a voice deeper than mine, but that is because as a girl her vocal cords sprouted nodules and she didn't have them scraped.

When Tim had the blues, which was about once a week, he'd invite me round to Wilton Row to play psychiatrists and have a quiet cup of tea. It was here that I properly met his elder sister, Lady Jane Willoughby, herself very intense, and her boyfriend, one of the most exceptional and prolific artists of the 20th and 21st century: Lucian Freud. Far more entertaining that his psycho-babbling grandfather. I'd much rather have been painted by Lucian than Dalí. That *would* have been fame and fortune.

These afternoons, our teas together were more precious to me than all the grand parties squashed together. Sometimes we'd go off for shepherd's pie round the corner at the Grenadier pub and watch the young guardsmen trading with the queens, which made Tim laugh and jollied him up.

Dear Julia Lockwood and Sarah Churchill were seriously involved with the theatre and moved in a completely different set when they moved at all. Julia took me to see her mother's new house in Richmond. It was the first time I ever saw a mink bedspread. It was blue mink, as deep blue as some of Tim's moods. Tim had a love of pleasure made all the richer because of the sense of tragedy and trouble around him.

There were difficult times to face for us all. I hadn't expected my life to get even more dramatic.

23

DEAR MARGE

*'I've been everywhere and done everything. I've eaten
caviar at Cannes, sausage rolls at the dogs. I've played
baccarat at Biarritz, and darts with the rural dean.
What is there left for me but marriage?'*

Iris Matilda Henderson (Margaret Lockwood),
The Lady Vanishes (1938)

I've said I followed the Boy Scouts' motto of Be Prepared. Well,
not for what happened next.

I'd had two blind dates in my life and they were truly
horrendous. I had sworn never, never again. But, for my old
friend and mentor Les Lee, I relented. A friend of his called
Louise said another friend was eager to meet me. Now, Louise,
although he had a woman's passport, was a middle-aged male
transvestite who had fathered children.

I explained that I'd given up blind dates with weirdos, but
Louise was persistent and I agreed on condition that the
appointment be for lunch, so that I could arrange an afternoon
audition as a getaway, and that lunch be at the Caprice.

I'd longed to eat at this famous restaurant ever since I'd seen
the wonderful Armenian millionaire Nubar Gulbenkian's car

outside it. This car, registration NG 5, was a customised London cab rebuilt by Rolls-Royce on the chassis of a London taxi, with carriage lamps and wickerwork panels let into the bodywork. I'd often see it around London. Gulbenkian had commissioned it because it would be tall enough for him to sit inside without removing his top hat. The master of quotations, his line about the taxi was: 'They tell me it turns on a sixpence, whatever that is.'

With my own unique logic, I reckoned that any man who would lunch with me at the Caprice could not be too bad. 'Don't worry about recognising him,' said Louise. 'I've given him dozens of photographs of you. He knows every hair on your head.'

On 19 November 1960, deliberately late, I went whizzing through the revolving doors and was immediately in a sea of expensive hats. The first person I recognised was Marjorie Proops, the *Daily Mirror*'s Agony Aunt. If only I had talked to her first. But a voice said, 'April? My name is Frank. What would you like to drink?' Frank was tall and thin and in his early forties. He was most considerate. I had a champagne cocktail, had another, and we went to eat. Frank had the same texture as Tim and that lot. The upper-class thing, quite at home in the Caprice. But why wouldn't he give me his surname?

Like Peter Finch, Frank was a natural charmer, skilful at putting one at one's ease. He was handsome in a bony-faced way. Soon we were lunching once a week, then twice a week, then every other day, and always at the Caprice, always very politely. This couldn't be all. Eventually it came: 'I think I can trust you, April. I want to tell you something. If I don't tell somebody, I'll go round the bend.'

'You like dressing in women's clothes,' I said.

'How did you know?'

'I guessed.'

'For years I've been doing it. There's a male brothel, I pay the boys to dress me up, then masturbate me. But now, here's the point, since I've been seeing you I haven't done it or wanted to. I think you've cured me. That's meant to be a compliment. It's something to do with knowing you were a boy, that you've had the operation, that it's a reality I can't compete with. You've stopped my pendulum swinging.'

It was the first time I'd heard about his pendulum. Frank explained that, having been brought up in a world full of grandfather clocks, it was the nearest he could come to describing the motion his personality sometimes took. Usually he was fairly normal – a job in the City, a healthy chauvinistic attitude towards the weaker sex – then out of the blue: SWING! He wanted to be a woman, to bind his hips in chiffon and sashay down to the boys in the brothel – 'those monsters', he called them. He was unable to resolve his conflict by surrendering to it and so make his life more tolerable. Until he met me, he said.

'My name isn't Frank, of course. It's Arthur.' Which sounded even more ridiculous. 'The Honourable Arthur Cameron Corbett, actually.'

Another bloody aristocrat!

'I want to tell you everything so that you'll understand my problem. My father's a Scotsman called Lord Rowallan. He used to be the Chief Scout. At the moment, he's the Governor of Tasmania. I'm his heir. My elder brother was killed in action in 1944. You can imagine the dreadful pressure on me never to do anything untoward. My father sees it as his duty to maintain a high moral tone. He would go bananas if he knew the real me.

'I went to Eton and to Balliol College, Oxford. My son Johnny is at Eton now. My wife's name is Eleanor. She's also from Scotland. We get on, but it's not what you'd call a passionate marriage – she lets me once a week, and that's my lot. I've three daughters too and we all live in Hampstead with a nanny, a gardener and a maid. Am I boring you?'

'Only a little bit.' He wasn't in the least; I was absolutely riveted, but I thought the kindest thing I could do was pretend that none of it was so very special.

The family's money came from Brown & Polson's Cornflour. Arthur's grandfather, Archibald, the 1st Baron, had married it in the form of Alice Polson. In consequence, the 2nd Baron, Arthur's father, had been desperately straight. Arthur's mother, Gwyn, was the sister of Jo Grimond, the one-time Liberal Party leader.

The family house was Rowallan Castle, an ugly Victorian heap near Kilmarnock with 7,000 acres. He had three brothers and a sister but the only member of the family he could really talk to was his aunt Elsie, a spinster of mannish appearance.

I told him I was having an affair with Tim Willoughby. Arthur was furious – and suddenly puritanical. He had rose-tinted vision of women, and put them on a pedestal, even when trying to be one himself.

'There aren't many 26-year-old virgins around any more. What do you expect me to do?'

'Marry him.'

Young as I was, and crazy as I was about Tim, I was totally pragmatic. 'Don't be foolish. Tim doesn't want to marry me; he wants an heir.'

'What would you say if I said I've fallen in love with you?' he said.

Not long after, Arthur rang me in the evening, which was unusual for him. Eleanor was having a fit. 'I've told her everything. I had to, darling.' The only thing between Arthur and me had been the lunch table, the talk. What was this *everything*? 'I told her I've been seeing you and I've told her who you are. I've told her about the women's clothes and the brothel boys. Once I started there was no convenient place to stop, I had to go on.'

Eleanor knew of Arthur's transvestite idiosyncrasy. She'd even zipped him up a few times. But she'd thought it was all in the past. Arthur said she wanted to meet me. This was something I hadn't expected. She obviously had guts, and I admired her even before I met her. Of course, I had nothing to be ashamed of. I'd never misbehaved with him. I'd never done anything with him. I'd never even held his hand. When we said goodbye, he always kissed me on the cheek. I had nothing to be ashamed of and felt I could face her.

Eleanor, née Boyle, was a cousin of the Earl of Glasgow. Her mother was born Mary Mackie, daughter of Sir Peter Mackie, the whisky baronet, and Eleanor was very rich in her own right. They were waiting for me at the Caprice. She was about my height, several years younger than Arthur, with masses of red hair, and dressed in Balmain. She was very Scottish looking. She was very nervous too. I felt a sham trying to convince her that Arthur was only a friend with a problem, when, in fact, without anyone wishing it, our lunches together had triggered in him something that meant disaster for her.

Eleanor was an overcontrolled woman and kept her passions hidden. Just before we went into lunch I said, 'I'm just going to pop to the loo.'

Eleanor said, 'Do you mind if I come with you?'

'No, Eleanor,' I replied, 'come on down.'

We went down to the loo together, and the moment we got in there, she fell apart. She grabbed my hand so hard I was in agony. She said, 'He's in love with you. You've got to help me save my marriage. We have four children.'

'Eleanor,' I replied, 'you have nothing to fear from me. I'm not in love with your husband. To me he's just a man I met through some strange person. I don't know anything about your husband.'

'Do go on seeing him if it stops him going off for the other thing,' she told me. 'The thought of that... I can't bear it.'

Over lunch, it was arranged that I should visit them in Hampstead on Sunday, and meet the children. The point of this was a hope that, if I could be somehow built into the pattern of their life, albeit discreetly and to one side, it might prevent the collapse of the family. What an extraordinary idea that was. And how forward thinking, how *modern* in concept for all these years ago. Eleanor was quite a woman.

I went for tea at the large undistinguished house in Wildwood Road, which overlooked Hampstead Heath. On the dot of 4 o'clock the door was thrown open and two nannies escorted four children in. Three little girls and a boy. The girls curtsied and the boy bowed. They were dressed in beautiful gowns.

I thought how cold everything was. Everything was so formal – and where was all the life in the children? I asked Eleanor, 'Can I take the children on the Heath for a little run after tea?'

The children immediately joined in with, 'Oh, Mummy, please, please, please.'

I took them on the Heath and before too long we were playing leapfrog and having a whale of a time. When we returned, Sarah asked, 'Oh, Mummy, can April come and live with us? We've had such fun.'

I went a few times and every time I went, of course, the same thing would happen. 'Oh please, Mummy, can April come and live with us?'

'Oh, Mummy, I love April – can she come and live with us?'

Eleanor must have been in turmoil inside.

Johnny didn't take to me very much. In fact, I got the impression that he thoroughly detested me. Perhaps he understood what was going to happen. He suffered much at school later on, as did his sisters. Tim was away, so once again I had no one to confide in. Eleanor went off to Amsterdam with the children and her concerns.

She'd given Arthur permission to take me out in the evenings. We went to The 400, the most respectable club I could think of. Princess Margaret and Billy Wallace had made it smart in the

1950s, but now it was coming to the end of its days. We talked. Inside, I knew that this was where I should get off, wish him well and hope that he would sort out his life in a way that didn't include me. But at the time I was going through acute anxieties of my own, which clouded my judgement. The chief bliss for a transsexual is to be regarded as a normal woman; the horror, to be outed as a 'freak'.

My true identity was not at this time generally known. Modelling London knew, to some degree. One evening at Roter Models, we had our feet up on the wall to reduce the swelling from walking up and down on carpet all day. All the models seemed to have problems. One was terribly in debt; one was hooked on pills, another on drink. Hildegard had her hubby's dimensions to haunt her.

Pauline Moore was beside me. Her boyfriend, Sid, was much older than she was and the age difference was a great worry to her. Maybe she thought she was a victim of gerontophilia, like the David Walliams character in *Little Britain*. A surprising number of people are. I decided to cheer her up. 'You think you've got it rough? Listen to me. I have news.'

Her feet immediately came down from the wall and she sat up. And I told her about my sex-transformation.

She gave me a wonderful reply: 'It's the loveliest thing I ever heard.'

Of course, some people in London did know exactly who I was. Or, rather, had been. There was my society crowd and also the more raffish of London – which, you must always remember, was a long way off from being the great metropolis of the 21st century. It was still something of a village and you could scream across town in 20 minutes. News, of course, travelled faster.

There were problems, like my time on *The Road to Hong Kong*. There were other hiccups too. Some might have called it hysteria. But there's no gain with hysterics.

24

HOLD THE FRONT PAGE!

'Christianity will go. It will vanish and shrink.
I needn't argue with that; I'm right and I will be
proved right. We're more popular than Jesus now.'
JOHN LENNON ON THE FAME OF THE BEATLES,
QUOTED IN THE EVENING STANDARD, LONDON, MARCH 1966

Someone earned a fiver to turn me into a freak show. How cheap it is to be betrayed.

It cost me £13 to become April Ashley. The then *Sunday People* newspaper paid £8 less to the person who 'outed' me. I metamorphosed into the equivalent of a circus attraction. I felt like a mutation, someone conjured up by PT Barnum. All for £5.

Overnight, I became a huge personality, a celebrity. Everybody recognised me. Everybody wanted to meet me. Oh my, people wanted to meet me. But not to have tea, or a glass of champagne and a chat. They wanted to stare. Even The Beatles had had a chance to get used to the idea of what was coming. Not me.

It was a Saturday and Della was away. There was an unexpected knock at the door. I opened it ajar and, as a man applied pressure from the other side, slammed it shut. I had no idea who he was, but he had the sinister aura of the suede shoe about him. Certainly, his foot was in my door.

'My name's Roy East!' he shouted.

'And so?'

'I'm a reporter for the *People* newspaper.'

Silence.

'Is it true you used to be a boy?'

My stomach hit the floor, blood flew to my head, my ears sang and my mouth dried up. I sat down and tried to work out what to do next. Taking a very long breath and moistening my lips with an adjacent Tio Pepe frappé, I yelled, 'Go to hell!'

'We know all about you.'

Silence.

'We're going to publish the story anyway.'

'I'll call the police!'

'Open up and make sure we get it right.'

'Whichever way you do it, you'll ruin me.'

When all my pleadings failed, I let this Roy East in and spoke as fully as I could. I discovered, sadly, that the paper had been tipped off by someone from Nevern Square days – he wouldn't say who.

It was only when he left that panic hit me. Tim was away, so I turned to Arthur. That was the secret of his success with me – he was always there. On Monday he went to see the editor. This made it worse. Barbara Back, a friend of his who was working on the paper after the death of her husband, tried to have the story killed. But now they were certain they were on to something fruity, something sensational.

It appeared the following Sunday under a banner headline: 'The Extraordinary Case Of Top Model April Ashley – Her Secret Is Out'.

The next day I called Signon and went in. She was frank with me: 'Those bastards! I'm sorry, darling, all your bookings have been cancelled. And there have been a lot of abusive calls from people who've used you in the past. I don't know why they bother. You realise you're finished, darling. You can forget England.'

I never denied who I was. I didn't advertise it, but I didn't deny it. People would say to me, 'Do you ever work in France?' I would say I did. 'Did you work at Le Carrousel?' I never tried to pretend. I didn't expect to have every single job that I've had cancelled overnight. Some photographers were furious, but my agents knew. All my friends knew. A lot of people I worked with knew. Every time they wanted their underwear modelled, they chose me, because I was very tall. I had lots of jobs booked for months in advance and every one was cancelled. Every single one.

Then, there was an audition for Bourneville Dark Chocolate. My agents told me, 'April, they've asked for you to give a reading.'

I thought, if I got the job, it would change things. Maybe there was a little chance for me after all. I did the reading and it went very well. What they wanted was a beautiful woman with a dark voice to imagine the dark chocolate and they had me read it six times. They applauded; there was a table of about ten people looking at me. About 200 girls were there too. They said they would let me know. I walked out... and then a wonderful, wonderful agent came running down the stairs after me. She was crying as she said, 'Oh, April. My heart is broken. They loved you. They said you were magic. But they will not give you the job – because Bourneville Chocolate say they can't have their name associated with a sex-change. I'm sorry, my darling.' In floods of tears, she threw her arms around me.

It was the same with Hush Puppies. I was perfect – then not.

A deb's delight invited me out for dinner. The boy arrived too early and pottered a while. When I came out of the boudoir he'd vanished. There was a call from a phone box: 'You'll think me the most awful shit, and I am, but I saw a photo of you in your room and suddenly recognised you. I'm sorry but I can't take you out. Oh, Christ, I am a shit.'

It upset me, but I felt sorry for the wretch too, because he'd suddenly been forced to face his own feebleness, to acknowledge that to be dissuaded from a heartfelt course of action by the disapproval of others is the most unmanly thing a man can do.

What did England expect from me? Nothing, it seemed. I was in the middle of a season for Roter Models but went home to hide, jumped into a bottle of sherry and pulled the cork. I was haunted by Monsieur Marcel's comment – 'You'll be back' – when I left Le Carrousel.

Would that be my only choice?

Then the dirty, harassing phone calls started. There was some respite from them when Julia and Sarah Churchill called to try to cheer me up. I felt under house arrest, afraid to go out.

Mrs Schroter rang. 'Where are you, April? We're missing our lovely girl. It's not like you to be late.'

'Mrs Schroter... you must know why.'

'I don't care about silly newspapers, my dear. For me you are just late for work. So I hope you won't be late tomorrow.'

The next day, I forced myself to go in. There was an embarrassed silence. 'Good morning, everyone.'

They broke ranks and gave me their sympathy in the best way of all – by hugging me. Even Mrs Schroter, normally so practical, joined in the mood. The door burst open and the Spanish and Greek women trooped forward to add their comfort.

But it was impossible. Beyond the dressing room was a carnival of gawkers. I was the centre of ridicule and terrible insults and cruelties. To this day, if I go to a party, people will shy away from me – and then, when they've had enough to drink, start queuing up to shake my hand. It's extraordinary. Life is so strange.

For me, London – where I had started my life as a woman – had collapsed overnight. Yet, I wasn't the only one whose circumstances had changed. Arthur told me that he and Eleanor had separated and he was moving into the Vanderbilt Hotel round the corner from my flat in Emperor's Gate.

In those days, you had to manipulate divorce. Arthur hired 'an intervener' and he and the woman spent the night together at the Grosvenor Hotel at Victoria Station playing cards. Just before breakfast was wheeled in, they hopped into bed so that the room-boy and the chambermaid could act as witnesses for 'adultery'.

There were many things about him that fascinated me, but what appealed to me most of all was that he was genuinely kind – not only to me but to many others as well. So, when he asked me to go and help him run a nightclub called the Jacaranda, in Marbella, which he had bought without me knowing, I agreed. I knew it was the correct move, especially after *The Road to Hong Kong* opened in cinemas. They'd removed my credit, the bastards.

Someone said something once about discretion and valour. I had suffered a serious reverse and it was advisable for the time being to withdraw with my shattered expectations. So, at the conclusion of 1961 I found myself with Arthur in a white Zephyr convertible he'd recently bought, with my Great Dane puppy, Mr Blue, half-asleep under my arm and en route to Spain.

Arthur was very chatty, excessively so. Nerves, I suspect. It was a new life for us all, including Mr Blue. In Madrid, they wouldn't take dogs at the Ritz, nor at the Castilliana Hilton. But the Palace Hotel was charming to Mr Blue, poor lamb. Apart from a little flatulence as we passed through the Home Counties, he had behaved like an angel throughout. Others did not.

Arthur and I had separate rooms, of course.

We went to the Patio Andaluz nightclub, flamenco cabaret, a mixed bunch of the international set gossiping among smoke and shrouded table lights, plus Arthur and I against a wall drinking champagne – and growing more festive, I felt.

I was walking briskly towards the Ladies when there was a yelp behind me. It was Paco, a Spanish dancer who'd worked at Le

Carrousel years before. We must have been chattering longer than I realised, because suddenly the figure of Arthur appeared, looking murderous. 'Whore!' he screamed. It was a word he often used when angry. It gave him a *frisson*. He threw my mink at me, followed at high speed by my handbag. 'Whore!' He dragged me out by the arm and hailed a taxi. I let him get in first. Then I slammed the door and told the cabbie to drive off – which he did, thank goodness.

I jumped into another cab. The driver told me that the real place for flamenco, where the Spaniards themselves went, was El Duende. The flamenco is a marvellous dance when you're furious. I became quite good at it in the flagrant style with a rose between my teeth.

The next thing I remember is Arthur standing over my bed waving his shirtsleeves about, ranting while my eyelashes slowly unstuck – how he'd been out of his mind with worry, what a mad thing it was for me to go wandering by myself around a strange city at night. I told him I didn't care, that I'd often wandered by myself around strange cities at night; that I wanted to go back to England; that I didn't want to go on to Marbella to do his bloody nightclub effort; would he please shut the door, there were people in the corridor; that it all seemed pointless, dreadful, draining; my nerves, my headache, oh God, etc… like something out of *The King and I*.

But what was there for me in London?

It was very quiet on the 12-hour drive to Marbella.

25

ROSEBUD

'Martinis are like a woman's breasts.
One is not enough and two's too many.'
THE SILVER BULLET: THE MARTINI IN AMERICAN CIVILISATION (1981),
LOWELL EDMUNDS

'And, darling…' It was dear old Prince Max von Hohenlohe-Langenburg, fat and twinkly in his decorations, sitting on my left at a gala dinner in the south of Spain. The room glittered with crystal and silver, pineapples, lobsters and champagne. The midnight Mediterranean was aglow and way beyond were the lights of Africa.

Max was leaning over me and looking downwards. 'Max, do spit it out!' I said finally.

'Well, dear, I was wondering what colour your nipples are. Brown or pink?'

I smoothed my delicate bosom, held by a band of ice-pink shantung, and said, 'The palest, Max, pink.'

He took out a Corona and began to tremble so violently that he set fire to one of his fingers, which was wet with brandy, and I had to light the cigar for him.

'Young cherries, sweet rosebuds, ah – you see that woman over there?' He indicated an American acquaintance who had inherited a large piece of Ohio and fled with it to Europe. 'Dried figs! Chewed up... but you, mmm, pink pips, my treasure, you are high-born, I think.'

High born, indeed! Were my Liverpool slum, coal in the bath, mother and George Jamieson ever farther away?

In 1961, Marbella – named by Queen Isabella for the beautiful sea it sits besides – was still only a fishing village of whitewashed houses with geranium window-boxes; generously protected by the Sierra Blanca mountains, it enjoyed 325 days of sunshine a year. That alone was a very agreeable invitation to the beautiful people.

There were many fishing villages like it, but what certified Marbella as *the* spot was the Marbella Club, then going through its most fashionable period before its 21st-century resurgence. Over drinks you met the Duke and Duchess of Windsor, King Juan Carlos of Spain, Ava Gardner, Audrey Hepburn, Gina Lollobrigida, Liz Taylor, an Onassis (Aristotle and Maria Callas were regulars) or a Khashoggi, maybe a Kennedy and a Monte Carlo ruler or a Saudi or African prince.

Most everything about the town and the club was – and is – marvellous. Cut by just a drop of creamy milk, the *café cortado* matches the Oriental mood and heavy perfume of the jasmine and oleander in the Andalusian air. From the cafés, there's always an intrusion to the scented air from the blended olive oil making the potato- and onion-rich Spanish omelettes, sizzling spicy sausage, flavouring the bread toasting on the grills.

There's also a feast in the architecture – which, like the majority of the glories of southern Spain, is the legacy of the Moslems who arrived from North Africa in AD 711. That conquest, which all but changed the course of European history, lasted for nearly 800 years and ended only seven months before Columbus set sail for discovery. Of course, some time after 1492, the bucket-and-spade families had every right to their invasion in search of sun, sea, and sangria, which like the bullfighting and flamenco of the region is that hallowed find, the real thing.

I got there before them.

Several years earlier, Prince Max had made over the 450-plus acres of seaside property to his son, Prince Alfonse. In 1955, Alfonse, aged 31, was married to Clark Gable's friend the 15-year-old Fiat heiress Princess Ira von Fürstenburg. After two sons, she hopped off with a Brazilian playboy called Pignatari, tried to go into films and flopped.

Alfonse buried himself in the business of hedonism and opened the property as a resort club for his rich and aristocratic connections. He ran it with the help of his cousin Rudi, Count Rudolf von Schonburg, who still remained a remarkable and refined presence at the club in 2005, and it was quickly established in the calendar of the jet and wet set.

It stands five minutes from the Old Town, off a modern thoroughfare, which when I first went was a donkey track. Count Rudi is a survivor of that era, a director of what has become the Marbella Club Hotel with luxury bedrooms, suites and villas linked to the sea by a crossword puzzle of walkways that always lead somewhere pleasant in the maze of subtropical gardens.

When I first went there, there was a square of orange trees in the centre of town; the main street was full of cafés, bars and shops; today, the fishmongers' stalls have shrimp somersaulting on the trays of ice while their big brothers – *gambas*, *langostinos*, *cigalas*, *carabineros* and *santiaguinos* – fight for space with soles and turbots and cod, oysters, crab, mussels and a catalogue of clams. There are short, silvery eels, blue-backed sea bass and pink fans of skate. Most intriguing among all this and the squid and the scallop shells, the langoustines, lobsters and crayfish, salmonetas, sardines, sole, bream, are trays of UFOs – Unidentified Frying Objects. It was at one end of this street, in the direction of Malaga, that the Jacaranda Club opened its doors at 9pm.

175

In the early days of Marbella, visitors who came for longer periods rented villas mostly on the sites of old farms and known as *fincas*. Arthur had rented a new villa on the *Finca el Capricho*. When we arrived, the house was damp and surrounded by mud and the log fire wouldn't catch.

Rogelia, the wife of Pepe the caretaker, brought us some supper. As usual, Arthur and I had separate rooms, which delighted her. For the Spanish peasant, 'separate bedrooms' was the last word in gentility. I had insisted on it, wishing for as much independence as possible. Arthur agreed, not being a rapist by nature, although he tried it on in Italy during the trip from London. He tried to rape me one night in the hotel and I just gave him hell. I said, 'Don't you dare ever try to do that to me. I'm your friend; I'm not your girlfriend. If you don't like it, I'll go back tonight.' I made it very plain to him that I wanted nothing to do with him sexually at all.

The reality was that he was curiously prim, and was prone to saying things like, 'You will never be my mistress, only my wife.' He once wrote to me in London, 'I have already said to my father and to Aunt Elsie that you would make the best and most beautiful Mrs Corbett and eventually Lady Rowallan. Of this I am sure and it is my life's work to convince you of it!' Oh my, Lady Rowallan.

Arthur wanted me on a pedestal, not on a barstool. My inability to remain on either thing was the cause of many rows between us. What enraged him most was when we were introduced as 'Lord and Lady Ashley'. He would splutter and suck his teeth ever so noisily at that.

Things began brightly enough in Spain. The sun was shining when we went down to explore the Jacaranda, zany tropical decor with a cool marble floor. Outside, through sliding glass doors, were orange and lemon trees and a plant called Dama de Nocke, which blooms on only one night of the year. Arthur always kept this flower for me by putting it in the fridge. Also in the garden was the jacaranda tree from which the club took its name. In the spring, this tree turned into a large mauve cloud.

Naturally, the staff were curious about me, especially when Arthur introduced me as his fiancée, but my notoriety was excellent for business. Everyone wanted to see me. It got around in two seconds flat about *the* April Ashley. People would come from far and wide to see me and the Jacaranda was the only nightclub in Marbella at that time. They all wanted to see me and Arthur promised to pay me for bringing in the business. I never got anything.

Jaime Parlade, who owned a local antiques shop, was the leader of the young, fast set. Gerald Brenan, lover of the painter Carrington, headed the older crowd. Bill and Doreen Godwin were news-agency correspondents for the region and became good friends, especially of Arthur's. My drinking partners were Sarah Skinner, an English girl living with a Spanish count; Rosemary Strachey, who lived in a tiny cottage with no electricity, was madly in love with Jaime and was a very good painter of cats; and Evelyn Locke, one of those dogged English women from Crawley in Sussex whom nothing daunts.

My intake of alcohol increased. Customers came to the club in the hope of witnessing a scene. Sometimes they were lucky. Certainly, I was unpredictable. This bewildered Arthur, who was both distressed and mesmerised by it.

Not long after our arrival, he had bought the villa, which I named 'Antoinette'. This he supposedly gave to me – minus the relevant documents. Neither the telephone nor the postman quite reached us at first.

The villa was plonked in the middle of a field and looked almost unseemly, like a virgin at a party. I soon threw up a low wall; Arthur planted a few trees and shrubs and put a palm tree on either side of the front gate. The outside of the villa achieved some presence.

The inside needed a firm hand too. All the rooms were different colours. I had the lot whitewashed. And, inspired by the Robinson Crusoe tomfooleries of the Jacaranda, I went bamboo. With wild prints for upholstery and rugs rioting on the floor.

Rogelia was established as our cook, Pepe as the gardener; their son Jose-Luis, who was at school, did odd jobs like splitting figs in the sun or delivering secret notes or swimming with me in the pool at the old farmhouse where his parents lived.

The only problem now was Arthur. I was 26; he was 42. There was much about him that I genuinely adored. I was his life. He lived, breathed and dreamed 'April Ashley'. Whereas this often led him to treat me with great tenderness and generosity, it could also become horribly claustrophobic. I made great efforts to understand the complexity of his feelings, but my own nature repeatedly rebelled against his attempts to project me as the miraculous resolution of his inner conflicts.

If the advantages of birth, education, influence and property were his, I believe that in the end the inner strengths, from my personality and all I'd been through, were mine. I think he knew it, which is why he both worshipped and resented me with a pathetic vehemence.

Arthur often needed uncloying. My disappearance now and again on one of the roads out of Marbella, in the company of a beautiful young man nearer my age, sometimes below it, usually did the trick. Not that I was unduly promiscuous. That came later. I was young and not as clued up as you might think about the sexual diversity of the human race. I'd seen plenty, but not it all, and probably still have not.

Arthur was two people. He was Arthur the man and also She Who Must Be Obeyed. 'She' would appear without warning. And 'She' was vile. A sidelong look would slither into Arthur's eyes. The spine would stiffen and the legs suddenly cross. The inevitable cigarette, normally wedged down firmly between his first two nicotined fingers, would slide up and perch effetely between the outstretched extremities. He would take short petulant puffs, cupping the elbow in the palm of his free hand – then, with forearm upright, the cigarette would twitch round to point backwards over his shoulder. A bitchy, accusing edge came into his voice, the mouth pursed, his bottom squirming among cushions… I never noticed it really until we got to Spain. We had always been together in public until then.

I never saw him in a frock in my life. I'd say to him, 'If you can ease the tension and stop driving me nuts, go and put a frock on.' He wouldn't. When he'd take me out and started buying me gloves and shoes, he'd be trembling from excitement.

He had been a Royal Artillery captain in the war and held the Croix de Guerre. Yet, he caused terrible scandals at Sandhurst. He would be in full dress uniform and would ride sidesaddle up the line in front of all his fellow officers. Now, in Spain, 'She' was with us on a regular basis. His 'pendulum' had started swinging again. I suspect it did until he died in 1993. Every single day 'She' would be there for the odd hour or two. I could tell immediately, by the way he held that cigarette, when 'She' had appeared.

And 'She' put on quite an act. The voice would go up a couple of pitches. The legs would become terribly overemphasised. Standing there and posing, Arthur would say that I was a whore and a prostitute and I'd gone to bed with this one and I'd gone to bed with that one. No. I'd just listen and I'd say, 'She's here, is she? Carry on, Arthur.' It didn't affect me. It wouldn't stop him – he'd just keep on ranting. Every insult that you could imagine was thrown at me. Yet never once in public.

It would almost be like a big orgasm, a big crescendo and then suddenly the cigarette would drop again and the knees would go down. The hands that were up here would drop. I'd say, 'Oh you're back again.' When 'She' had gone, his line would be: 'If only you'd marry me, I'd be cured!'

I was so young, and it took me ages to work it out that there were three people in our relationship. Before I met him, he used to pay all these boys money to go and dress up with them. Then there would be mutual masturbation; he was quite open about it. Yet, it was mind-boggling to see him sitting there and then, suddenly, the man that you know becomes somebody else. 'My pendulum was swinging and I'm sorry,' he'd say.

I'd shoot back that it was very nice to be called a whore and a prostitute and to be accused of sleeping with this one and that one. 'It does make me very fond of you, I must say. You wonder why I'm beginning to dislike you. Well, just ask HER.'

It was a famous but fragile friend who helped me escape 'Her' for a little time.

26

BORGIAS AND BEDROOMS

'The rain in Spain stays mainly in the plain.'
PROFESSOR HENRY HIGGINS, PYGMALION (1938)

Arthur was a pain – but what of me? I was beginning to wonder if I could ever have a proper relationship. My emotions were flying in every direction. People carry baggage in their lives, but I was overweight long before check-in.

I was always trying to understand myself. Had the sex-change also changed *me* as well as my body? Searching back, I suppose what I wanted then was security; a sense of place, a sense of being. Arthur was offering some of that – but, my, he had lots of baggage too. And when Arthur slipped into a grotesque parody of me, I was at a loss. Was there ever going to be an answer?

For the moment, Sarah Churchill provided one. She'd arrived in Marbella to visit Henry Audley, who had a house nearby. She had moved into the Villa Santa Cecilia and told me, 'Sweetheart, come and stay with me until your nerves slacken.'

I leaped at the opportunity and spent several weeks there. Sarah loved to write, but I believe her greatest talent was for acting. She could have become a great actress if she'd concentrated on it instead of letting her energies seep out in so many different directions. She had trained for the ballet as a girl and would often get up on her toes after a few drinks. Later, Arthur changed all the Jacaranda tabletops from wood to glass because of Sarah's penchant, and mine, to dance on them.

Lord Audley – Henry – cabled frequently. He had been crippled by a stroke. Well, Sarah got him out of his wheelchair and made him throw away his walking sticks. It was a remarkable transformation, accompanied by growing affection and furious rows, and with that they soon found themselves married.

Arthur wanted me back at the Villa Antoinette. Sarah had bumped into him in the village talking April this, April that. She suggested that, since he claimed to have given me the house as a grand gesture, he should do the chivalrous thing: move out and stay out until I chose to invite him back. This wasn't impossible, since there was a small unused flat available for him at the Jacaranda. He acted on her advice and covered the walls there with photographs of me. I returned to the villa and planted a hedge. I urged it to grow quickly because by now I was becoming one of the tourist attractions of the region. Strangers would drive up the dust track and leer at me.

I don't know why but 'She' stayed away, and Arthur and I, left alone as it were, got on much better. We became regulars at the Marbella Club, where one night we met the Duke and Duchess del Infantado. The Duke was grim, as befitted a man descended from the Borgias.

He had three sons. My eye fell on the eldest, Inigo, the heir, but not before his eye had fallen on me – in fact, both his eyes, the biggest I'd ever seen, too big to fit in his head. He was 20 years old, slender, solemn, sensual.

I asked him to visit us at the Jacaranda. He did. We danced and smooched. Arthur told me to lay off or else the family would be down on us like a delivery of coal, close the club, have us deported – his imagination ran away with him, although the Spanish aristocracy can be desperately parochial compared to the English. He accused me of sleeping with Inigo. Incorrect.

But not for long.

After the holiday, Inigo had to return to Madrid with his family. Every day he telephoned me and then he called from Seville, from another family palace. He said we would be alone there to make *amor*.

I went with seven suitcases and Mr Blue. I was full of hope.

Latin noblemen christen everything, even the flimsiest bungalow, a palace. But this one was genuine. Inigo drove me through high wrought-iron gates and up a short drive flanked by birds and love-seats sculpted from yew to the house, where a retainer took the car away. Mr Blue was led downstairs and I upstairs.

Inigo was a very old-fashioned young man. He hardly spoke at all. When we did, it was in French. We made love forever, day after day after day. It's all he wanted to do. Me too.

Our passion was secretive and moody and exciting.

And brief.

Papa telephoned. He threatened to have me deported if Inigo didn't return at once to Madrid. Inigo suggested we flee to North Africa, but I was older and wiser and couldn't place my future in the infatuation of a boy with very noble prospects.

He took the plane to Madrid. I booked into the Alfonso XIII Hotel. Arthur rang. He was extremely sweet at exactly the right moment and met me at Malaga Airport in the white Zephyr.

As usual, when I returned from one of my crazy escapades, he had filled the Villa Antoinette with flowers. They were not the only fragrant thing of that moment – I was offered work too. Hallelujah! It was a season of fashion shows in Madrid for the House of Rango. They proved a success and back in Marbella the Jacaranda was thriving. The snag was, we were surrounded by ex-pat British who lived in a sort of PG Wodehouse fantasy. The English widows were a treat, though. They were immensely respectable in rose-print frocks, came to the Jacaranda for their cocktails and ended up dancing with the local bloods. These lads, constantly frustrated by their own good Catholic girls, would make up to the English women by asking them to dance, very close – and a young Spaniard doesn't have to press against much to get an erection.

I always knew when this had happened because the trotting matron would suddenly go bright red, become confused and girlish and rush to the table to swallow off what remained of her drink. The women often made arrangements with the boys – who weren't gigolos, but only wanted somewhere to put themselves – and I thought it was good luck for all of them.

By chance, I also had some good fortune. One evening, a car turned up to take me to an impromptu party organised by the movie producer Kevin (*Thunderball*) McClory and the heiress Bobo Sigrist. They had rented a property belonging to General Franco's daughter, Carmen.

The Villa Verde was a tremendous clifftop pile inhabited by a mad gang. I was handed a vase of a cocktail topped with fruit and sat down beside a thin blond man.

'Haven't we met before?'

'Have we? I'm Peter O'Toole.'

He wasn't famous then. I had first met him at Duncan Melvin's in London.

'You've changed,' I said. Where was his big nose? The mousy hair?

'I'm doing this David Lean thing about Lawrence of Arabia. I'm playing Lawrence.'

'Is that why they've straightened and dyed your hair?'

'Yes, and a nose job as well. It was in the contract.'

'Peter, you look divine.'

And he did. I watched him on Michael Parkinson's chat show in December 2005, and the twinkle he had in his eyes that night in Spain was still there. He is one of the great characters of life. That night, he looked at me over our brimming glasses of alcohol and asked, 'Do you know Omar? We call him Cairo Fred.'

Peter strolled over and dragged the man back. Omar Sharif was then at the height of his beauty, powerful and delicate with stunning eyes. He turned 74 in 2006 but remains a busy actor and still looks wonderful, despite a heart bypass and a bad back – with which I can sympathise. But that night, he was not only the most beautiful but also the most sober man in the room, cast straight from Egypt and on his first international picture.

The three of us partied until dawn. Then, Peter's studio car, one of those long black American ones, suddenly to be seen rolling all round the unmade roads of Spain, took the three of us back to the Villa Antoinette, where Peter and Omar decided to spend the remainder of their time off from the movie. We went bananas. Peter especially. Whenever he had time off, he'd dive headfirst into a bottle.

King Saud of Saudi Arabia was in the area attempting to ensure that his country was not maligned in the movie. He invited Peter to dinner, but Peter stayed with me instead. The following day, Omar and I saw the King at the Malaga bullfight, creating an extremely good impression by distributing gold wristwatches to all the *toreros*. That evening we came across a clutch of royal princes in a nightclub. One of them told me he was a motoring enthusiast – he would buy a Cadillac, drive it into the desert and leave it there when the petrol ran out, return by camel, and buy another one. He was thoroughly put out when I explained that these machines are designed to be refilled with petrol.

When Peter and Omar returned to the location in Seville, they invited me along and I put up at the Alfonso XIII. For *Lawrence of Arabia*, Seville had been turned into a convincing pastiche of Cairo. The Military HQ scenes were being shot either at the Military Academy or at the Duchess of Medinaceli's palace. During the shooting at the palace, a cable snapped, swung down and demolished an important-looking statue. How could they tell the Duchess? Since she liked Jack Hawkins, he was delegated to break the appalling news. 'Don't worry,' she said, 'it's only Roman.'

Pedro, the Marqués de Domecq D'Usquain, was opening a new *bodega* in Jerez de la Frontera. It was my last night with the actors and I made a drop-dead entrance in emerald satin, Peter O'Toole giggling on one arm, Omar Sharif smouldering on the other. Flashbulbs popped endlessly about us.

Pedro had laid on a gruelling feast, a different sherry with each course, followed by cabaret, dancing and mixing. After an hour or so of flirting with the grandees, I was told by a footman that Mr O'Toole was howling for me at one of the bars.

'Peter, what on earth is it?'

'Oh, darling!' he wailed and hugged me. 'How can you bear the pain?'

'What pain? I haven't got a pain.'

'You know, the pain... of it.'

That evening, people had gossiped to him about me, but it was nothing that he didn't already know. He was always upset about the distress the sex-change must have caused, but now he was drunk and maudlin. I said we should leave.

On the way out, I hit one man in the face – he'd made some lewd remark. Peter took a swing at another. Back at the hotel, undressing in my room, I heard a nearby door slam – Peter was heading for the lift. Naked except for my coat, and clattering along in mules, I flew after him into the rain.

He'd almost made it back to the *bodega* when I caught up. It wasn't easy to turn him round. Incoherent, fighting drunk, he was obviously looking for a brawl. Instead, we went back to bed together. It insured against him making a fool of himself in public.

The next morning he went back to being Lawrence of Arabia and his studio car took me back to Marbella.

27

TITS AND TARTS

Domino (Claudine Auger): *'What sharp little eyes you've got.'*
James Bond (Sean Connery): *'Wait till you get to my teeth.'*

THUNDERBALL (1965)

I was big news. The Fleet Street newspapers wanted my story.
The money on offer was tempting. I demanded more. They
were in heat for me because of my links with the aristocracy and
a compromise of £10,000 was reached. The *News of the World* got
a lot of scandal for their money – six weeks of sex, drugs and
violence, a sensationalisation of my short but seemingly
intriguing life. (I had a manager, Ken Johnson, who we agreed
could have £3,000 of my fee. It wasn't a good omen.) The
newspaper wanted to protect their interest in me and I was to be
flown to London. I spent a lot of time with the newspaper's
writer Noyes Thomas.

One thing that got everyone going was that I had the nerve to
associate with the 'upper classes'. How dare I? It was all so
unbelievably ho-ho. Just like the country itself. In those days, people
were expected to stay in their place. But where was my place?

Arthur's divorce from Eleanor had been finalised and, before I
left Spain, we became engaged to be married. I had been

convinced that this was the right move, probably by Arthur's extraordinary insistence that this was the case. Yet I insisted, in turn, that it be a long engagement. The family's jeweller, Mr Hardwick at Asprey's, helped me choose an engagement ring. I must have given Arthur that ring back a hundred thousand times, but he would always put it back on my finger. He repeated each time, 'I love you enough for both of us.'

I said to him, 'You know Arthur, when you're 25, it's very nice to be loved but it's not very satisfying if you don't love back. When you're young like me, you need to do the loving because it's much nicer to love someone than to be loved. It's all right to be loved by friends, but you don't want someone in love with you, when you're not in love with them.' He didn't care about any of that. He was simply obsessed with me, with April Ashley, or possibly the *idea* of April Ashley. Arthur's father had cut him off – he'd lost a £5 million fortune to be with me – and all the wealth would go to Johnny.

It was a weird world I was in. Some treated me like a movie star, others like a shit. I never knew which way it would go. When I reflect now, I wonder if I was looking for the security of an identity in being Lady Rowallan. Did I want to become someone proper? Was that what it was all about? At the time, life was too hectic for self-inquiry.

My manager announced he'd committed me to a cabaret tour to capitalise on all the press and fanfare around me. Cabaret? My whole life had been one. But off we went at it. I took some singing lessons. And some dancing lessons. I had one week's rehearsal. What a mess. The plan had been for Des O'Connor to advise on the show, but his asking price was too high.

My contract was for a one-week trial with a five-week option at the Astor Club off Berkeley Square in London, which attracted the black-tie crowd and tarts in similar sorts of numbers.

I swanned it down the stairs at the Astor to the theme tune

'April Love' on to a stage clouded by dry ice, the chorus stretching their arms towards me in something between salutation and supplication. It was all pretty corny. The songs they'd exhumed were no better. 'A Good Man Is Hard To Find', 'An Old-Fashioned Millionaire', 'Lola Lola' was the level of it. I did my week and broke all Astor attendance records. But I loathed it. Mistaking the nature of a five-week option, I had already bought my ticket for Spain. When it was explained to me that the option was the Astor's, not mine, I was forced to stagger on.

After another three weeks, I went to the manager and said, 'Listen, darling, this is a crappy show. Let's ditch the last two weeks. It's so *bad*.'

'But you're pulling more people than Shirley Bassey!'

'I know. I'm the biggest freak in town. But I don't like what I'm doing to myself.'

'Miss Ashley, do you realise that if you went out there and said, "Shit" they'd still come to see you?'

The next night I went on and said, 'Ladies and gentlemen, I hear from the management that even if I only said "Shit" you'd still come to see me, so – SHIT!'

And I walked off.

There was absolute silence followed by both booing – and cheering. The management were horrified, the cast delighted.

'I've been wanting to say that to them all my life,' said Jackie Irving, one of the chorus. She was a sexy creature who'd worked on *Summer Holiday* with Cliff Richard. She'd been hoping to have an affair with him, but he didn't go in for sleeping around. She eventually married Adam Faith – a talented singer and actor who was to die much too early.

The Astor season came to an abrupt end. And a new career as an Agony Aunt, which goes on today, began. As a result of the newspaper series, I had received thousands of letters. People wanted to know all about the sex-change, wanting help on sexual matters, some of them with horrifying problems. I felt obliged to deal with them all. I knew only too well what it was like to be alone with such terrible concerns.

The abusive letters, and there were plenty of them too, I simply ignored.

My manager had signed me to appear in Manchester, Dudley and Weston-super-Mare. We were tied by contract and he was beginning to get on my nerves. I didn't even have proper stage costumes – one has to be able to move about in them without falling over.

I got in quite a state. At one point, I shouted at the manager, 'It's so tacky. "A Good Man Is Hard To Find" – that's every drag queen's number. I'm not going to do these shows...' He said that if I didn't he'd sue me for everything I had. I had moved into a flat in Queen's Gate Terrace in London and I didn't want to be thrown on to the streets. So, to Manchester and the Northern Sporting Club, cabaret then bingo then cabaret then bingo. I looked a dream and sang like murder; it was awful.

On to the Dudley Hippodrome, where they billed me as 'The Sensation of the Year'. For this show, they had signed up a stripper called Miss Fifi. During the finale, she upstaged me by letting her left tit drop out as I came down the stairs. It was very effective, because in 1962 tits on display were rare. After two nights of this, I'd had enough of this forerunner of Janet Jackson.

'Fifi, dearest, I may not be very good but I'm good enough to know when someone's upstaging me. That's two nights you've dropped your tit. I don't want to see it again. If I do, you'll have to take the consequences.'

On the third night, I sashayed down the staircase. Plop. There was that tit again. I leaned over and, like Dracula, sank my teeth into it. There was a short scream and, oh my, we didn't see that tit again.

Next was the Arena Club, Weston, where I was billed as 'The

Most Talked-about Woman in the World' – one week, twice nightly. We were all staying in a boarding house. The landlady refused to send up my breakfast so I went down to find out what was going on. The cast had rampaged the previous night and were still drunk, swearing, fighting each other, being sick. I was blamed for leading them astray. Eventually, we ended up in a couple of caravans between the city's abattoir and the gasworks.

I wasn't even speaking to my manager by now, but when it was over I announced I was returning to Spain to recover from the ordeal. 'Well, you can't go for long,' he said. 'I've signed you for shows in South Africa and Australia. And I'm cooking something in Las Vegas.'

It didn't happen. And, heartbreakingly, Tim Willoughby vanished. In the summer of 1963, Tim called from his house in Torremolinos. He owned a nightclub there called Lalli Lalli, which he insisted was Polynesian for 'Penis Penis'. He sounded low and asked me to go with him and his valet Jorgen to Tangier for a week or so.

Tim became wildly romantic on the ferry across. We plunged straight into the Casbah and stopped at the door of an Arab house. It was opened by Hetty-on-the-Jetty McGee, who'd gone ethnic in a big way. She had picked up her nickname years before on the jetty of Ibiza harbour where it was her living to concoct mammoth cauldrons of stew and sell it for 25 pesetas a bowl.

The house was typically Moroccan – inward-looking, a large room on each floor. Tim's depression returned; he and Jorgen sat all day long on cushions listening to tinny Moroccan pop music on the radio and smoking hashish. They gave me some and I was sick. As a child, my father had caught me with a cigarette and forced me to finish the whole packet – I never touched a cigarette again. However, I subsequently learned to accommodate myself to a little hashish.

The days passed, Hetty kept us fat with her cooking, but there were no visitors. We didn't go out at all and I was bored, bored, bored. So I decided not to stay on. Tim saw me off in a daze and said he was planning to visit Corsica and would I go with him? It was left that he would collect me on his return through Spain to France.

But he didn't. I have no idea what his subsequent movements were. Some weeks later, in the middle of August, I heard that he was missing. Apparently, he'd been drinking in Cap Ferrat with a chum called Bill and – against advice – decided to put out for Corsica in bad weather in a small motorboat. Bill was a sailor but they never arrived. No trace of either of them was found.

The speculation in Marbella was that Tim had arranged his own disappearance and dropped out to Tahiti. He'd visited it during the filming of Marlon Brando's *Mutiny on the Bounty* and often said he wanted to buy an island in the South Pacific, where he'd run amok sexually and populate it with his offspring.

Tim's sister Jane hired a plane and spent days flying low over the area. Nothing. He'd simply vanished. Like the Lucan vanishing, with no physical remains, there were reports of sightings for years afterwards. His spirit survives and, years later, during my own voyage to Tahiti, I believe I encountered it. Back then, it was a bizarre and tragic end to a dynamic personality. Tim could be very haughty at times – what he called the 'Nancy' coming out in him (Nancy Astor being his maternal grandmother). There was no heir to the £15 million Ancaster heritage. Tim's father founded a multi-million-pound trust to maintain Grimsthorpe and Drummond Castle for the general public. Jane, who has no children, inherited the Willoughby de Eresby title, which dates from 1313, and it will die with her.

A little bit of me died with Tim too. He was such a wonderful friend and champion for me.

28

SEX, SCANDAL AND MARRIAGE

Arthur (Dudley Moore): *'I'm going to take a bath.'*
Hobson, the butler (John Gielgud): *'I'll alert the media.'*
ARTHUR (1981)

Fleet Street were after me again. But this time, because of another scandalous lady – Christine Keeler. She and some others linked to the Profumo Affair had arrived in Spain and the newspapers were after them.

I'd been seen in Madrid with Noyes Thomas of the *News of the World* and Kim Proctor, who was following leads on Christine and Mandy Rice-Davies. The journalists added two and two together and got five. In London, they were making much of Christine's disappearance, using it as a way to link her with Profumo. They believed I was harbouring her on the Costa del Sol. Indeed, though unknown to me, Christine and her friends had tried to rent an apartment near the villa but it was too much money and they moved on to the fishing village of Altea. Nevertheless, the press laid siege to the Villa Antoinette; day and night, reporters would pop up from behind bushes when I least expected it and start ranting at me.

So when I was woken up one night by a rumpus in the garden

I was inclined to dismiss it as 'journalism'. Then I made out singing voices. 'I've got a dog, his name is Blue.' Peter O'Toole and Omar Sharif, at the time unquestionably the world's two most beautiful men, had come to stay.

Peter and I often slept together on these occasions, on the divan in the sitting room in front of the log fire – chastely. He didn't like my bedrooms. Peter had his quirks. He didn't like daylight much. He loathed sunlight and writhed out of chairs whenever it struck him. Apart from his face, neck and forearms, which were deeply tanned from filming, he was a deathly colour. His flesh looked blue with cold, like an emaciated El Greco. Another thing he didn't like – there was such a list of them – was the sight of blood, so I was seconded into taking his father to the bullfight in Malaga. Blood, I knew about.

Sian Phillips, Peter's hugely talented wife, came over to the house with their daughter Katie on the girl's second birthday. She knew of my association with Peter but wasn't disturbed by it. Nor had she any reason to be.

With Omar, however, it went a lot further. We had lunch and he talked about desire. We understood each other. Perfectly.

That night I waited in front of the fire for Peter to pass out. He seemed to take forever. Finally, he slumped and I tiptoed away and opened Omar's bedroom door.

Omar lived up to all my exotic expectations. We were mad, passionate lovers. I think we had both known it was going to happen and the anticipation only added to all the pleasure. And it was quite something to be making love with one of the most desired men in the world.

With my head resting on his damp brown chest, we were together until the sun came up and then I crept back to Peter. As I slipped between the sheets and lay back feeling pleased with myself, Peter stirred.

'Traitor,' he said, and we fell asleep laughing.

To my very great surprise, I later discovered that Omar knew nothing of my sex-change.

It was the company of such wonderful, talented men that made me decide to become an actress. I was still engaged to Arthur, who was living at the Jacaranda, so I lent the villa to Lionel Bart and Lionel Blair for a month while I pursued my new dream in London.

Sarah Churchill had introduced me to the actress Ellen Pollock, who agreed to prepare me for an audition at the Webber-Douglas Academy of Dramatic Art. I also made contact with Signon from my modelling days. She tried to help but explained, in the nicest possible way, that people still thought me too weird.

At my audition, I did two pieces, Lady Macbeth's 'Unsex me here...' and a snatch from *The Seagull*. They stopped me halfway through and said they'd let me know. It was clearly 'don't call us, we'll call you' time. And I got the message.

I flew, in every sense, back to Spain – to the Jacaranda, Mr Blue and, of course, Arthur, who was beaming with a present: very pretty pearl earrings. I went to Madrid to work again for Rango and there got the bad news that Henry Audley had died from a cerebral haemorrhage at the Alhambra Palace in Granada in the middle of a motoring tour with Sarah. He always said that his time with Sarah was by far the happiest and most exciting of his life.

I lost myself in an affair with Simon Munro Kerr, great-grandson of John Martin Munro Kerr, the man regarded as the father of gynaecology. The first night with Simon, I couldn't believe a man could be so golden, so handsome. We made love violently.

My jetting around hurt Arthur. He threatened to kill himself. At such times, he would hand over to me his keys and his will. One morning he appeared with these at my bedroom window. He said he was going to drown himself.

'Arthur, if you are going to put an end to yourself, why are you carrying a weekend case?'

Sarah Churchill showed up with him a few hours later. She'd found him wandering along the Gibraltar road looking wretched. I brewed some tea, returned the keys and the will, and the incident was buried. But Sarah was angry with me. She thought I was being cruel, so I went to a drawer and produced several suicide notes, which I had kept instead of throwing them on the fire as they deserved. She was sensitive on the subject of suicide. That year, 1963, her sister Diana had killed herself, unable to cope with the disintegration of her long marriage to Duncan Sandys.

Sarah's brother-in-law Sandys was part of 'The Man without a Head' scandal. This anonymous figure featured in a notorious photograph of the time in which Margaret, Duchess of Argyll, wearing only a string of pearls, is seen performing oral sex on a man whose head is not visible. It was produced as part of the evidence during the Argyll divorce case in Edinburgh in March 1963. Sandys, one of Harold Macmillan's ministers, felt obliged to provide a photograph of his penis to show it wasn't his distinctive organ the Duchess was having her fun with.

I wasn't having much fun. I felt lost, going from one thing to another, but not getting a proper result from anything. When Arthur asked me to set a date for our marriage over dinner at the Marbella Club, I agreed to 10 September 1963.

Hold the front page! Again?

The telephone at the Jacaranda rang all day, every day. Lord Rowallan wrote from hospital, where he was having treatment for throat cancer, and pleaded with Arthur to come to his senses. Arthur's brother Bobby Corbett, the fifth and youngest Rowallan, who was a great friend of the Queen Mother's, sent a telegram saying, 'Can I be a bridesmaid?'

Arthur was furious, but I said that I found it rather funny. I said, 'Tell him to put a frock on and come.'

All my friends were disgusted with me. They knew I didn't love

Arthur and saw it as a cold act of self-advancement. Sarah didn't mention it at all. Arthur and I fought as usual. I wanted to back out at every minute – but I did not.

I felt guilty about Eleanor. I felt guilty about the children and I felt guilty about his father dying of cancer. Arthur was always blackmailing me mentally about his father, and said his father was getting ill because of us and if I were to marry him everything would settle down.

He had great allies. Bill and Doreen Godwin would say, 'Oh, April, you should marry him. He loves you so much. He loves you beyond words.'

When we first decided we were going to get married, we went to see the Bishop of Malaga to see about adopting six children. Then, suddenly, 'She' started appearing again all the time and I told Arthur, 'Forget about adoption.' I knew I could not inflict this mad man on children.

Legally, my passport was sufficient to get a marriage licence in Gibraltar. My birth certificate had never been altered.

And 10 September 1963 arrived.

Even as the car went down the driveway, I turned around to him and said, 'You know, Arthur, I think this is an awfully bad idea. I don't love you. In fact, I've come to the conclusion that I don't even particularly like you any more. I used to adore you but I don't like you these days. I'm sick of "She" appearing. I'm sick to death of you misbehaving. You've haven't paid me one single penny for three years' work. You pay my maid and you pay the electricity, it's £12 a month. What are you doing? This is a very bad idea. I don't love you.'

'Oh, darling, I love you enough for the two of us,' he replied.

When we got to Gibraltar, we were about 20 minutes late and the Registrar had gone off for lunch. Evelyn Locke, Nicolette Meirs and Bill and Doreen Godwin were the witnesses and we all drank whisky until the registrar came back.

I went through the ceremony anaesthetised I was so drunk. When we came out, the whole of Gibraltar was there. I can't remember much about the day, apart from the fact that I drank a whole bottle of whisky and got married! Married in a £3 coat and a £1 hat – a huge black picture hat. It all looked very nice. Well, so I'm told.

Everyone thought I'd married for the title, but if I was going to marry for a title I would have gone for a real one. I would become a duchess. Not a bloody one got from Lloyd George. Not on your nelly. I didn't give a damn about the title.

I was amazed by the size of the crowd that had gathered. Sarah, who'd been married by the same man in the same place, warned me that this tended to happen – what with Gibraltar being so small and having a very efficient bush telegraph.

As if by second nature, I started to give royal waves, the white glove fluttering like a bird then going up and down. Well, I remain a fervent royalist. I have a picture of the Queen and Queen Mother on my fridge. Always. Wherever I am.

So there I was, white glove fluttering, the Honourable Mrs Arthur Corbett.

Oh my.

29

THE HONEYMOONERS

'AM ARRIVING WITH THE MARQUIS TOMORROW STOP.
PLEASE ARRANGE STANDING OVATION.'

GLORIA SWANSON'S 1926 POST-MARRIAGE TELEGRAM TO ADOLPH ZUKOR

My husband moved into the Villa Antoinette, a development that gave me enormous concerns. What *would* happen?

I know it was all very peculiar circumstances but I believed we had established some good ground rules. The plan was that I would commute to Spain from London and Arthur would do the reverse. We should adopt children. He would grant me an allowance of £2,000 a year.

Importantly – for me, certainly – he would be fitted with a new set of false teeth. The ones he had were old and green; he had an irritating habit of sucking on them to keep them in, because his gums had shrunk. Maybe I'm offering too much information, but it's the little things, like the straw and the camel, that can cause trouble.

I started as I meant to go on and went to London, where I found a flat in Cheyne Walk in Chelsea. Arthur wrote several times a week: '*Poor Sarah Churchill is in dire trouble again but I haven't seen any mention of it in the English papers. She has been fined*

5,000 pesetas and recommended by the Governor for deportation from Spain for being "drunk and disorderly" in Malaga and also because she nearly killed two workmen who were on top of a wall she knocked down with her car.'

Arthur decided to sell the Jacaranda after an impressive offer from developers. Carmen came to London with him and belatedly we exchanged wedding gifts. From him, an oyster mink coat. From me, gold cufflinks set with pearls.

But our relationship nose-dived. Our lovemaking was not a success. For three years, Arthur had been gearing himself up for the great moment, but his fantasy – and everything else – collapsed in bed. It was all fumbling and fiddling and no good for either one of us. Then everything else began to turn into thin air. It was nobody's fault. Just the truth at last.

After a week of dismay, Arthur left for Spain and I moved on to a flat in Lennox Gardens, where I was burgled of my jewellery. I had promised to spend Christmas with Arthur. With no club to go to, he was smoking more than ever. We argued and argued. Then, on one fateful occasion, his spine suddenly stiffened, he petulantly crossed his legs, the cigarette shot up to his fingertips and 'She' appeared.

Enough was enough was enough.

This time something detached itself and fell away inside me. I packed my bags and called a cab. At Malaga Airport, I waited all day long for an empty seat to London. I had plenty of time to think. It was dark, wet and freezing cold when I fell into Lennox Gardens. I sat down and wrote to him:

A letter from me. A none too happy one, I'm afraid. I have thought and thought, not slept for days. But from all the pain and torture in my mind, I see one thing very, very clearly. That is, I will not ever be coming back to you. I don't know what I will do, I don't know how I will live. But I know I won't be back...

I am paying dearly for my sin of marrying you. The worry and the anguish I have felt in the past three years is making me ill. So the only thing I can do is try to cut you out of my life completely. Then all I have are my earthly problems. A job, a less expensive place to live. Arthur, don't think I expect money from you. I don't. Because I know I should never have married you...

It's so funny but I felt so much more (although I never really did) secure before I married you than I did after. Then you denying what you had promised made me feel so sick in the stomach, I could never have stood myself, let alone you, afterwards. Then I seem to remember you trying to convince me of other lies of yours in the past. I don't want to sound bitter, but I suppose I am a little. At the moment my life seems a wreck all over again. I hope this time I have a little more strength.

I hope you sell your land. In brief, Arthur, I hope one day you find happiness. Although my heart is breaking, I think you had better have Mr Blue.

God bless you,

April.

Arthur's response told me to stop being a silly cow and return to being his wife. He had no understanding whatsoever of the situation. It made me even more determined.

I sank into some splendid habits during the long nights at Lennox Gardens. I would telephone The Caprice at 1am and ask them to send around two dozen oysters in a taxi. They arrived on a silver plate covered with lemon wedges. A welcome luxury, though it was a lifestyle I knew could not continue. Urgently, I needed a cheaper place to live. I thought that as every other oyster slid down my throat.

In Spain, I had become friends with Cecilia Johnson. She looked like Elizabeth Taylor, had the same haunting eyes, and had endured a terrible time during the Second World War. Cecilia was born in Shanghai and had been interned in a concentration camp there with her family. Her health was poor because of it – but it never showed in her attitude to life. I moved into her basement flat in Shawfield Street just off the King's Road in Chelsea.

We became a couple of girls on the town. She loved gambling, I loved clubbing, we both loved parties. Cecilia said Oliver Reed was a wonderful lover and they certainly enjoyed themselves together. I can't comment on her love life too much, but mine was astonishing at the time. I became wildly promiscuous.

While she was seeing the writer Anthony Haden-Guest – they called him 'The Beast' and Tom Wolfe put him in *The Bonfire of the Vanities* – I got involved with Sir Peter Osborne. He was Jenny Little's brother – her husband Tony Little and Peter are the decorating duo Osborne & Little, who are on the King's Road in Chelsea in 2006 – and I adored him. I used to go to tea with his mother Lady Osborne, the formidable 'Lady O' whom the Duke of Devonshire said had 'the mind of a Borgia and the body of a cook'. I liked her very much but she was wily, like John Aspinall, her son from her first marriage. With Sir George Osborne, she had three children, Jenny, Anthony and Peter. I had a great crush on Peter. I was even prepared to get up at some awful hour around dawn to go riding with him in Richmond Park. We were ardent lovers for a time.

I am quite good with horses, but one morning I was badly thrown. As I pitched into the air, I put my hands out in front of me to break my fall. It was the end of the romance, I told him I'd lost all my fingernails and getting up at 6am was doing me no good at all.

He's had tremendous success and I'm sure his son George, who was the Tory Shadow Chancellor at the start of 2006, will go on to do wonderful political things with David Cameron. George certainly has an intriguing background with Lady O as his grandmother and John Aspinall as step-uncle. He's even related in a roundabout way to the television presenter Donna Air, who is married to John's son Damian. Six degrees of separation indeed. Oh my, what a village it all is.

And certainly was for Cecilia and I. We roared around London. For a rest I would go to Wips, Tim Willoughby's old club at the top of Charles House in Leicester Place. Its best feature was a veranda running all the way round, overlooking London. It was very quiet there after he died, a ghost club. I'd feed strips of my steak to a tank of piranha fish and think of Tim.

It was a difficult time, but enriched by new friends: I met Denny Daviss and Al Mancini at the Establishment Club. Denny was the curvaceous daughter of a South African shipping magnate and an opera singer. Carol Coombe was another delight. She's been married to Ronald Armstrong-Jones – father of Tony, who married Princess Margaret – but had divorced him and married Pepe Lopez, an Italian lawyer. They divided their time between London and Rome.

Eventually, Cecilia and I decided we had been putting ourselves about so much that we chose to call a halt and behave ourselves. Instead of saying yes to any man who phoned, we agreed to accept the invitation only if we genuinely liked him. But in our current mood we didn't like any of them; we ended up sitting it out in the local, the Chelsea Potter. We rented a television to occupy our evenings. I became hooked on TV, which has been a companion and tranquilliser ever since. But TV or the Chelsea Potter – it was hardly grabbing life by the horns. So to speak.

Maggie Simmonds, now the Countess of Kimberley, broke the monotony: 'Molly Neville and I are starting up a model agency. Will you come on to our books?'

'Honestly, Maggie, I don't think there's any point.'

'We disagree. It's been years since the story broke. And now you're the Honourable Mrs Corbett. We'll get you heaps of work.'

She was a kind friend. But wrong. There was no reaction at all.

I applied for work at Simpson's of Piccadilly. 'Wanted, to sell men's ties, a girl with personality.' That was me. But they thought not. This happened with Fortnum & Mason, Harrods, Harvey Nichols... My celebrity was of no help whatsoever.

My only job at this time came about through Sarah, who put me up for the position of assistant stage manager in a revival of *Fata Morgana* at the Ashcroft Theatre, Croydon, in April 1964. What fame! The play's about a femme fatale (Sarah had that role, naturally) who seduces a young man – David Hemmings before his star-making turn for Antonioni in *Blow-Up* with that awful bore Vanessa Redgrave – on a hot Hungarian plain. David – I was so sad when he died in 2003, and just after he was so good in *Gladiator* and enjoying a renaissance – was half-naked most of the time, and when he wasn't rehearsing he played the guitar and wrote verses. All very Sixties, but he enjoyed an evening out.

Sarah had tried to keep me low-key. 'I will introduce you as Jane (as in Plain) Spencer (as in Churchill) and I'm sure there'll be no problems.'

On the first day of rehearsals, David Hemmings came bowling through the door and said, 'Christ, April, you were pissed last night.'

'Was I? Where?'

'At the Establishment.'

'Extraordinary, I don't remember being there at all – I mean, no, my name's Jane Spencer.'

It was no good.

Ellen Pollock directed the play and she often came to Shawfield Street and got excited watching the Saturday-afternoon wrestling, and listening to Kent Walton on television.

Edina Ronay – Egon Ronay's daughter, who was living with Michael Caine at the time – was also in the cast, as well as a beautiful young actress called Lyn Ashcroft. We rehearsed in Soho and my job was to dish out coffee, help people with dialogue lines, tidy up, brush the wigs – but nothing like Joan Collins's fringe.

Sir Winston and Lady Churchill came for the last matinee. They sat in the front row, detectives setting the parameters with the press, accompanied by their granddaughter Edwina Dixon and her husband Piers. Each time Sarah had an exit, I heard Sir Winston's voice booming, 'Where's she gone? What's Sarah up to now? Why has she walked off?' Or, if an episode took his fancy: 'That was a jolly amusing bit, yes, very good.'

The audience waited for his remarks. After the show, he came on to the stage. Sarah had put a table and chairs there, a large glass of his favourite brandy and a fat cigar, and everyone was presented. It was too much for me; I ran and hid, but Sarah pulled me out and introduced us. As Churchill got up to leave, the two bodyguards went to support him under each arm, but he pushed them away and shuffled out on a stick. He died the following year.

I was so glad that – even if only for a moment – I'd met someone who'd been such an important part of history.

30
LA DOLCE VITA

'As the gin slips down your throat, and the dim electrics
shine on the potted plants and on Muriel's lurid colour
scheme of emerald green and gold, you feel like the fish in
the tank above the cash register — swimming aimlessly
among artificial water-weeds, mindless in warm water.'

COLIN MACINNES, ON MURIEL BELCHER'S COLONY ROOM CLUB,
ENCOUNTER MAGAZINE, 1967

Supposedly, that most wicked area of the metropolis, Soho, got its name from a medieval hunting cry – Soho! It was more tally ho! for me.

I'd run around Soho on my first visit to London but had moved on from cafés and coffee shops through my affair with Tim Willoughby. He had taken me to Muriel Belcher's Colony Room Club in Dean Street. It was there that I met Francis Bacon and Lucian Freud, Dan Farson and John Deakin, Jeffrey Bernard and George Melly.

Bacon had a boyishly good-looking face topped by short dark curls. If he'd been shot through a Doris Day lens, he'd have looked 18, but in reality his features were already blitzed by the

207

booze. My first impression was that he was drunk, and until he died it remained my impression of him.

Muriel herself was a treat. A banshee, a howling, foul-mouthed butch bisexual, she spoke in homosexual slang learned from Kenneth Williams. It *was* a carry-on. She called all the men 'her', yet was kind to her favourites. Poor Dan Farson, now gone, who used to take photographs in the Fitzroy Tavern, told the story of how a pair of rats strayed into Muriel's from a horrid restaurant downstairs. She shouted at the two pairs of red rodent eyes, 'You two can fuck off!' Her voice dropped, Farson said, and she pointed out, 'You see, I've called last orders. Anyhow, you're not members.' Yet they were probably more civilised than some of the people who drank at what was always called Muriel's. Francis Bacon had once painted Muriel at full screech, but even his genius could not capture everything about her.

It was a protégé of Bacon's, a New Zealander called Peter, who led me to my gigolo, a proper one in Italy. One evening at Muriel's, he invited me to spend a week in his studio in Positano. The town is built vertically on to a cliff face; you have to walk up and down everywhere, and everyone is permanently purple-faced.

Peter's friends were an arty lot, but fortunately included Jessica Mason, whose husband had written the great William Holden film *The World of Suzie Wong*. Jessica had no ankles. Her feet were stuck straight on to the ends of her legs, but from the knees up she was exactly like Joyce Grenfell.

On the beach was an open-air nightclub full of stone lions. Everyone seemed to have boyfriends except me. Then I spotted a prospect. Niccolo asked me to dance and dance we did.

'And what do you do?'

'I'm a gigolo.'

'How much do you charge?'

'Depends.'

'Come and have a drink.'

'April, how could you?' whispered Peter. 'He's a gigolo.'

'I know – isn't it fun?'

After a few drinks, I said, 'Niccolo, can I hire you for the night?'

'For you, a special rate. Nothing.'

'Done!'

He came from Naples and he wanted me to meet his family; I hired a car and we drove there. Naples is a city of extremes, all squalor and glamour. The Neapolitans cannot resist a beautiful woman. They fall apart at the seams, they become like children, they sigh and they swoon. In the streets, they shouted and whistled at me.

I had to return to London. Niccolo begged me to take him with me because Naples was unreal for him too. London was where things were happening. But I couldn't afford him. There's only ever one freebie.

I didn't hang about in London. The Italian fashion industry was flourishing. And it was like Hollywood in Rome with the Cinecittà Studios booming. *Ben Hur* was made there, and *Cleopatra* in 1961. It was all hustle and bustle at the cafés on Via Veneto and the shops on Via Condotti. Liz Taylor, Deborah Kerr, Sophia Loren, Gina Lollobrigida, Claudia Cardinale, Marcello Mastroianni, Rod Steiger, Stewart Granger and Richard Burton were among the many stars to be seen in the city.

It's still a thriving spot for the movies; in the past few years, Anthony Minghella's *The Talented Mr Ripley*, Martin Scorsese's *The Gangs of New York* and Mel Gibson's *The Passion of Christ* were filmed at the Cinecittà Studios. And then there was that all-sex-and-strumpets BBC soap posing as history, *Rome*.

When I got there back in the Sixties, it was like joining the cast of Fellini's *La Dolce Vita*. The Hotel d'Inghilterra off the Via Condotti, which Jessica Mason had recommended, is in a part of Rome packed with palaces. I arrived with a long string of luggage and several candy-striped hatboxes, so the hotel treated me well.

The Italians go for display. Unlike the English, who delight in hiding wealth and distinction under an old darned pullover, the Italians like to give it all out in the first act. A Roman holiday is the finest cure I know for a tight arse.

The first night, I walked along to the Spanish Steps. I had no idea about Roman men but I knew where I wanted to go – Piazza di Spagna, Piazza del Populo, Piazza Navona, all those piazzas. I walked along the Via Sistina and was harassed. It is a narrow street lined with tarts, and the men were all over me like a plague. A rash I could have coped with.

I hopped into a cab and said, '*Trastevere, per jauore.*' Trastevere is the equivalent of Paris's Left Bank, except that it has the Vatican City too. Deciding to fall in love with the Piazza Santa Maria, I sat down at a café and the *ragazzi* began to hover round. I thought that, if this was how it was to be, I might as well go the whole hog and see what all this *dolce vita* was about up on the Via Veneto.

Outside the Café de Paris on the Veneto, sipping an Irish coffee chased by a bottle of Guinness, I did my best to be grand but it was hopeless, it was like trying to fight off the weather; so I went back to bed to rethink how a lady does Rome on foot.

Next morning I telephoned Jessica, who invited me to meet the puppeteer Ginny Campbell-Becker and Jill St Amant – who was later to ask me to be matron of honour at her wedding. Jill was what we then called a fast girl, and when her mother arrived in Rome for the wedding she said, 'Jill, don't tell me – what weirdos are coming to the wedding?'

'Well, Mummy, the only well-known one is April Ashley.'

'Oh dear, she's got such large hands.'

And when I met the mother she said to me, 'I've read in the newspaper that you have huge hands – where are they?'

Jill had warned me and I'd worn white gloves to make them look as large as possible.

'But they aren't huge,' she said. 'Why did they describe them as huge?'

'My hands aren't petite, but they're no larger than many other women's.'

It was a regular thing for me. If you are a sex-change, you must go through something like this at least five times a week. And, even if people don't say it, you know they're thinking it. It is horrid to be the object of constant scrutiny for the telltale signs. I was always quick to deal with it by being myself, being who I am.

Apart from Jessica Mason, my other number in Rome was that of Carol and Pepe Lopez. They had a magnificent apartment occupying a whole floor of a palazzo on the Piazza Santa Maria in Trastevere. Carol had become *persona non grata* with the Royal Family when Tony Armstrong-Jones married Princess Margaret in 1960. She had committed the cardinal sin of selling her story to the newspapers; it was all good insider stuff.

Carol had fine blonde hair and even in middle-age looked staggering in a bikini. Pepe was big, burly and Latin, and always making passes at the girls.

It was at one of their parties that I first met a most exceptional, most extraordinary man – Captain Lenny Plugge. He was short and tubby, and wore thick, round spectacles through which he peered at me. He was 70-something, but bursting with eagerness.

He'd invented two-way car radio and made a fortune; he'd also been the Tory MP for Chatham in Kent. The club Les Ambassadeurs off Park Lane had once been his town house, run by a staff of 30 footmen in powdered wigs. He'd had a house in the country, a flat in New York, a yacht in Cannes, but by the time I met him all this had shrunk disastrously to a house in Lowndes Square, two flats in Dolphin Square and a tower in Rome.

His wife Anna he adored, but they hardly ever lived together – their recipe for a long marriage. Lenny was something of a philanderer and loved the company of beautiful women. He had a son, and a twin son and daughter. (The twin son was killed in a car crash.) The daughter, Gale Benson, was murdered by Michael X in the West Indies. Michael X was convicted and hanged in 1975 for the murder of Joseph Skerritt, a member of his Black Liberation Army. Gale, who was also known as Hale Kimga, had been found buried on the grounds of their commune.

Lenny and I saw a great deal of each other in Rome. He adored fancy-dress balls and would dress up as a cardinal because he said it was such a thrill to bless all the women who rushed the car whenever it stopped at traffic lights.

We would meet for lunches of calamari at the Piccolo Mondo, where I introduced Sarah Churchill to him and he told her, 'Everyone, just everyone, says I remind them of your father.' Sarah had none of that. But Lenny was Lenny and didn't care. That's what he believed. He always kept in touch with me; he was part of the good life.

On one occasion, Lenny took me to the last night of the Bolshoi Ballet at Covent Garden. When the curtain calls came, he began pulling flowers out of a carrier bag and chucking them at the stage. He'd pulled them up by the roots from the garden, but hadn't removed the clods of earth. 'I find a little weight helps them to travel,' he informed me.

These dangerous missiles bombarded the stage. Did the ballerinas dance!

31

HIGH SPIRITS

'Good directors often make bad films.
Bad directors always make bad films.'
GORE VIDAL (1999)

S arah Churchill lurched on to my skyline in Rome.
I'd rented a flat from an English couple, Bob and Anne
Tannock, in the Via della Chiesa Nuova around the corner from the
Piazza Navona; it was right at the top of the building with a roof
terrace and five large comfortable rooms, all for £36 a month.

'The only problem,' said Anne, 'is that a young man called
Geoffrey Aquilina Ross goes with it.'

I took a look at him. Geoffrey would come in handy as an
escort. It would be possible to go out in the evening without
being savaged.

I'd hardly unpacked all my shoes when Sarah turned up. She
complained that 'they' didn't want her in Spain – 'One doesn't
deliberately drive into walls, does one?' The friendly thing to do
would have been to invite her to move in with me, but we knew
it would be disastrous. We were both big personalities; we'd have
been crashing into each other morning, noon and night.

Sarah moved into the Hotel Sistina; if she went on special

binges, she'd invariably end up at the Hilton, miles away, and I'd get a call in the morning: 'April, darling, be a brick and bring me over some day clothes – I'm at the Hilton again – my evening dress is a write-off.'

I'd travel out to the Hilton on its hill with an extra blouse and a pair of slacks and join her for breakfast – Bloody Marys followed by a sauna bath. This was my introduction to saunas. 'Don't cop out, we'll try it together,' Sarah told me. 'They say it's very good for you.' Once inside I got the giggles.

'I know you're laughing at me.'

'I'm not, Sarah, I'm just a bit nervous.'

'No, you're not, you're laughing at me.'

It was because she had a typical redhead's complexion and went brilliant purple in the plunge pool with a little ginger muff. If only they'd got a photograph of that, for the press were on to us immediately. 'Sarah Churchill and April Ashley have brought back the *dolce vita* to the Via Veneto,' said the *Daily American*.

They kept getting it wrong. 'Lady April Corbett *ex-capitano di marina*.' Another claimed I was born Edward Ashley and underlined it with a photograph of the Eton Wall Game and the speculative me arrowed in the scrum. The European press kept asking me if I were the son of Lord Rowallan.

'Mandy Rice-Davies *si e esibitaper qualche sera in un night all'aperto alia presenza di* Sarah Churchill *e dell'ex-marinaio* Lady April Corbett.' The Profumo scandal had been amusing Italy, and Mandy was taking around a cabaret act while the iron – and she – was hot.

Then, I had my Lana Turner moment. I wasn't spotted at Swabb's coffee shop on Sunset Boulevard, but on the Via Veneto. Carol Lopez had gone with me to the Max Factor Studios to try for a job that they wouldn't give me and we were being served trays of Guinness at lunchtime on the pavement of the Café de Paris.

Carol had to dash but I stayed and Denny Daviss and Al Mancini walked by. 'We're on our way to see Fellini. He's casting a new film, *Juliet of the Spirits*. Why don't you come along?'

The casting girl, Paola, recognised me right away from one of Jessica Mason's parties. The maestro arrived in an extravagant manner, bellowing and smiling and winking and twirling his fingers in the air like an elephant who'd had ballet lessons. I saw Paola whisper the low-down on me. He clapped the other portfolios shut and came across. Taking my face in his hands, he gave me a smacking kiss on each cheek and said, 'You must be in my film.'

While I waited for news of the film, Billy Wantage arrived from London with his girlfriend Sonia. I suggested we all went to Capri for the Assumption of the Virgin August Bank Holiday.

I was relieved to bump into Niccolo, even though he threatened to leap off a cliff if I didn't become his lifelong partner. I said fine, but added that I'd love to meet him for a drink the following day on the terrace of the Quisisana Hotel.

When I arrived there, Niccolo was late. I ordered a cocktail and began to flick through a magazine. The island was jammed with tourists and some of them began to gather round me. I was used to this by now, but, even so, whole families seemed to be stopping and staring at me. I flicked ever faster.

Then someone must have identified me because a loud buzz ran through the crowd; groups of ordinary Italian holidaymakers were turning into a mob. The road was completely blocked. I was on my feet; everywhere I turned, faces were babbling at me, and when they smelled my fear I began to be jostled. This was dangerous. I was in a panic. A waiter saw what was happening, grabbed me by the arm and ran towards the dining room. We scrambled inside and he threw across the plate-glass door and locked it on them.

I turned round to see the glass completely covered with faces and hands pressed against it, more pushing from behind, all yelling for me to come out. It was horrifying. What did they want from me? What could I give them?

I thought the glass was going to give way. The waiter led me along an underground tunnel, which led to my hotel. I was in a desperate state when, behind me in the street, I heard someone say, 'April, is that you?' It was Shirley MacLaine and her husband Steve. The last time I had met her I'd been in a car crash in Spain. Now this. I didn't know where to look and just said, 'I'm going to bed.'

There was no sleep until I fled Capri. In Rome, I called Paola, who cautioned me to be patient with Fellini. I fretted, for I knew that, if I got work from him, all could be well.

I'd discovered Sonia's good side and we went off together to Santa Marinella, a village on the coast north-west of Rome. We booked into a hotel on the ugly rocky sea front and went to watch the dancing in an open-air café next door.

Two strangers walked in, one wildly good-looking in the Mediterranean way, the other studious in horn-rimmed spectacles. I told them to get lost and refused the drinks they sent to our table, but they persisted all evening. Sonia succumbed at midnight. The dishy one, Alberto, whisked her on to the dance floor and I thought, 'Hell, now I'm going to be landed with Spectacles.'

The first thing he said, in excellent English, was: 'I've never heard a woman say "fuck off" before.'

'Go away, you drip.'

'But I think you're the most wonderful woman I've ever met.'

'Drop dead.'

'You're magnificent – you must know that. I want to tell you how magnificent you are.'

'Piss off, Four Eyes.'

'You drive me crazy! What's the matter with you?'

'Look, I don't want anything to do with you. Go and chat up

that one over there, she looks your type, the one with the knickers round her knees already.'

'*Mama mia*, I love you! At least let me buy you a drink, yes?'

He sat down and I thought, 'Right, we'll have champagne.' But I still refused to dance with him. He grew huffier and more aggressive, casting looks at Alberto who was doing very well by comparison, escorting Sonia round seventh heaven on the dance floor with his hands all over her bum.

Then Massimo – that was his name – did the loveliest thing. He began to pelt me very gently with geranium petals, making a light popping sound with his lips. The gesture was so ravishing I had to respond, and so I removed his spectacles – he was transformed.

I accepted Massimo's invitation to drive to Milan where he lived and worked as an industrial manager. The first few days were a great pleasure. We played houses. But everyone in Milan wanted to know who I was, where I'd come from. I held back on the truth because the anonymity, the ordinariness, was such an adventure.

Things developed quickly. Massimo started to tell me to wear less make-up. And one day he rang from the office to say, 'I've some business colleagues in town – will you cook dinner for eight tonight?' I went to the grocer and bought all the goodies and began chopping in the kitchen. Then he rang again, cancelled dinner and said we'd be going out to eat; he'd collect me in 20 minutes – would I be ready, please. Would I be ready, please! Is this what it meant to be married to an Italian? Passion all night, bullshit all day? What would be next? His laundry?

I left a note and flew back to Rome. When I walked into the flat, Geoffrey said, 'Hi, love. We were wondering how long you'd be. He's phoned, of course.'

He phoned again. 'What are you doing? Why aren't you here?'

'I'm not cut out to be an Italian Momma, Massimo, so there was no point in staying.'

'But I love you. Isn't that enough?'

Almost. I'd certainly became emotionally entangled with him and ended up making flying visits to Milan. Suddenly his phone calls stopped. A few weeks later, he called again: 'April… I don't know how to say it. Look, I was told the most incredible story about you. *Stupefacentel*. I wasn't going to ring. But I must know if it's true.'

'I can guess what it is.'

'Is it true? Were you?'

'Yes.'

'I don't know what to say. I'm astonished.'

He was very upset. And his *machismo* had been hurt. I don't think it was the fact of my sex-change exactly. When it comes to sex, most men are capable of going 360 degrees. It was that he felt he'd been hoodwinked – not only in his own eyes but in the eyes of others too.

'I know, Massimo, I should have told you. I don't want to hurt you, so I'm going to put the phone down. Call me later or don't call – whatever you decide, I'll understand.'

I should have told him. I don't tell every man I meet, but I do when it begins to get serious. It was such a luxury to have that man love me for myself, without the intrusion of all the other business. So, I'd put off telling him when I should have. It is always such a dilemma for me. My status would later become something of a dilemma for the Italian authorities when I was arrested. Would it be men's jail or the ladies' prison?

In Rome, I saw less of Sarah Churchill because she was living with a painter called Lobo whom I didn't like. But, even without her help, I was socialising frantically, splashing through the fountains of Rome – very Anita Ekberg – until the early hours of most mornings.

A policeman pulled me out of one in the Piazza del Popolo, but I explained I was English and intolerably hot and he let me climb back in again. The police were to show up on another occasion in a rather less agreeable fashion, though.

It was on a drive with two Englishmen, both called Tony. As their car turned into the Via Veneto, the driving Tony put his foot down and we shot forward. Police cars were on our tail and I hollered to be let out, having arranged to meet them in Dave Crowley's Bar.

I'd walked only a little way when I was swung round so violently I thought I was being attacked. I found myself confronted by yet another good-looking, pint-sized Italian. I wasted no time and slapped his face.

'You're drunk!' he shouted.

'Fuck off,' I said.

He was a policeman.

Next thing I knew, I was arrested – along with the two Tonys. A little bribery at the police station appeared to settle the moment. But the copper I slapped demanded a public apology. It was a hissy-fit moment.

'He attacked me first,' I said. 'But I'll be happy to apologise to him if he apologises to me.'

He wouldn't.

The two Tonys, who were set free, begged me not to be stubborn, but I saw no reason for abandoning my principles in a crisis.

'If you don't apologise, you'll have to go to prison.'

'Right – let's go!'

Then there was the question of which prison. One of them said, 'This one's famous because she's a man really.'

'When you cart me off, can we go out the back way? Because I know the *paparazzi* will be waiting out front.'

They took me out the front way, where the photographers clicked to their hearts' content and I yelled '*Stronzi! Stronzi!*'

Think *The Shawshank Redemption*. But not as long. The prison governor was curt and the women's section where I was sent after being examined was run by nuns. The first night, it brought the horrors of St Theresa's Primary School, Liverpool, but without the uniform. I was on remand, so they couldn't force me to wear jailhouse clothes. I clung to my sleeveless gold-lamé dress and mink stole.

The sanitary arrangements were frightful. I couldn't bring myself to use the lavatory, apart from a little pee, and so ate nothing, deliberately constipating myself. This wasn't difficult because the food was inedible pasta slops. I kept myself going with a few sips of water every 20 minutes or so.

Behind the cells was a collection of zoo-like pens giving air. While pacing my cell I heard a hissing. My neighbour in the next-door cell was gabbling away in street Italian, saying, 'You must be very expensive, you must be Via Veneto stuff; I bet you charge a lot.'

Fat chance.

A nun asked me if I wanted to do some work. I was escorted by the governor and his officers to a larger pen. As soon as I entered, I burst out laughing. Half a dozen women were sitting in the sunshine sewing labels on to mailbags. I had thought that this sort of thing happened only in the movies.

When the governor had gone, the women turned peculiar. They started to touch me, feel my clothes, wanted to try on my handmade satin shoes. I thought I was going to be assaulted again. But I sat down and started sewing the mailbags; the tension cleared. Soon I had all their stories. Most of them were prostitutes and petty thieves and were being fed by their relatives because the prison diet was so bad. One thief had been in there nine months without trial.

On the fifth day, my things were returned and I was told I was leaving for the law courts. As I went out through the prison doors into the police van, I was overjoyed to see Pepe waiting. He explained that we had to go before a magistrate. The policeman would explain his side of the case; Pepe would offer mine. But he warned me that in Italy it was not thought wise to find for a visitor rather than a local, especially a local policeman.

My evidence was given through an interpreter. I didn't understand a word of the proceedings. Pepe said nothing as we came out and faced the flashbulbs. But in the car he explained that I could either leave Italy within three days and remain banned from the country for five years or I could pay a massive fine and do a stretch in jail.

The only chance for appeal was if Fellini would give me a contract. I asked Paola if that was a possibility. She was frank: 'Can't really help there. Fellini doesn't give out contracts. Sometimes not even to the big stars.'

And I was a falling star.

So, it was *arrivederci* to *La Dolce Vita*.

But only the Italian variety...

32

WILL HE STILL LOVE ME?

'There is only one thing in the world worse than being talked about, and that is not being talked about.'

THE PICTURE OF DORIAN GRAY (1891), OSCAR WILDE

They say – too often – that if you lived through the Sixties and had a properly good time you can't remember them. I can see it all now. In Technicolor. And hear the action as if listening through a Bose sound system.

It's big screen, big sound, astonishing memories of an astonishing time – especially on the King's Road, Chelsea, London SW3. Who would have wanted to be anywhere else at that moment?

Those who sought and got most attention flaunted themselves and swaggered along the King's Road. And, oh my, I lived there, just around the corner from the Chelsea Potter, which, thankfully, has remained an oasis on that singular London thoroughfare reaching from Sloane Square to World's End. What a place for adventures.

On arrival from Rome, I was all over the newspapers again because of my time in that filthy Italian jail. Mrs Guppy, a masterpiece of calm in a twin-set and trilling voice, owned the building that housed the flat in Shawfield Street. She was not upset with me. She believed abroad was simply frightful.

In turn, the King's Road was a marvel. I walked out on it; it was the beginning of winter but felt like spring. Everything simply gushed at me. The clubs and restaurants and shops, Quorum, Alvaro's, Mary Quant, the Casserole, Hung On You, the Pheasantry. And the people – the street was like a catwalk. Miniskirts, op-art dresses, Vidal's geometric haircuts, Mary Quant lookalikes, men with hair over their ears wearing striped blazers, chiffon scarves, white shoes, purple trousers. The Picasso Café was full of Mods, beads, bandanas, boots and boys like dolls, girls with orange lips, white faces, black Dusty Springfield eyes; The Beatles and all the glorious others were singing out of boutique doorways.

It's Michael Caine, I think, who tells the story of taking his mother along the King's Road to see what all the fuss was about miniskirts. 'This girl walked by with a mini up to *here*. She goes by and my mother looked at her. We walked on and my mother never said a word. So, I said, "What do you think, Mum?"

'She said, "If it's not for sale, you shouldn't put it in the window."'

Of course, most of it was.

Certainly for rent.

Everywhere I went there were faces from the newspapers. In the Chelsea Potter, Joan and Shura Shivarg, Charlotte Rampling and Jeremy Lloyd, and the rather worrying Ozzie Clark; David Bailey, who'd be so kind to me, lunching with Jean Shrimpton at Alvaro's; Sir Mark Palmer and Catherine Tennant in silver shoes and pea-green stockings; Michael Fish – I've still got a designed something somewhere with his imprint 'Peculiar to Michael Fish' on it, but it seems to have shrunk! – in the middle of the road and handing out sweets to strangers. Michael took his inspiration from Greece for his design of Mick Jagger's outfit for The Rolling Stones' famous concert in Hyde Park some years later. Lots of people, including pub-quiz masters today, put it down to Ozzie Clark, but it was Michael.

It was the thing to go to the opera on the arm of your hairdresser, interior decorator, fashion designer, photographer, plumber. It was Le Carré time: tinker, tailor, soldier... anything went. Hairdressers had the shortest vogue of the lot and lasted about three months; plumbers the longest.

The Avengers with the evergreen Patrick Macnee – who loved to play tennis naked – and Honor Blackman was on television; Harold Wilson was in Number 10 Downing Street; Tony Armstrong-Jones, by now Lord Snowdon, had discovered Carnaby Street; and the King's Road gossiped about which heiress had eloped with a road sweeper and other general sex matters in our favourite haunt, the Aretusa Club. It was like living in a gossip column. April Ashley's Diary would have shamed Bridget Jones's as far, far too tame.

Sarah Churchill rang from Rome wanting to know if anything had appeared in the English papers about her and Lobo. And there had been something in one of the evening papers too. Her sister Mary, Lady Soames, telephoned me to say the family were all concerned about Sarah. I told her I didn't like Lobo a bit. There must have been a family tiff soon after because Sarah got it into her head that I'd rung her mother and ratted on her. I would no more have called Lady Churchill than I would the Queen; Sarah would not listen. I began to see more of her sister-in-law, June Churchill, Randolph's wife.

Annabel's was still the big attraction for a particular set, but all the time new clubs appeared – such as the Pickwick in Great Newport Street. That's where I swapped sweaters with Kim Novak, who was wonderfully movieland and had just set pulses racing in *The Amorous Adventures of Moll Flanders*. Kim was a delight and I hope my low full bosom did justice to one of Hollywood's greatest sweater girls. It was a fun place, the Pickwick. Hermione

Gingold didn't mind at all when I stuck an electric back-scratcher up her skirt. She giggled in her unique way.

Clubs lasted longer than hairdressers, but Tim Willoughby's haunt Wips in the West End had been taken over by Brian Morris and, as the Ad Lib, become the most fashionable club in London. I can't think of a name who didn't go there. The crowd included the Bedfords, Sandie Shaw, Rollo Fielding, Patrick Lichfield, Anita Pallenberg, Terence Stamp, Chris Stamp (Terence's brother and co-manager of The Who), PJ Proby, Marianne Faithfull – a full house of the Sixties.

I chose my spot carefully and adopted a table by the door where I would not be crowded but could see everything – just everything – that went on. One evening my place was occupied by a bunch of boys. I demanded, 'What are they doing there?'

Brian Morris took me aside and said, 'But they're The Beatles. Do you mind? Just for once?'

A few nights afterwards, they were in it again. We had to come to some arrangement. First come first served was no good. They were such early birds. There were negotiations. We agreed to alternate. Their spokesman was John Lennon. And he was outspoken.

From then on, every time I arrived I would here John's voice: 'Here comes the fucking Duchess...' He said it with a smile, though, and would always offer me a drink. I could have gone to bed with all of the boys, but it was Paul McCartney who I believe really had his eye on me.

During another night at the Ad Lib, the lads called me over for a drink. 'Come on, Duchess,' said John before parading a tiny strange-looking lad with wonderful skin front of me. 'Duchess, this is Mick Jagger.'

'Who?'

'C'mon, April, you know Mick Jagger.'

'What?'

'Of The Rolling Stones.'

'The Rolling Pins?'

I promise I was not trying to be clever, but John was seriously bemused by this. Mick Jagger was seriously pissed off; it's always struck me that perhaps he thinks his arse is a perfume factory. But I'd been in Europe and was out of touch; and in the Ad Lib you couldn't hear yourself speak, never mind John Lennon – who was having himself a very good time indeed.

We all were. I used to visit dear Diana Dors, who had a flat in the King's Road above Safeway's supermarket, for drinks. She was friends with the wonderful Mexican actress Linda Christian who was married to Edmund Purdom, having left Tyrone Power, when I first met her in Rome.

I'd always loved Diana – in the 1950s she would turn up in a powder-blue Cadillac with 'DD' monogrammed on the doors; I could never work out whether she was boasting about her startling cleavage or her initials. Her big rival for vehicular show was Lady Docker, who had a cream-and-gold Daimler upholstered with the skins of six zebras because she said mink was too hot to sit on.

At Diana's one afternoon, Linda Christian began teasing Charles Peacock; he was a Chelsea Potter regular and always staring at me. I'd told him, 'If you're going to stare at me like that, you might as well speak to me.' Charles was the first man in the King's Road to wear a flowered tie, which he made himself. Once, he tore his tropically themed curtains down in order to make costumes so that we could run off to Tahiti together. He was confused and I found out why when he asked, 'I want to see a doctor about changing my sex. Will you dress me up?'

Chelsea was such a mixture. I could look down Shawfield Street and see an official limousine drop Princess Margaret off for tea at a house on the end, while in a council house with no electricity opposite lived the MacNamara kids, all sleeping in one

227

damp room. The four of them – Terry, Rita, Gary and Little Jed – would spy on me through the railings, and one afternoon I overheard the girl saying to her friend, 'She's a witch. My mum said she changed from a man into a woman so she must be a witch.' The father was Irish, the mother half-Indian, and the racial combination made them fabulous to look at; my favourite was Gary because he was the naughtiest and had a slight squint. There was something Freudian about that – and I don't mean Lucian.

Mrs Guppy approved of my foster-mothering enormously. She was less taken by a red lamp I'd put in the window. It made the sitting room very cosy, but Mrs Guppy had other ideas. 'Apreel,' she fluted, 'don't you think you might risk possibly giving the wrong impression with that lamp?' This was her phlegmatic English way of controlling the roost.

When, one very hot afternoon, I sat outside in bra and panties and sombrero, she offered, 'I really do think there's a chance, Apreel, dear, of your catching a chill if you sit outside the house with no clothes on.'

London might have been the capital of the country but it was the King's Road that had the world's attention. It was no surprise that Peki appeared on such a swinging scene. She'd been working with Ricky Renee at the Chez Nous Club in Berlin, billed as 'Ein Marchen aus Tahiti', a fairytale from Tahiti.

She went through terrible indecision about having her sex-change – 'Operation Pussycat' she called it. I'd offered to pay for her to go to Casablanca in the early 1960s, but she said no; a German baron was courting her, money wasn't the problem. He paid for it, in 1963 I believe. I don't know exactly what course her treatment took – she was very secretive about it. By the time she arrived in England, she'd had 'Operation Pussycat' and was living as a woman and wanted to build a new life.

Her ambition was to be an English lady with a British passport. She loved its air of distinction beside which all other passports look like dog licences, its size, the board binding, the Royal Coat of Arms in gold on dark blue. *Her Britannic Majesty's Principal Secretary of State for Foreign and Commonwealth Affairs Requests and Requires...* well, we all loved that. So they did away with it.

Her search for grand British status and respectability began rather badly. She changed her stage name from Peki to Amanda, picked up some whips and leather gear, and started as a stripper at Raymond's Revue Bar in Soho. I thought not, and told her so. She was so much better and sophisticated doing Marlene Dietrich – who, if her Carrousel visits were anything to go by, would have enthusiastically approved.

Amanda listened when I said, holding back a smile, that the Passport Office might not approve of her evenings as a Miss Whiplash taking her clothes off in provocative fashion. I suggested marriage to an Englishman was the quickest way. We went to the Chepstow pub in Notting Hill for drinks. There was a crowd of gay boys there and I went over to one. He looked not too rich, not too difficult.

'Hello, what's your name, then?'

'Lear.'

'You're English, Mr Lear?'

'Scottish.'

'He's Scottish, Amanda.'

'What a shame.'

'Scottish still counts; they have the same passports.'

I turned to little Mr Lear, the target. 'Mr Lear, do you want to earn £50? Would you marry my girlfriend Amanda who wants to stay in the country?'

About a week later, on 11 December 1965, we drove off to the Chelsea Register Office. Amanda, then 26, married architecture student Morgan Paul Lear, aged 20. She was described as a fashion model.

I'd borrowed an open white Mercedes as a wedding wagon.

After the ceremony, as we roared down the King's Road in it towards Sloane Square, I felt sentimental. 'Oh, marriage, it's always so romantic – don't you feel somehow different, Amanda?'

She scowled at me.

I continued, 'Since I'm already paying for this spree, let me treat you newlyweds to a wedding breakfast at the café in Peter Jones.'

'A wedding breakfast?' Amanda's eyes unslanted. I'd never seen them go like that before. 'Give him the money and tell him to fook off.'

'Sorry, Mr Lear – no breakfast for you today.'

We dumped him. It was a shame. The Peter Jones top-floor café did a terrific Full Monty English breakfast – bacon, sausage, eggs, tomatoes, Heinz beans, the works. Sad, but I gave Mr Lear his £50 and he had to fook off. I know it was an arrangement but I still think it rather humourless of Amanda. Charm did not seem her great asset. She was pragmatic.

Immediately after the wedding, she applied for the passport and within a few days was Amanda Lear everywhere she went. She would go on to become a millionairess and disco queen of Europe, and a popular talk-show host in Italy in 2006. Her Italian career began in 1982 when Silvio Berlusconi had her host a prime-time variety show; he's certainly done more for Amanda's future than he has for Italy as prime minister.

Amanda moved into the Hotel Constantine, a curious establishment near South Kensington Tube station that wanted to be London's equivalent of New York's Chelsea Hotel. She added style to her Eurasian beauty and – to everybody, except me it seemed – her mystery background. She was to become Dalí's long-time muse, as well as one of Ozzie Clark's favourite models. She joined an illustrious set. Ozzie and Celia Birtwell met David Hockney in 1961 and both men went on to study at the Royal College of Art in London. When Ozzie and Celia married in

1969, Hockney was their best man and painted them in their Notting Hill flat; *Mr and Mrs Ozzie Clarke and Percy* is one of the best-known Hockneys.

I had a great deal of fun with them. It was a time when everybody knew everybody. Ozzie was called the 'King of the King's Road' and, although useless with money and relationships, he became world famous for his outfits. I had one and so did Marianne Faithfull, Jimi Hendrix and Patti Boyd. He created jumpsuits for Mick Jagger, silk dresses for Bianca Jagger and dressed Eartha Kitt in snakeskin. Liz Taylor, Brigitte Bardot, Eric Clapton, George Harrison and Andy Warhol all wore his designs.

And Amanda, once a man called Alain Tapp, alias Peki d'Oslo, was in this crowd. She could reinvent herself for every opportunity. It was the music world she wanted to conquer, though. She was engaged to Bryan Ferry for about 12 months and is the model with the black panther on the cover of the Roxy Music album *For Your Pleasure*. She was David Bowie's lover for about the same amount of time. He wanted her to sing, and she did, on his *Midnight Special*, shown on America's NBC in 1974. Yet at first, she was deeply involved with Brian Jones of The Rolling Stones.

Over time, I began to hear less and less from her. She telephoned when she was depressed or wanted help, ringing me three times a day, every day. When you've had so much to do with someone and then that happens, it is terribly sad. She became strangely bloodless, like someone who's been marinated in haemorrhoid cream. Maybe she saw me as a threat, but I was never that.

Once, she was arrested because she could not explain the pills she had in her handbag. She telephoned a doctor in Germany, who explained they were on prescription, and the charges were dropped. But before all that could be done she had to appear in court at Marylebone in London. She says Brian Jones bailed her out. Actually, I bailed her for £100. Brian Jones loaned us his chocolate-brown Rolls-Royce to go to court, so we arrived in style. But I bailed her out. Strange, how time can change facts.

Of course, sometimes things are not as they seem at the time. I always had concerns that Brian's death in 1969, when he was only 27 years old, was not a simple drugs overdose. There were so many conflicting things about the events; there were suspicions but no evidence. In that clever 2005 film *Stoned*, director Stephen Woolley suggests that poor Brian was killed by his builder Frank Thorogood – and he makes a good case.

Brian was another tragedy of excess, no matter how he died. It was a time when many people went too far. Thankfully, I have so many happy memories of that time too.

33

GHOSTS

'There are more things in heaven and earth, Horatio,
Than are dreamt of in your philosophy.'
HAMLET, ACT I SCENE V, WILLIAM SHAKESPEARE

Although I did not want to frolic like Amanda, I rather regret not going to bed with Paul McCartney. It might have been nice. In fact, I could have slept with all of The Beatles.

I turned Paul down. We were at the Aretusa Club in the King's Road and I did a very naughty thing. He wanted to go to bed with me and kept asking. He was persistent. He always seemed to get the girls he wanted.

Well, I decided he wasn't having me, much as he clearly wanted to, and one night I said, 'Get rid of the entourage.'

And he did.

While he was paying the bill, I went outside and got hold of a taxi. I knew every taxi in town at the time, and said to the driver, 'When I say, "Go", go very quickly indeed.'

We waited and Paul appeared. I said, 'Go' and we went. Paul was running down the King's Road after me and shouted, 'YOU FUCKING BITCH…'

It was a hoot. I could have gone to bed with them all, all the rock stars. Every time I turned around, there was some famous face slobbering about me. I was very tall and very glamorous. I looked like a star and just about everybody was a star-fucker. Even the stars themselves. A little bit incestuous, you might think.

At one time, I was taken home most nights by Keith Moon. We would sit in the back of his Bentley or white Rolls-Royce, whichever one was on call, sipping huge whiskies. Keith's passions were drink and schoolgirls. One evening when he'd been at the whiskies, he said to me, 'It's about time you found some young girls.'

'Oh no, darling,' I replied, 'it's time you found me some nice young men. I'm working too hard.'

He looked over at me from deep in the seat of the car and said, 'Well, let's have another drink. A large one?'

He was adorable and such a wonderful drummer with The Who – before Keith, drummers just drummed, if you know what I mean. It was excess again, but it was ironic that he died in 1978 of an overdose of pills that were intended to help his booze addiction.

At about the same time, I embarked on a sad love affair. At a wedding reception at the Hyde Park Hotel, I was introduced to Clive Raphael, a gregarious and overweight Jewish man passionately close to his parents. He owned a string of garages in the Midlands and offered me a lift home.

A few nights later, he called in his Bentley, a massive cigar sticking out of his face and in his buttonhole a red carnation the size of a cricket ball. We ate at the 21 Club and went on to Annabel's. He said he was 28 years old.

'But you look 45!' I couldn't help it. And I was rather irritated by his constant efforts to impress – not me especially, but the world, and most of all himself. Underneath the playboy act, he was so insecure that he began to interest me. I decided to educate him: 'Clive, yes, I'd love to go out again. But the Bentley, the cigar, the carnation – two of them must go and I don't care which two.'

Fortunately, he kept the car and we became a couple, usually at Shawfield Street, because his own house, in a mews behind Harley Street, looked like a nightclub in Tel Aviv. We used his house only to give dinner parties for his business friends. Clive's commercial interests were wide and murky. He called himself a 'wheeler dealer', with a smirk. When we went out, he spent money like water; money ruled his and his friends' lives because it was the only thing they had.

His favourite recreation was flying. He had a pilot's licence, and I believe he found peace up there alone, away from all his social paranoia. I'd go along when he went up to collect the money from his garages. In Leeds, he asked me to marry him and suggested we fly to Mexico for a licence.

Legally, I didn't know how things stood with Arthur – no one did – so I suggested we go to Manchester instead to visit my mother, whom I'd had no contact with. I don't know what I was thinking. It was just some sort of knee-jerk reaction.

When I telephoned, she said, 'What do you want?'

'To see if you want to go out for lunch.'

'Just a minute and I'll ask Bernie. Hey, Bernie, can I go out to lunch with our April? He says it's all right if I'm not long.'

Clive and I arranged to collect her. As we crossed the Yorkshire moors, we passed small police huts and policemen digging. It was chilling: they were searching for the corpses of children tortured and murdered by Ian Brady and Myra Hindley.

Mother was wearing a beaverskin coat down to her ankles. Since she was tiny, it made her look like a molehill travelling on white high heels. She snuggled into the back of the Bentley and all but disappeared. 'Aren't these American cars big?'

'Where do you want to go for lunch?'

'Once a week, Bernie and I go for a Chinese. I'd like to go there. It's very posh – we'll get good service. They know me there.'

'Hello, Mrs Cartmel. We have a nice table for you and your friends.'

'I told you they knew us, Bernie and me.' And with a big smile of false teeth she started to tuck into her Woodbines.

Mother never introduced me as her daughter.

Clive and I moved into the penthouse of Montrose House, a block of flats he had bought behind Belgrave Square; it wasn't as wonderful as it sounds. Clive was a strange character, a man of dark moods and probably even darker deeds. He badly beat me one night. Afterwards, he burst into tears, said he didn't know why he'd done it, bought me a Jeep as a peace offering and suggested we go shark fishing in Cornwall. We went with Stewart Granger's son Jamie. Clive didn't enjoy it. He spent the whole time in dark glasses.

We tried Majorca, but Clive punched and hurt me again, and again said later that he didn't know why. I thought it was something to do with his inferiority complex and suggested he visit a psychiatrist. But it was the end. I didn't want a man who knocked me about.

Not long after we split up, Clive married a beautiful young model called Penny Brahms, but that didn't work out either. I saw him shopping in Beauchamp Place one day. 'My wife's left me. Will you have dinner? Come up to the flat.'

It was the Montrose penthouse. He was alone and unhappy with two Dobermans and panoramic views across London for company. Without speaking, he began to play a grand piano. I sat at the opposite end of the room on a long dark sofa until I couldn't stand it any longer and left.

I heard nothing more of him until March 1972. While he was piloting his parents and girlfriend across France, his aeroplane exploded, killing all four of them. There were all sorts of strange stories about the incident, and I could believe any of them. The chief one was that Clive, who was a shady entrepreneur, had upset fellow gunrunners to the Middle East and that they had done away with him.

At first, his will seemed to be as inexplicable as his death. Apparently, it left Penny four nude photographs of herself and a shilling (five pence). 'The Shilling Will' case at the Old Bailey was front-page news. In the end, the will was proved to be a forgery and the perpetrators were jailed. Penny inherited the £500,000 from her late husband's estate and married Michael 'Dandy Kim' Carbon-Waterfield.

I wasn't so well off in matters monetary, though. Finishing with Clive had thrown me back on to my own financial resources and I discovered that I had none. I sold the mink.

In the Chelsea Potter, always an oasis, an American GI told me he was driving down to Ibiza and would happily give me a lift. Ibiza would be cheap. Cecilia was now Mrs Richard Lewis and living in New York and, although Mrs Guppy offered to drop the rent, I could no longer afford Shawfield Street.

Now, this was not the Ibiza of the 21st century. It was just being 'discovered' back then, and when I got there was somewhere between 'bohemian' and 'Society' in its evolution. The first person I made friends with was Major Teddy Sinclair, who took a great pride in his figure and marched up and down the beach every day in shorts, eyeing the girls. 'I've been offered a house in Talamanca, just across the bay,' he said. 'Why don't you share it? Nine pounds a month.'

When we arrived, the cottage was carpeted with a thick layer of dead black beetles. There was no electricity and the water had to be drawn from a well, but it was right on the sea. Teddy and I didn't crowd each other. He liked the English Bar and I preferred Arlene's Bronx Bar. He had a stream of girls passing through and I had Klaus Schmidt.

Klaus was a German painter with excellent English. Tall and dark, he loved cracking jokes and he cracked them in the English style, because, 'A German joke is no laughing matter.' Although it was the middle of summer, he insisted on wearing a black suit, shoes and tie, and a white shirt, just like an undertaker. He also detested the sun and the sea. To put himself through it in this way was part of his theory of art.

Another part of his theory was that in order to be a great artist one had to be celibate for long periods, to drive the energy up into the imagination – 'So there will be no hankie-pankies, please.'

Teddy said, 'I don't approve of Krauts as a rule, but your Schmidt's OK.'

We didn't do much – lazed around, ate paella, drank red wine thinned with *gaseosa*. We couldn't afford to do more. Even so, I was forced to sell some more jewellery. At the end of August, Klaus had to return to Nuremberg; when the boat went out there was hardly a loo-roll left in Ibiza. We waved until we could no longer see each other. I suddenly felt immensely lonely and burst into tears. But his departure forced me to be more adventurous. Which I've always liked to be.

Sandy Pratt's Bar at Santa Eulalia del Rio was the hub of a showbusiness colony where the loudest mouth belonged to Terry-Thomas. Oh my, was he vulgar. I couldn't stand him. But there were lots of far more interesting residents – and visitors. Diana Rigg – Mrs Peel, though not yet a Dame – turned up with David Warner, who'd been such a big hit as the nasty rival to Albert Finney's eponymous hero in *Tom Jones*. Happily, he's back in fashion again. Back then, he was dutifully rehearsing *Hamlet*, modishly the Prince of Denmark as a Sixties dropout – and spent his time running around with his head in the text. He'd recite at anyone he bumped into.

Hamlet. A very insecure young man.

Polly Drysdale had a large place on the island. She gave only

This was the top end of fashion when
I began modelling in London after
Casablanca. I worked with Sandra Paul,
now Mrs Michael Howard,
Bronwen Pugh, who married Viscount
Astor, Grace Coddington and Sue Lloyd.

A studio shot in 1975 and (*inset*) there I am with lovely dark hair – not a hint of grey! – in California some years later.

Ready for my close-up, Mr De Mille (*top*) and dressed to kill – getting a bite out of acting as Countess Dracula at the Collegiate Theatre in 1974.

Top left: With husband number one – me and Arthur in the swim, for once, at Finca el Capricho, Marbella, 1961. Notice my passport – The Honourable Mrs Corbett!

Top right: Arthur with the telltale cigarette when She Who Must Be Obeyed took over.

Bottom: Too much of La Dolce Vita – on the tiles in Rome with Sarah Churchill in 1964.

A darling. Husband number two
Jeff West. Jeff had the right looks for
Hollywood, a real leading man. He also
had fabulous contacts – that's him at his
Santa Monica club with David Bowie
and his wife Iman.

With the wonderfully supportive Julia 'Toots' Lockwood in Juan-les-Pins in 1957 and making a point to Peter O'Toole at a party in Jerez de la Frontera in 1962.

Above: Dressed for dinner with the kitchen crew at AD8 in 1974. I see the hint of one or two martinis in my smile...

Below: The First Lady with Alan Jay Lerner of 'My Fair Lady' fame. And (*inset*) at the screening of Rudolph Valentino's 'Blood and Sand' which was re-released in May, 1973.

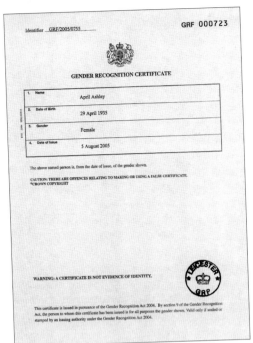

I am April Ashley – officially. This is the certificate recognizing my status as a woman. And that's me today – not a hint of a dark hair I'm afraid! (*Below*) Bon voyage – before I sailed the Pacific. Me with Shirley Ann Field and (*centre*) Peter Finch's daughter Anita.

intimate dinner parties, not cocktail parties. I'd first met Polly with Arthur in Marbella when she had floated into town on her yacht, the 365-ton *Hiniesta*, with her first husband (the Comte de Mun), her current husband (the Hon. John North) and her future husband (Stephen Drysdale) all on board at the same time. Polly was American and always had plenty of money. Her mother was Caresse Crosby (aka Mary Phelps Jacob), who invented and patented the first modern brassiere and who married the handsome multi-millionaire poet-murderer-suicide Harry Crosby, founder of the Black Sun Press in Paris in the 1920s. Among other things, Polly's mother left her a huge cinquecento castle in the Sabine Hills, Rocca Sinibalda, built in the shape of an eagle – including beak.

Equally impressive, the home of the Baron and Baroness van Pallandt, then known everywhere as singers Nina and Frederick, was by far the most beautiful on Ibiza; an old farmhouse carefully restored and lighted completely by candles. When they gave a party, it was like going into a cathedral. I went with a friend of mine, Shura, and during the party asked him to play the piano. Everyone groaned and carried on talking.

But one by one they stopped, because he was the world-famous concert pianist Shura Cherkassky. Shura was a methodical man and did everything by numbers – just *four* prawns, just *two* potatoes, just *six* strawberries, just *seven* hours' sleep. Sometimes the numbers were quite arbitrary but he stuck to them as an exercise in self-discipline.

Totally maddening, of course. Especially for his wife. Oh my.

There were even crazier people on what I now considered my island. And, it seemed, everywhere I ventured.

34

FRAMED!

'People who are very beautiful make their own laws.'
KAREN STONE (VIVIEN LEIGH), THE ROMAN SPRING OF MRS STONE (1961)

In 2006, Nina Van Pallandt was back on Ibiza leading, I'm told, something of a reclusive life. She'd had a fascinating time getting involved with the Howard Hughes literary hoaxer Clifford Irving and then making movies in Hollywood.

They were beautiful people, but the cute material of Nina and Frederick didn't fit the reality of the couple. They were always kind to me and Frederick was a wonderful sailor. Once to everyone's dismay, including his wife's, he brought his yacht into harbour perfectly, with a spectacular manoeuvre in rotten weather. He was always what we might call today, laid-back. That was probably due to the drugs he was inhaling. He was as high as his sail at sea that day.

Nina and Frederick split up in 1969; Frederick was murdered in 1994. He was involved with a drugs cartel, transporting large amounts of cannabis in his own boat, and clearly upset some people with the tragic consequences.

What brought all these people to this orbit at the same time as me is one of the quirks of my life. When I first got there, Elmyr de Hory ruled the island. He was a tiny, precious Hungarian who painted forgeries of Matisse, Renoir, Chagall and Modigliani. He eventually became known worldwide as one of the most talented and greatest art forgers of all time. Even long after his death, Elmyr's work still attracts attention.

His fakes sold for fortunes in Europe and America through the dealers Fernand Legros and Real Lessard. Elmyr was quite shameless – about both art and sex. He would go down to Ibiza harbour to meet the boats, holding a big bag of money in one hand and a big bag of dope in the other, and ask the young men if they needed a place to stay.

I met him in the Bronx Bar. 'I have ze Viscount Maugham coming to stay and he'll be staying viz me for some time, I sink.'

'Robin! How lovely.'

'You know zis Viscount?'

'I met Robin years ago when he was Mr Maugham and I was – oh, years ago.'

'Then I sink you must come up for a drink.'

Robin used to come to Le Carrousel but there was no need for Elmyr, a monumental snob who loved titles, to know that.

Robin Maugham so fell in love with the island that he asked Sandy Pratt to find him a house on it. This was Casa Cala Pada, not large but it lent itself to glamour, overlooking gardens of pine, palm and oleander that spread down to the sea. He later added another floor and then, thinking it too big, sold it – to his subsequent regret.

Going up to Elmyr's one night, Robin and I were stopped by policemen with machine guns. A boy had rung Elmyr to say he was coming over to murder him. We were allowed through only after the police had telephoned the house.

When Robin was asked, 'Do you think it's true that Elmyr painted all those forgeries?' he replied, 'Good God, no, the man can't even paint his face properly.' Which was true. Elmyr went out in far too much rouge and powder. He also dyed his hair. Yet, he also painted rather tremendous art 'masterpieces'. The scandal broke in 1968, with Elmyr declaring, 'I've been framed!'

The thing he dreaded most about his subsequent imprisonment in Barcelona was that he'd be unable to dye his hair. When he was released it had grown through grey, but he decided this was wonderfully distinguished and didn't dye it again. He went free on a technicality. Although he had painted the pictures, someone else in the conspiracy had signed them with all those famous names.

Oh, who will I be today? Let's be Picasso. It was a wonderful story.

Clifford Irving, a failed New York novelist but successful Lothario in sandals, was living on the island. He persuaded Elmyr to collaborate on his story – *Fake!*. But Clifford made his infamy with a fake of his own, the bogus 'authorised' biography of Howard Hughes. One of the most brilliant literary hoaxes of the last century, it forced even reclusive billionaire Howard Hughes out of hiding in order to refute it – but not before Irving had hoodwinked everyone else. I knew he had an eye for the ladies even when his wife was present, but didn't realise how much he was chasing the main chance.

Robin became the centre of my social life on the island. He modelled himself on his uncle, Somerset Maugham, but his one major success was *The Servant*, and that mostly resulted from the movie with Dirk Bogarde and my old sparring partner Sarah Miles. Yet his title – he was the son of the 1st Viscount Maugham, the Lord Chancellor – worked well on Ibiza and he was a grand host. I acted as hostess at many of his parties there, one a month in the summer.

His guests included Alan Searle, his uncle's secretary. When Somerset Maugham died in 1965, Alan lost whatever stuffing remained in him. Fat, friendless, alcoholic, his hypochondria turning increasingly into genuine diseases, but with skin as fresh and pink as the belly of a sow thanks to Dr Niehans's Rejuvenation Therapy, he wandered purposelessly through the old haunts. His search for someone who might acknowledge him – around his neck an old Etonian tie he was not entitled to wear – remains a gruesome warning to all kept boys.

Robin told me many stories about people I was later to meet, especially Sir Michael Duff, the Lord Lieutenant of Caernarvonshire and Lord Snowdon's godfather. One day, he suddenly remembered this fact and sent the boy a teddy-bear. But Michael had forgotten about time and the thank-you letter was written from Cambridge, where Tony Snowdon was an undergraduate.

There was an occasion when he had to give a dinner to the local dignitaries of Caernarvon and decided to start with liqueurs, fruit and meringues and end up with soup and rolls, the entire meal being served in reverse. So intimidated were they by Sir Michael that not one of the councillors made a single reference to it.

I never thought of him as eccentric. His effects were too calculated for that. He was more of a practical joker. One of his favourite pranks was to dress up as Queen Mary and pay surprise visits in a royal car – until he bumped into Queen Mary in a neighbour's hall.

Robin wanted to write my life story and we agreed to talk about it at his house. His first question on the subject was unbelievably tactless. 'How often do you masturbate?'

'Mind your own bloody business!'

Robin went into a tantrum of epic proportions. I was banished from the main house to a cottage at the back. It was a short-lived exile. He often threw tantrums, especially after drinking too much.

He had an outstanding war record, had been terribly brave against Rommel in the desert, but had survived with a piece of shrapnel in the brain and this could well have had something to do with his ill-assorted humours and bouts of amnesia. But, as far as his writing my life story was concerned, that was that. I went back to hostess duties rather than literary ones. I suppose I could have contacted Clifford Irving, but by then he was being hounded by unhappy publishers and police.

Anyway, would he have told the truth as I'm doing now? Which includes my wonderful friendship with Viva King, who was one of the grand eccentrics of the last century; a truly historical figure in bohemian legend. I first met her at a party given by the painter Martin Newall and the first thing she said to me was: 'Take your hat off.'

'I can't take my hat off, my hair's in a bun, it's full of pins.'

'I won't pay any attention to you until you take your hat off.'

All my hair fell down and she said, 'That's better. Now we can talk.'

I was determined to make friends. Viva was born in Argentina in 1893, the daughter of an English railway manager. Her exploits in 'upper bohemia' began in the 1920s when she was secretary to the celebrated – and often celebrating – painter Augustus John. She told me she went into his study one morning to find him beating the desk with an erection, shouting, 'No, no, no, no, no!' Which, I suppose, showed a little more maturity than the usual 'Yes, yes, yes!'

There was nothing boring in knowing Viva. She taught me much about friendship, loyalty and eccentric ways.

And vice versa.

35

VIVA VIVA

'To dance, one must be a little mad.'
ANTHONY QUINN IN THE TITLE ROLE OF
ZORBA THE GREEK (1964)

Viva was a society hostess who seemed to me to have nothing but fascinating friends. I never knew her husband, Willie King. He died in 1963, just before I met Viva, leaving her a handsome house, full of Victorian paintings and signed first editions, in Thurloe Square opposite the Victoria and Albert Museum, where he had been the Keeper of Ceramics.

They had no children. Viva said that she had had an abortion when young, the baby of a great celebrity (I suspect Paul Robeson), and led me to believe that she couldn't or wouldn't become pregnant again.

She and her friend Nancy Cunard were the first women in London to have public affairs with black men, Nancy with the pianist Harry Crowder, Viva with the musician Hutch; he was rumoured to have had most of the titled ladies of Britain. But the only man she ever really loved was Philip Heseltine, who composed under the name Peter Warlock. He had gassed himself

247

to death in 1930. After Willie's death, his friend Gerry Wellington (the 7th Duke) proposed to her three times.

'Gerry says being a duke is like having a birthday every day.'

'So why don't you accept him? I'm dying to say, "My friend the Duchess of Wellington". You're mad to refuse him.'

'I'm not mad at all. You've no idea what I had to put up with from Willie all those years. I don't want to marry ever again. I've got my freedom and I'm enjoying it.'

She was having an affair with a man 50 years her junior. She explained her reluctance about becoming the Duchess of Wellington this way: 'It's a great tragedy for a woman to discover sex at the end of her life. I don't mean banging. I mean proper sex.'

'It's better than never discovering it at all.'

'Do you think so? It's made me terribly fretful over my lost opportunities. I'd have had a much happier life if I'd cottoned on to sex at the beginning instead of at the end. Willie was hopeless. He preferred the boys, of course. I've always been a passionate woman but, now that I'm no longer ashamed, it's too late.'

Viva was the Hollywood image of the elderly English lady: white hair, china-blue eyes, the skin of a young girl, the house with 18th-century furniture, the stick, the memories, the sharp tongue that would suddenly melt into intimacies and good nature. From 1964 to 1974, Viva's birthday present to me was a party in her house. At one of them, I met her nephew Richard Booth, who has made Hay-on-Wye a geographical landmark on the world literary scene.

Lady Diana Cooper, renowned in her day as the most beautiful woman in Europe and *Time* magazine's cover girl of February 1926, was a regular. She came to a party in a cream trouser suit and an enormous cream stetson with a rolled brim. As I was talking to her, she raised her arm and pulled from behind the brim a cream Chihuahua and chatted on while tickling its neck. I adored her and she was always running after me to say how good it was to see me. She seemed accepting of everything; whatever happened and the people around her she always thought 'agreeable'. Maybe it was her way of dealing with difficulties.

Her husband Duff Cooper, who had died in 1954, had given her a marital run-around but she stuck with him. Astonishingly, it was only made public in January 2006 that he had an illegitimate son, fathered when he was Ambassador to Paris. Diana was 93 when she died in 1986. She knew all about the affair, and the son, but never said a word – quite remarkable restraint, don't you think? I couldn't have kept my mouth shut.

Which was something Viva was guilty of. She and I had become very close. While staying in Florence, she had slipped and broken her collarbone and had spent the rest of her holiday in stiff wadding from the waist to the neck. I rescued her from that. I'd had a touch of my recurrent bronchitis and Viva said to me, 'What we both need is a holiday. I'll treat you.'

For some reason, we decided on Malta. On the plane, a middle-class English couple started chatting to us. They were going out there to retire. The woman said to me, 'I'm sure I know your face. Do you mind my asking your name?'

'Ada Brown. I used to be quite a well-known model.'

The plane broke down in Rome and we had to spend the night at a hotel in Parioli. I wasn't at all sure I shouldn't be arrested on Italian soil. Going through passport control, Viva, who knew all about my stay in jail there, was even jumpier than I was. She kept hanging back.

'What the hell are you doing, Viva?'

'I'm getting ready to grease his palm.'

'What with?'

'I've got a thousand-lire note.'

'That's about ten bob. It won't get us anywhere. Now pull yourself together and stop attracting attention.'

At the Parioli Hotel, the couple appeared again. 'Can we join you for dinner?'

How could one say no?

And, as expected, the woman didn't stop playing with her artificial pearls all through the meal. 'I know I'm going on a bit. But it's nagging me dreadfully. I can't help feeling that I know you. In fact, it's driving me mad.'

'Don't let it do that. You've probably seen me on a lot of hoardings.'

Viva was twitching, playing with *her* pearls (plastic poppers), dying to tell.

'You dare, Viva,' I muttered, 'you know how I like to go unremarked when abroad.'

At long last, we arrived in Malta. The hotel put us in an annex, far from the main building. You gained it by climbing over the swimming pool on a bridge with only one railing. Viva, though moderate in all her habits (except sex, and that only late in life), was no stranger to the bottle and it was likely she'd fall in at some point.

The only other room was up three flights of stairs. We tried it but after the first flight Viva was already expectorating.

'Is this really the best you can do?' I asked the manager.

'I'm afraid it is.'

'Then would you be so good as to call us a taxi.'

'Why?'

'Because we can't stay here. And will you fetch our bags while you're about it.'

'But you've already booked in.'

'Then you'll have to unbook us. Mrs King is an old lady. She can't climb skyscrapers last thing at night.'

Viva looked daggers at me. She detested being described as an 'old lady'. She tugged my elbow. 'What are you up to now, April?'

'Don't interrupt, Viva.' We'd been bickering since Rome. 'When it comes to hotels, I know what I'm doing.'

We bundled into the taxi and I said, 'To the Hilton, please.'

'To the Hilton!' Viva exclaimed. 'The Hilton, good Lord! It's me who's footing the bill! I can't afford the Hilton.'

'Yes you can. Five days at the Hilton will do us both far more good than a fortnight in that pit!'

On our first morning at the Hilton, we went down to the coffee shop for breakfast. It was full except for one table, which we grabbed. And who followed us in, with nowhere to sit except at our table? The retired middle-class couple.

The woman started up: 'I hate to be a bore but I can't get over the feeling that I know you.'

Viva said out loud, 'Can I tell them? I want to.'

'You say one word, madam, and you'll regret it. I told you in Rome, now I'm telling you in Malta – shut up.'

By now, the couple's tongues were lolling out. 'Oh, do tell us, do!' The woman's pearls were all twisted up in her knuckles.

'I'm sorry. I'm on a private holiday with my –' I sniffed in the direction of Viva '– friend, Mrs King here – who keeps opening her big mouth.'

Then Viva looked up with the devil in her eye. 'She's the famous sex-change!'

Wicked creature! The couple died of embarrassment, simply *died*. The woman was choking herself, then the pearls snapped and shot all over the coffee shop. I stormed out. I'd checked in as the Hon. Mrs Corbett, as it got one marginally better treatment. Now it was round the hotel in ten seconds.

Twenty-four hours later Viva and I made it up with tears and champagne in the discotheque. It seemed that no matter what happened or what we encountered we remained friends.

It was at a Viva party that I met James Bailey. He introduced himself and then fell over in an alcoholic coma and had to be carried up to one of the bedrooms. He became my great opera partner. Very tiny, very fat, very effeminate, James nonetheless had the knack of commanding people's respect. As a young man, he had come under the influence of Oliver Messel, Tony Snowdon's uncle, and had designed for La Scala and Covent Garden. But he was ruined by the drink – he would check into a clinic and have himself put to sleep for three days solid in order to give his liver a holiday. His other vice was uniformed policemen. He tended to importune them while they were on duty.

James also suffered from absent-mindedness. Having inherited a house in Scotland, he forgot he was having one of the bedroom floors replaced, walked in and fell through it to the floor below, breaking his nose.

His moods were utterly unpredictable. About three times a year, he would clap his hands together and say, 'Isn't it time I bought you a frock?' and he'd go off to Thea Porter or Yuki or Bill Gibb to choose one. One mouth-watering jacket of cream ostrich feathers I idiotically gave to Liza Minnelli in Tramp discotheque in a fit of drunken generosity.

When we went to the opera, he would hire a limousine and we'd both dress up. One evening in 1965, he called at my flat to take us to Verdi's *Don Carlos*.

We were about to go down when the phone rang. 'Mrs Corbett? This is the Fazakerley Hospital calling...'

36

SONS AND DAUGHTERS

'Signor dottore
Che si può fare?'
[Honoured doctor
What can be done?]

Cosi Fan Tutte (1790), music by Wolfgang Amadeus Mozart,
libretto by Lorenzo da Ponte

M y father was dying.
He was the one family I had truly loved growing up and now his sad life was ebbing away. Ironically, although now a woman, I was the only one of his born sons to attend his funeral.

The voice from Fazakerley Hospital had been straightforward: 'Your father is here. He's dying.'

'Thank you for letting me know.'

I had said nothing whatsoever to James. The opera went ahead as planned, and the next morning I caught the train to Liverpool. I hadn't seen my father since 1961. It was in the same hospital and he had said, 'I always knew, darling. I'm proud of you.'

My sister Theresa was at the hospital. 'You won't recognise him. *He* certainly won't recognise *you*.'

Tuberculosis had shrunk my father to nothing, but I took

253

him by the hand and said, 'Hello, Dad.' He gave me the most wonderful smile. And he did recognise me. Three days later, he died.

I phoned my mother, who said there was an insurance policy to cover the funeral expenses. With help from the hospital, I managed the arrangements.

Theresa was furious that I'd called my mother. She hated her and they hadn't spoken for ages. Now Tess said that, after the burial, she wouldn't speak to me either – and she didn't, for 12 years. Apart from me and Tess, the mourners were Aunty Frances (his sister-in-law) and Aunty May (his sister), who was sweet. I liked her. My brothers could not be found.

Like my father, I've never been sentimental about death. It happens a lot. Like my father too, I'm soft-hearted. Yet, at the funeral parlour, I told them not to go over the top with some elaborate coffin. Father would prefer the cash spent on oysters and mushrooms, gently warmed in cream, and Guinness.

The undertaker came through and said, 'Does anyone want to see him?'

Aunty Frances jumped up and said, 'Yes, I'd love to.'

But I put my foot down. 'None of that nonsense – let's get this thing done.'

Between Fazakerley Hospital and the Roman Catholic cemetery, there was a humpback bridge. As the funeral car approached it, Aunty May said, 'Do you know what happened there?'

'On that bridge?'

'Yes, that's where your grandfather went. In the old days, hearses were pulled by horses with black plumes on their heads. It used to take hours and hours to cross Liverpool by hearse, so there would be stops at pubs along the way.

'Father – your grandfather – was burying your uncle, your father's brother who died young. Father had a drink at all the stops. And in those days, did they drink! Like open sewers they were. By the time they reached the graveside, your grandfather was fully drunk.

'As they came out of the cemetery, he decided to climb up on to the pillion to join the coachman. Going over the hump-bridge, the hearse jolted. It threw him off the top. He landed bang on his head.

'And that was that. That's how your grandfather died, burying his son.'

I wore a dazzling canary-yellow suit to bury my father. It would have appealed to him – bubbly and exciting. Which was more than can be said for the ceremony. The Catholic funeral service had been changed from Latin and the use of English gave the feeling of the priest's boredom with funerals, certainly with this one of a man whose engaging smile and love he'd never known. He sucked his teeth throughout the service. It reminded me of Arthur.

Soon after the funeral, my mother married Bernie. I would have bought them a Chinese meal had I known anything about it.

37

SLAP AND TICKLE

'Include me out.'

HOLLYWOOD MOGUL SAM GOLDWYN

I was at a loss, but I was back in London. I stayed with friends and hoped for work. Then, into my life arrived slim, good-looking Edward Maddock. I'd met him through his brother Peter, who was a friend of Robin Maugham's, but now he turned up penniless at my door.

We were both floating around and I suggested we share a place as brother and sister. We found a slum room in Elm Park Gardens, where we slept together for warmth because it was winter and the gas meter ate more than us.

At one point, there was so little cash we had nothing but boiled potatoes for three weeks. I couldn't find work and refused to go on social security. What money we had came from me pawning jewellery.

When a lovely and talented call-girl said we could use her place at weekends; it was like finding treasure. Her flat was in Nell Gwynne House in Chelsea on the eighth floor. This floor was notorious for working girls.

There were peculiar calls from her clients. I'd pick up the phone and say hello in my husky voice and off they'd go into fantasyland. Edward would put his head on my shoulder and listen in. He became so excited by one of the calls that he made love to me there and then on the floor. Which is how we became lovers.

But the other flat was awful. Strangely, it was Amanda Lear who got us out of that pit. She went off to Europe to work and rented her flat to us. It was tiny but it was warm and inviting, with a draped bedstead and endless hot water.

Harvey Sambrook, a friend from the Chelsea Potter – if only I had had shares – asked me to help out at the Gasworks – by day a junk shop, by night a junk restaurant. My wages were less than a couple of pounds a night plus tips. Post-op, I mastered the idea of being a woman with a formal, groomed and gracious look. It was just the way I wanted to be, the way I wanted to carry myself. It didn't always help – certainly not at the Gasworks. As I served the customers in a black crepe evening dress and two ropes of pearls, I never saw a tip.

Joan Shivarg did the cooking, Harvey waited upstairs, I did downstairs, and between us we'd fend off Joan's would-be lover, who tended to burst in and hit her halfway through the evening. Joan was born a Wyndham, and had she been born a boy she would have inherited Petworth House in Sussex. As it was, the house went to the National Trust and she went to the Gasworks. When Harvey left, Edward came in to help and loathed every minute of it. He got a kick out of picking old salad out of the dustbin, wiping it with a dishcloth, and serving it to the customers. Then Joan left and the place began to fall apart.

Edward began studying law, and we calculated that, if Micky Mullen, a school friend of his, joined us, then Robin Maugham's flat opposite Foyle's in Charing Cross Road would be cheaper to rent than Amanda's. Micky followed Edward everywhere.

At Shaldon Mansions, I was the housewife with two men to

cook for. We went to parties but not if we couldn't afford a taxi, which was quite often. It's no fun going to parties on a bus. At first, Edward loved the fact that I was a celebrity, that we attracted all the attention. Robin Maugham said to him, 'Going out with April is worse than going out with Marlene Dietrich.' But Edward came to hate it when we were introduced as 'April Ashley and her boyfriend'.

Edward's parents strongly disapproved of our living together. His father was a self-made man from Preston in Lancashire. One night I was going to a hippy party and wearing a crazy pink get-up and a pair of outrageous Roman sandals with straps and chains all the way up the legs. Edward announced his parents were to visit. I left before they were due. But I realised I'd left my purse behind and went back. There they were, he standing in tweeds, she sitting in pearls.

''Ow d'ye do,' said the father in a broad Lancashire accent. His only remark about the incident would be to another member of the family: 'I've met April. She 'ad chains on 'er legs.'

Edward and I had decided to find a flat just for ourselves. But, just before moving, Edward said, 'I've got something awful to tell you.'

'Awful for you or for me?'

'Awful for you, I think. What I want to say is – I'm not going to make love to you any more.'

'Why not?'

'Because that part's over. I'm not going to pretend.'

If it had been *EastEnders* or some American soap opera, I would have had hysterics. But I knew Edward well enough to know that if he had made up his mind there was no changing it. He didn't want to stop living with me, but he wanted to stop loving me in a physical way. It was a terrible shock, because by now I was deeply committed to him.

But I couldn't live with him in that way. As I prepared to move out, he said that he would probably kill himself. I was hurt. 'It's all very well for you to tell me coldly in the middle of the street that you don't want to make love to me any more, but that you'd like me to stick around to play nanny – what can you think of me, Edward? I'm not going because I decided it but because you did.'

'You don't care what becomes of me? Whether I try to kill myself?'

'Yes, I do care.' How I cared. 'But it's a risk we'll have to take.'

The world has slapped me in the face many times and I say this not out of self-pity but because it is the case. Sometimes I found I have to toughen then soften very rapidly, something that probably has contributed to the volatility of my behaviour. I was always determined not to take these slaps lying down, but just as determined not to become an embittered old bat. I think I won that one.

But then, I'm a natural optimist; I have a terrific zest for life that frightens me even now. And perhaps suffering is the consequence of this. The more roads you cross, the greater the risk of being hit by cars.

Being single can be such a responsibility day after day, year after year. People imagine that to be single and childless is to be free and unaccountable. Superficially, this is true. But it is also another test of endurance. The burden of individuality for single people is exhausting. It requires you to employ stratagems and draw on reserves of energy you never thought you had. As a result, single people are exceptionally strong and to choose the unmarried life can give a person great power. To be lumbered with it, however, can be painful.

With me, loneliness was never an acute problem. I'm never bored. Some people become very jittery if left to their own devices. Sarah Churchill was rather like this; so was Arthur. A genuine eccentric he turned out to be. Looking back, I cannot see how on earth he and I could ever have made a go of it – or ever imagined we could. All told, we spent no more than ten days together as man and wife.

While sweating it out in that bed in Casablanca, I was convinced that after the operation life could only be marvellous. But isn't it maddening? You move one mountain only to find yourself at the foot of another.

What made me able to survive these abrupt switches of fortune was wonderment at my own transformation. Whenever I looked at myself in the mirror, it was not in self-admiration or self-congratulation but in disbelief. Yes, I looked beautiful. I was told this so many times that it ceased to affect me. That is not quite the same as saying it was unimportant. Many people, including Viva, felt that my chief weakness was an excessive pride in my looks – and Viva said so in her autobiography, *The Weeping and the Laughter*. If it is true, I have always felt it to be a relatively ludicrous failing, comparable to eating too many Maynard's wine gums. The great gift is to feel beautiful.

I never felt beautiful before the operation. And after it? Even approaching five decades on, rarely a day passes without my being astonished and exalted by what was possible for me. I resist the temptation to thank God – although maybe I should have – just as I resisted the temptation to deify Dr Burou, as too many sex-changes develop God fixations on their surgeon.

Nonetheless, the fact of my transformation remains a continuing source of strength and a way to help others. And was, I believed, my most powerful weapon when I decided to try to enforce my claim on the Villa Antoinette.

I was very broke and had understood that the house had been given to me; although I had no deeds in my possession, I had been led to believe that these existed in my name among the papers in Arthur's safe.

My manager's solicitor was Terry Walton. He had worked his way up the hard way, had plenty of drive, was open and unaffected, and I felt I could tell him anything, so I asked him to handle my case. He wrote to Arthur in Spain but there was no reply.

There was the problem of jurisdiction with Arthur in Spain and me pursuing him in the English courts. After months of stonewalling, we decided to initiate proceedings for maintenance as a substitute for a direct claim on the villa. In this, the question of jurisdiction would not arise because of the assets held by Arthur in England.

Arthur was eventually advised that the best way for him to resolve the dispute was to seek an annulment of our marriage. In May 1967, he filed a petition for a declaration that the marriage was 'null and void and of no effect because the respondent [i.e. me] at the time of the ceremony was a person of the male sex; or in the alternative for a decree of nullity on the ground that the marriage was never consummated owing to the incapacity or wilful refusal of the respondent to consummate it'.

I countered by seeking 'a decree of nullity on the ground of either the petitioner's [i.e. Arthur's] incapacity or his wilful refusal to consummate the marriage'.

Legally, lots of long words, and a long time. In human terms, it was sensational. And utterly heartbreaking and humiliating.

And savage, like the Devil's work.

38

CONFUSION IN COURT

'The Devil I safely can aver,
Has neither hoof, nor tail, nor sting;
Nor is he, as some sages swear,
A spirit, neither here nor there,
In nothing — yet in everything.'

PETER BELL THE THIRD (WRITTEN 1819; FIRST PUBLISHED 1939),
PERCY BYSSHE SHELLEY

For me, this was a public battle about my personal transformation that would involve a rerun of all the horrors of my early life, which I had endured so much to escape. For others — the public, the press, the law, the medical profession — it was compelling; it was unique. It was the first time an English court had been asked to decide the sex of an individual.

Arthur's argument was that, since marriage is a biological relationship between a man and a woman, and as biological sex is fixed at birth at the latest, I could not be regarded as a woman for the purposes of marriage.

My contention was that, since the scientific definition of sex is not clear-cut in all cases, and since marriage is also a legal and social relationship between a man and a woman, I should be regarded as a woman for the purposes of marriage because, as a result of my operation, I could function in no other way. Today, looking back, that seems straightforward enough. It wasn't, not by a long, long way. The law took charge.

I was granted alimony of £6 a week because Arthur was working as a barman in Marbella at an estimated £18 per week; if his assets had been taken into account, he would have been counted still a rich man, despite having been cut off from his inheritance.

I was subjected to a series of physical and psychological examinations, firstly by the medical inspectors to the court, then by the doctors for my defence. They were Dr CN Armstrong, consultant physician at the Royal Victoria Infirmary, Newcastle-upon-Tyne; Professor Ivor Mills, Professor of Medicine at Cambridge University; and Professor Martin Roth, Professor of Psychiatry in the University of Newcastle-upon-Tyne.

I went to Addenbrooke's Hospital in Cambridge for a full physical examination. I almost ran out. Indeed, when I drove past that hospital at Christmas in 2005, I gave an involuntary shudder.

'Miss Ashley,' said Professor Mills, 'do you realise I'm on your side?'

'Then why all these dreadful questions about my body before the operation?'

'Because we have to be able to explain you and your body in court. Now lie down. I'll leave you and come back in about ten minutes. Think about it. I'm on your side but I have to know everything.'

After these examinations, I was in a frightful state. I'd just finished with Edward. Everything seemed unreal. It was as if my life had been a fantasy.

All attempts to communicate with Dr Burou failed. He answered none of the letters from all those professors with alphabets after their names.

I was examined all over again by the three doctors on Arthur's side: Professor John Dewhurst, Professor of Obstetrics and Gynaecology at Queen Charlotte's Hospital; Professor Dent, Professor of Human Metabolism at the University College Hospital; and Dr John Randell, consultant psychiatrist at Charing Cross Hospital. Professor Dewhurst performed the three-finger test, which is the standard method of determining whether the vagina can accommodate a normal-sized penis. I passed that one.

The terrible effect of all these medical examinations was to bring me face to face with my almost forgotten pre-operative self. I had to confront George Jamieson again. When they asked me about my penis, it freaked me out. That wasn't me. I was April Ashley, beautiful, transformed April Ashley. I had only pursued what I rightfully believed was mine and now I was the star of my own horror film.

Then, Terry Walton asked me to enlist the help of my mother. Mother! He explained that her evidence about me as a child, as George, could be vital in my case. I should have known better.

My mother and Bernie were now running a corner grocery shop at Denton on the outskirts of Manchester. They'd achieved their ambition of moving into a bungalow. I rang the doorbell in Frederick Street, Denton.

'Hello,' she said. 'When are you leaving?'

'Tomorrow morning.'

'You won't get Bernie's name in the papers, will you?'

'Mother, they're not *interested* in Bernie.'

'Oh, that's good. Do you like the bungalow?'

'Yes, it's very nice.'

'It's lovely.'

I'd taken bottles of rosé. After the second bottle, she relaxed more and more, but I didn't. I tried to explain to her about the divorce, its implications, but she couldn't take it in and preferred to enlighten me about Theresa's awfulness, how Theresa wouldn't speak to her, how Marjorie came to see her only when she wanted something, and how the boys were much better only she didn't see much of them either.

I ended up having a polite battle with a mother I didn't know and a person I couldn't reach. The more we talked, the more I realised that she was much fonder of Arthur than she was of me. And that she was a scatterbrain and would be anybody's under cross-examination.

I'd gone to see if she could and would testify on my behalf, and came away terrified that she might.

I was staying with my friend Joan Foa and her husband Giorgio at their house in Holland Park. She knew Roger Ormrod, a possible judge in my case. He was also a doctor and we thought he would not only understand the case but even be sympathetic towards me. When the letter arrived saying he would be hearing the case, Joan and I did a little dance of joy around her kitchen.

My leading counsel was JP Comyn QC, assisted by Leonard Lewis. They both had their work cut out in a field where even the experts did not agree. Mr Comyn was one of the most persuasive and feared advocates of the time and was extremely fashionable.

But I think he underestimated the complexity of the argument that would have to be mounted in my defence and the force with which it would have to be presented if we were to succeed. He held too much faith in putting me in the witness box and letting my appearance as a tall glamorous woman do the job for him.

By contrast, Arthur was represented by Joseph Jackson QC, a thoroughly rude and unpleasant man – and one of the best divorce lawyers in Britain.

Judge Ormrod, hopefully my champion, confined deliberation to my original biological classification, disregarding the psychological factor. 'Since marriage is essentially a relationship between man and woman, the validity of the marriage in this case depends, in my judgment, on whether the respondent is or is not a woman.

'I think, with respect, that this is a more precise way of formulating the question than that adopted in paragraph two of the petition, in which it is alleged that the respondent is a male. The greater, of course, includes the less, but the distinction may not be without importance, at any rate in some cases.

'The question then becomes what is meant by the word "woman" in the context of marriage, for I am not concerned to determine the "legal sex" of the respondent at large.'

Who was I?

Or, more alarmingly, *what* was I?

This was going to be debated in front of the whole world. Thousands of people like me, or people confused and troubled by their sexuality, had their rights – in some cases their lives – resting on Corbett v. Corbett (otherwise Ashley) in the Probate, Divorce and Admiralty Division of the Royal Courts of Justice in London's Strand. The evening before the trial, I worried about what to wear, distractedly watched some television, got a takeaway chicken vindaloo and munched a couple of Mandrax tablets in an attempt to sleep. They didn't help.

On 11 November 1969, drowsy from lack of sleep but shaken awake by coffee and the need to get going, I put on a black velvet maxi-coat and a fox hat. It was a tough decision. If I had been too severe, I would have been called too butch; too feminine and they'd say I was trying too hard.

Friends had arranged a car, which took me back of the court to avoid the press. Silly thought, the reporters knew all the tricks and swarmed across the courtyard. I was ushered across the famous Great Hall, and Terry Walton and Mr Comyn were outside Number Two Court.

Arthur was there with his lot. He was in a dark suit and tie, and looked much older than I had expected. 'How silly,' I thought, 'that I can't go over and greet him.' More than all the probing questions and fingers, this simple fact made me realise that I was now in the grip of something inhuman.

Just as frightening was the thought of going back to the past, to the days when I could never look in the mirror because I felt a total freak, someone supposed to be one thing but turning into another. Now I had surrendered my soul to the lawyers and would have to watch while they kicked it about among themselves.

39

LEGAL X-RAYS

'Just the facts, Ma'am.'

DETECTIVE SERGEANT JOE FRIDAY (JACK WEBB),
DRAGNET (1954)

At times inside Number Two Court in the Strand, it sounded like some hospital soap opera, an episode of *ER*. The plot was just as perplexing. The world has changed, but only so very recently in the 21st century have the laws that affect many, many thousands of people around the world managed to catch up. Yet one factor will never change. Nature often plays games, cruel tricks that mix up hormones and chromosomes, those scientific mysteries – certainly, to most people – that shape our lives.

In my divorce case, this is how it was. Abnormalities of sexual identity are divided into two broad categories: the psychological and the physical. Of the psychological, two main abnormalities are recognised – the transvestite and the transsexual, although transsexualism may possibly have some physical origin too.

A transvestite is someone with a strong desire to wear the clothes of the opposite sex. This is usually intermittent and not accompanied by the corresponding desire to live and pass as a member of the opposite sex. Transvestite males are frequently heterosexual.

The transsexual, on the other hand, desires to become to the fullest possible extent a member of the opposite sex. Transvestitism and transsexualism are both far more common among males than among females.

While disagreeing strongly on where the emphasis should lie, the medical witnesses on both sides agreed that there are four fundamental criteria for assessing the sexual identity of an individual. These are:

Chromosomal sex. Normally, a person has 23 pairs of chromosomes in his or her ordinary body cells. All ova carry the X. There are two varieties of spermatozoa, one X, the other Y. Fusion of the ovum with an X spermatozoon produces an embryo of XX chromosomes and eventually a normal female. Fusion of the ovum with a Y spermatozoon produces an XY embryo and eventually a normal male.

Gonadal sex. This refers to the presence of either testes or ovaries, and the hormonal ratios that they regulate.

External body form or genital sex. The presence of a penis and scrotum or a vagina, plus secondary sexual characteristics.

Psychological sex. The standard here is the Terman-Miles Test, an extensive questionnaire that the patient is asked to complete.

For most, there is no problem. All four will be congruent. But naturally there are exceptions. There can be errors at the stage of chromosomal fusion resulting, for example, in an XXY chromosome pattern or an XO (i.e. single X). The XXY gives rise to Klinefelter's syndrome, an undermasculinised male with atrophied testes and some breast enlargement.

At puberty, the secondary sexual characteristics fail to develop in the proper way. The XO is Turner's syndrome. An X goes missing, producing an individual with the external appearance of a female but no ovaries and, again, failure of the normal changes at puberty.

The development of a normal male or female is not governed exclusively by the chromosomes. The correct chemical balance in the embryo is also critical. For example, the adrenogenital syndrome, in which the chromosomes are XX but the external genitalia may appear to be male. What has happened is that abnormal enlargement of the clitoris has produced the appearance of a penis and fusion of the labia the appearance of a scrotum. But there are no testicles and further examination reveals the deception. In most cases, hormone treatment and surgical intervention enables the woman to live as a normal fertile female.

Alternatively, a subject has XY chromosomes and testes but the external genital appearance of a woman, with well-formed breasts (testicular feminisation syndrome) due to the tissues being insensitive to male hormones. Testes are usually found in the abdomen. Surgical resolution of this problem is far more difficult, since it is always easier to remove an excess than it is to supply a want.

All the doctors agreed that the above examples, which are not very uncommon, would be classified as 'intersex'. The physical criteria fail to agree. Many doctors, including Dr Armstrong, define intersex as the state in which any of the criteria, including the psychological, fail to agree.

But because society demanded that we be either male or female, the medical profession had to assign the subject to one sex or the other. As Professor Dewhurst put it, 'We do not determine sex – in medicine we determine the sex in which it is best for the individual to live.' So what about me? Could I be classified as intersex and therefore be reassigned to the female sex as being that in which it was best for me to live? That was the medical consideration.

And, were I not to be classified as intersex, would my post-operative transsexual status nonetheless entitle me to be classified as a woman for the purposes of marriage? That was the legal consideration.

Of my chromosomal sex, there was no doubt. Professor Hayhoe found it to be XY: male.

Of my gonadal sex, there was no evidence, although it was presumed male at birth. Professor Mills and Dr Armstrong thought that I was a probable case of Klinefelter's syndrome. This occurs in the case of XXY chromosomes but occasionally in XY too. They accepted my statement of spontaneous breast development and small testes and generally feminised figure prior to the taking of oestrogen, underlined by the report from the Walton Hospital in Liverpool.

Professor Mills attached much importance to the reference to 'little bodily or facial hair'. His examination of my body found no evidence of male hair growth whatsoever, either on my face or elsewhere, and, once such hair develops, evidence of it can never be entirely eliminated. An endocrinologist, he felt that subjects with a decidedly abnormal ratio between male and female hormones might also be candidates for intersex.

He referred to a chemical test carried out on my urine, which indicated that my hormonal balance was strongly female in character. Another test produced a more ambiguous result. Neither test was allowed in evidence, because they were not carried out under legal supervision.

Of my genital sex, it was now female due to vagino-plasty, though male at birth.

With regard to psychological sex, I took the Terman-Miles Test. The average male scores 65+, the average female -31. My score was -15, the conclusion being that my psyche was emphatically female in orientation. Unfortunately, this test was also inadmissible because it wasn't carried out under legal supervision.

Dr Armstrong and Professor Roth felt that transsexuals could not be classified as properly male or female and could only be usefully described as intersex. All their attempts to broaden the discussion along these lines were cut short by my fading champion, Ormrod. He agreed with Professor Dewhurst and Dr Randell that, in questions of sex-determination, little regard should be given to psychological factors when chromosomal, gonadal and genital sexes are all the same.

I tried to understand all this in my numbed, incredulous state of mind, as I sat in the front row of my very own freak show. After all of it, I felt once again like a circus act, gazed down upon from the public gallery by the sort of people who paid to see the Elephant Man. It wasn't like Le Carrousel, where I made a choice. In this, as I saw it, I had no choice.

The one person who did not look me in the eye was Mr Justice Ormrod. Through his little spectacles, he glanced furtively in my direction and mumbled his references to me with, I sensed, distaste.

I felt stripped, denuded and humiliated in front of the world. I thought I was going to die. I wondered if maybe I should have. But I quickly lost that thought, for it would have been the ultimate surrender – and I had long overcome that.

40

MRS CORBETT

'Whom God wishes to destroy, he first makes mad.'
EURIPIDES

Maybe it was an omen. One of the first things to be discussed was what to call me. I was happy with 'April Ashley', but they settled on 'Mrs Corbett'.

Mr Corbett and I sat on the front bench with our solicitors and the QCs one bench up behind us. Everyone stood for the entrance of Mr Justice Ormrod, whom I felt didn't like me. I mentioned this to Terry and Professor Mills over lunch in the basement of the courts and they laughed it off. But I knew Ormrod was disconcerted by me. His behaviour towards me was contemptuous. Judges are the absolute rulers of their domain, and can play at being God, a temptation they do not always resist.

I thought it rather ironic that the man led – Arthur's case was opened first. He was very frank and clever about his personal life. He explained that he had had sexual relations with many women before, during and after his marriage to Eleanor. He also

275

described his sexual deviations. From an early age, he had experienced a desire to dress up in female clothes. In the early stages of his marriage, he had done so in the presence of his wife on a few occasions. Subsequently, he had dressed as a woman four or five times a year, keeping it from his wife, but the demanding urge continued. He eased it with pornography.

He openly gave evidence that he then went to male brothels in London and had frequent homosexual encounters with many men. He said he didn't indulge in anal intercourse. He did become more and more involved, and interested, in sexual deviations of all kinds, though.

When he dressed as a woman and looked in the mirror, he said, 'I didn't like what I saw. You want the fantasy to appear right. It utterly failed to appear right in my eyes.'

From our first meeting at the Caprice, he said he had been mesmerised by me. 'This was so much more than I could ever hope to be. The reality was far greater than any fantasy. It far outstripped any fantasy for myself. I could never have contemplated it for myself.'

It was explicit, hot and honest stuff. As far as I know, he held nothing back, although some famous titled names were kept out of his revelations about the male brothels. I hadn't known about how much gay sex he had indulged in.

And suddenly, I realised what he was doing. So did my medical and legal advisers. Arthur was emphatically presenting himself in vivid, sordid detail as a deviate. By adopting this very ahead-of-its-time confessional approach as the contrite pervert, he cast a pall of depravity over our entire relationship. It was an attempt to say our marriage was no more than a squalid prank, a deliberate mockery of moral society perpetrated by a couple of queers for their own twisted amusement.

By implication, I too was a deviate, and no more than a deviate. Certainly not a woman, physically and emotionally. He appeared to be apologising in court – and got sympathy. I was not apologising for being myself and sympathy wasn't forthcoming.

It was the first turning point of a case that was now revealed as something quite different from an objective consideration of my status for marriage purposes. I now had to defend myself against an all-purpose stigma of indecency, against the prevailing opinion, led by Arthur's testimony, that our marriage was a shameful joke because I myself was a shameful joke.

At one point, Ormrod suddenly asked if it were necessary to continue wasting the taxpayers' money. Both Arthur's lawyer and mine protested that it was important to hear the evidence in full and Ormrod grumpily agreed to go on. In the face of his alarming lack of interest in the debate, my counsel began to look very worried indeed.

There was another concern, as Professor Mills explained, 'There is a great deal of snobbery in this case, April.'

I suppose it *was* another example of what John Prescott would call the 'class war'. Us Vs Them. I assumed Professor Mills meant not only the obvious prejudices against transsexuals, but also a more subtle association between Arthur and the men around him. Why should they have any truck with someone who, born in a Liverpool slum, not only refused to stay there but also had the damn nerve to change her sex into the bargain? And, not only that, but more, cheek of all cheek, had the impertinence to marry into the peerage as well? I felt they saw me as an *arriviste* and so in their eyes not worthy of serious consideration.

Dr Randell's psychiatric examination was, to say the least, curt. At one point, I had my head X-rayed because Professor Dent said it would show male characteristics. He was wrong. Dent, by far the friendliest of the opposition, seemed to regret having been caught up in the affair – as, later, did Professor Dewhurst. The provisional nature of his conclusions spotlighted themselves under cross-examination.

They say that if your shoulders are wider than your hips it is a sign of masculinity. My shoulders were half an inch wider than my hips.

When the discussion turned to the question of my beard, the subject was raised of the races of the world who do not have hairy faces – Orientals, Mongolians, Red Indians. I longed to cry out, 'I'm not a fucking Red Indian!' Both men and women have hair on all parts of their bodies except the palms of the hands and the soles of the feet. This varies in amount and character according to sex. My face is quite downy, but of female type, and my pubic hair is in the classic female pattern. I used to worry about my legs and would have them waxed. My beautician said to me, 'Miss Ashley, if you think you've got hairy legs, you should see Elizabeth Taylor's shoulders.'

And the past came back into court; Dr Vaillant was subpoenaed by the opposition. He was still head of the psychiatric department at Walton. But I was shocked when they brought him in because he was in a desperate condition, a terrified man. He said he suffered from vertigo and they had to all but shove him into the witness box.

The judge said, 'Mrs Corbett, will you please stand up.'

I stood rigidly to attention.

'What do you think of the respondent now, Dr Vaillant?'

He screwed up his face and his eyes started out on stalks. He hissed one word: 'Mincing!'

After extracts from the Walton report were read out, they let him go. Vertigo? A few feet up in the witness box? It was cruel to bring him in. He had no useful testimony to offer.

Jackson tried to imply that I was a gold-digger and had conned Arthur into marriage. Arthur said he knew all of my history at the time of our marriage and that he felt for me the love that a man feels for a woman. The judge said he thought this was all part of Arthur's fantasies.

'But,' said Jackson, 'you received and accepted many presents from Mr Corbett?'

'Yes, every single one chosen by my husband and never asked for by me.'

Then, the moment I'd been dreading arrived. I could understand Dr Vaillant's fear a little better. They asked me about my body when I was George. It was a horror of horrors to be quizzed about the anatomy of my body before the operation. I broke down. I cried.

For any transsexual, this is the most distressing memory of all – we bury it, we try to forget it, we push it further and further into the recesses of the mind, and so it remains the centre of insecurity.

It's scarier for me, for I like everything in the open; no secrets with me, no blanking out. Let's shout and scream and have a tantrum and then be friends again. But don't hide the problem.

I have already described my male genitals as meagre, and that is exactly what they were. To my eyes, my appearance was otherwise more female than male. I couldn't be more specific in court, more clinically precise, and I think that went against me. There was no helpful detail in the Walton report. This made it difficult for my doctors' belief in an XY case of Klinefelter's syndrome to be taken into account.

If you had the basic security of knowing if you were a man or a woman, it would still be abhorrent to have the details of your sexual mind and body cavalcaded in court, in public. So, how did I feel? It was horrible. I wanted to scream for help. I felt I was in an asylum. Yet having been forced to meet George again, to confront my previous self in public, it freed me. It took a long, long time, but this courtroom catharsis was a new beginning. I emerged a stronger individual, having acknowledged aspects of my past that in my weakness I should have preferred to regard as simply not being there.

An analogy for that time would be the working-class boy who works his way into the middle class, his biggest problem is coming to terms with his origins. My working-class origins never bothered me in the slightest. They were completely upstaged by my more fundamental and harrowing transference from male to female.

Some transsexuals are no happier after surgery, and there are many suicides. Their dream is to become a normal man or woman. This is not possible, can never be possible, through surgery. Transsexuals should not delude themselves on this score. If they do, they are setting themselves up for a big, possibly lethal, disappointment. It is important that they learn to understand themselves as transsexuals and, if they find this difficult, various groups and associations are there to help them. (See Appendix 2: Help and Advice Contacts.)

For post-operative transsexuals, the greatest test is accepting totally what it actually means: *that they were never natural males and can never be natural females either*. That is the trauma we live with every day. On these grounds alone, it seems to me, we are the most obvious of all intersex types. Far too simple, of course.

After 17 difficult days, the trial concluded on 9 December, but there were to be more nervous weeks. Judge Ormrod would not deliver his judgment until 2 February 1970.

Arthur, with whom I had hardly exchanged a glance, flew back to Spain, but not before Terry Walton had chased him down the Strand and slapped a writ on him, seeking a court declaration that Arthur held the Villa Antoinette in trust for me.

A happy thought as Christmas approached.

The only one.

41

THE NIGHTMARE

First witch: *'When shall we three meet again,*
In thunder, lightning, or in rain?'
Second witch: *'When the hurly-burly's done,*
'When the battle's lost and won.'

MACBETH, ACT I SCENE I, WILLIAM SHAKESPEARE

I was now, of course, famous around the world. Or notorious. It all depended on the point of view. I was also a nervous wreck. I had lost about 30 pounds in weight and was now hovering around seven stone. Painfully thin for me. But clinging on. Only just. And my past returned again, but this time to help.

Just before the trial ended, I was leaving the courtroom when there it was, standing in the corridor in boots and a full-length black mink and heavy dark glasses. The return of Rita. I was in a state and, at first, only thought of her as Gigi from Paris, but across the road in a teashop it all came back. She had four children but had divorced Marcel. Time shifted out of the way and it was like the old days. She drove me back to Holland Park, where we brewed endless pots of tea and talked and talked.

I hadn't seen or heard anything of her for 12 years. Apart from a broader American accent, she hadn't changed at all. Yet, in its very different way, her divorce had been almost as traumatic as mine was being, because it had clearly taken a similar toll on her self-assurance and sense of identity.

When we'd last met I had been Toni April. But she had recognised me from the newspaper photographs. She'd been unable to trace Joey. I told her that he'd gone to Canada and bought a boat.

We were partners in trouble. And I was also a junior partner – thanks to Edward Maddock's brother Peter – in a restaurant near Harrods at 8 Egerton Gardens Mews.

After Edward Maddock and I separated, through one of his friends, I took off, sweeping my chinchilla cloak around me, and found refuge in Oxford with lots of high-living undergraduates in velvet and lace and ruffles, like Count Adam Zamoyski. I was always surrounded by handsome young men and I went to bed with every one of them. The Oxford balls weren't considered a success unless I was there. Or the picnics in Magdalen Fields. I went up again to that most marvellous city, to a dancing party at Lady Margaret Hall. Rita came with me. She took to the place directly and her high spirits awed them. She could party all night, have one hour's sleep and be as fresh as the morning milk for more excesses the following day.

The beautiful undergraduates were fine therapy, for they were less interested in the trial than in their own exotic affairs. Richard Doyle, great-nephew of Sir Arthur Conan Doyle and a novelist himself, paid me exquisite attentions at a time when my self-esteem was at its most vulnerable. His letters were a help during that nerve-racking winter.

As were the pots of tea with Rita, who was that human bridge between my past and present and future – which, in the form of 2 February 1970, arrived quickly. It was indeed the Day of Judgment.

I had lost another seven pounds in weight and was down to six and a half stone. A skeleton. But I was in better shape than Arthur. At 9am that morning, he was found in a coma at the Villa Antoinette, which further fattened the headlines. He was discovered face down on the sitting-room floor by the maid, who had come in to take Mr Blue for a walk. They reported he'd been unconscious for at least 16 hours and had missed his flight to London. His doctor said he'd hurt his head in a fall.

Without Arthur present, Judge Ormrod delivered – and it was worse than the worst: '*I hold that it has been established that the respondent is not, and was not, a woman at the date of the ceremony of marriage, but was, at all times, a male.*

'*The marriage is, accordingly, void...*'

It was like having a bucket of ice thrown all over me. I was totally chilled. To the bone. These were moments that seemed to last a year.

Looking through his full judgment all this time on, it still makes me shake and want to scream at how cruel it was. I wasn't the only one upset by the attitude. My lawyer friend Peter Maddock was with me in court. He grabbed my arm and said, 'We're going – you don't have to listen to this.'

I left the court. But it was running away. For, even if I didn't listen to it, I had to accept it.

The press were outside and were told, 'If you want to speak to Miss Ashley, there will be a press conference in half an hour at 8 Egerton Gardens Mews.'

As we went there, the consequences of Judge Ormrod's ruling began to sink in. Any consideration of intersex was discounted by the judge, who in some instances had evidently not believed the testimony relating to it and in others had held it to be irrelevant. The psychological sex, he said, would have importance only when the biological criteria were not congruent. Transsexuals around the world therefore lost all marriageable rights, and were subject to needless and petty discrimination, for more than 30 years. Not since the Oscar Wilde trial had a civil matter led to such socially disastrous consequences.

As for my villa – forget that.

I recall very little of the press circus. They asked me what I felt about Arthur's coma.

'I'm sorry about it. But I shan't be flying out to see him. That part of my life has ended.

'Yes, I'm still to be regarded as a woman for social purposes – woman's passport, woman's prison, woman's national insurance, woman's hospital...'

'What are you going to do now?'

'Carry on. What else can one do?'

They never asked how. I did. Ormrod, with his cruel judgment, had dealt with me, with this *arriviste*. How better to slap me down for my cheek than to deliver a verdict denying I was a woman at all?

That night I lay on the bed and wept myself, finally, to sleep. The next day I kept my promise – I carried on.

In Britain at the time, the biggest talk-show host was a friendly enough, smiling lad called Simon Dee. I was asked to appear the first Sunday after the judgment. I said I could only do it if I had a large glass of whisky to have on the set. Eventually, they relented. A TV first.

John Lennon and Yoko Ono were on with me, talking about their bags. What I would have given for a Lennon 'Here comes the fucking Duchess'. But he was in the thrall of Yoko. She seemed to pull all his strings. And they talked about their bags. They would climb into them and stay there. Bag for Peace. Bag for Love. Bag for Whatever. They kept climbing into these bags.

I thought of the circus again and, oh my, we were all clowns together.

If it were all happening in today's world, I would be offered all sorts of counselling. I don't want to get into my views – yet – of the politically correct world we live in, but I just had to cope. It was not an easy time in my life and there had been some grim times in the past.

I was in a state of shock. As I came out of it, I went into a deep depression. The judge's words went round and round in my head provoking ugly nightmares and the physical sensations associated with fear. I felt guilty. Hideously so.

My pride had taken a beating from which it has never fully recovered. I confessed now that to this day some of that trauma is still with me. Judge Ormrod did a devil's job, like a witch's curse.

I had been proud of escaping from the Liverpool slums; I had been proud of finding by myself the solution to my problems of sexual identity, and now it was just thrown back in my face as worse than nothing.

Nervous wreck? I was a physical wreck too. I was completely run down. I checked into the Forest Mere health farm in Hampshire, where I spent most of the time alone. I had to face people, but I couldn't. I didn't know what to say to them and they didn't know what to say to me. Ava Gardner was there, preparing for a film. I wanted to introduce myself, but all my confidence had been erased. Meals were served in my room.

My mental state was horrific. Why was I alone? Why had I no family to help me? When your confidence in yourself as a person is knocked completely away, it produces uncontrollable feelings that amount to suffering from acute claustrophobia and acute agoraphobia at the same time. Everything was out of control.

I was frightened of hurting myself. Since Casablanca, I had never done this but my aloneness increased the apprehension that I might do something silly by mistake; not because I sought death, but rather escape from the torture.

Self-control was my answer. I'd brought a bottle of Remy Martin to help me sleep. Each night I stared at it, longing to crack it open and swallow the lot but knowing that if I did the cognac would destroy whatever drive remained in me.

It was one of the modest challenges I set myself, which kept me sane by giving my willpower something specific to deal with. I love reading but couldn't manage it. I decided to put the television on and leave it on all the time just for the noise. I often slept through it. I kept nodding off or cutting out. The awful thing about depression is losing the powers of discrimination.

I was staying in a row of chalets, the walls between which were very thin. In the adjacent chalet, a man was on the telephone and I heard him say, 'You'll never guess who's in the cabin next to mine – that monster April Ashley.'

At that moment, the feeling of loneliness was never more complete. More than an anguish of friendlessness, it was a bleak and limitless conviction that I was outside humanity altogether and therefore that humanity was meaningless and had no existence.

This lasted for, oh my, some moments. Then I became angry. Bloody angry. I was angry with the man next door. I had gone way beyond the confines of self-pity, towards insanity, but my anger brought me back from the edge.

I tried the sauna bath. It was crowded with overweight women. I looked like something out of a concentration camp and was embarrassed by my body which, after the court case, was the object of their uneasy curiosity. They were embarrassed too.

Big Blonde Betty gave me a massage every morning. I asked for as much oil and cream as possible because my skin was out of condition and flaking off. Followed by a steam bath, more oil, beauty treatments, my daily walk, rabbit food, TV, dozing, fitful sleep. But I didn't want to stay at Forest Mere forever. I was scared that if I didn't rejoin the world immediately the depression would settle on me and that would be the end. That was progress in itself.

Yet I was apprehensive about leaving this cocoon. How would people react? Wonderfully, there were many people secure enough in themselves not only to accept me, in all my vivid headline sinfulness, but also to champion me. Close friends like Viva weren't bothered in the least, except for my welfare.

Looking back, I should probably have forgotten the health farm and gone to some sunny spot in Europe and made love with abandon. Whatever. I don't know if it was wiser to do what I did, but things will be what they will be. Sometimes we do have no control over them.

Strangers reacted in all sorts of ways. There was the usual screwed-up minority who made a point of referring to me as 'him', especially if I were within earshot. Some poked me in the breasts to see if they were real, or pulled my hair to see if it were false. What amazes me is that in other respects these were normal people. Sex cases seem to bring out weird secret obsessions in such individuals. They acted as if they had a perfect right to humiliate me in this way, as if my past meant that I surrendered all rights to the basic courtesies.

Generally, though, people were unexpectedly kind and went out of their way to boost me. One woman who had attended the trial every day ran across me in the street. In Sloane Square, I felt a tug on my sleeve and turned round. I recognised her at once. About 60 years old, very slim and smart. 'Miss Ashley, do you remember me? I hope you won't take any notice of that idiotic judgment. You would be foolish to do so. Live your life, be wonderful. I watched you. You are very brave.'

I mumbled something and ran off. It was terrible, running away from her like that, but I felt the tears coming. Right up until that moment, I'd kept it all in. I'd read the letters alone with the odd little tear. But now this woman in Sloane Square had simply reached across and touched my heart and had almost triggered the flood.

I wanted to sob it all away. I should have done. But I held it back – just. It was a long time before I recovered the courage to let myself go in this respect. Crying is not given to us for nothing. It is a release for distressed emotions.

There were many letters, of course, mostly from women, mostly kind and encouraging. Only two were truly abusive. 'You're a bloody man, get back into trousers, who do you think you're kidding?' That kind of thing. And they could get lost.

Now I had to consider whether I could go through it all again with an appeal. The lawyers thought there was a good chance. Terry Walton was so convinced he offered to help fund such a venture; money was the problem. I had received legal aid for the case, but it is not granted for appeals.

The *Sunday Mirror* had paid me £5,000 for my side of the story. My Egerton Gardens Mews partners suggested I invested it all in the restaurant, otherwise it would be swallowed up in costs: legal aid had to be paid back if you got money within seven years.

The cost of the appeal was assessed at £7,000, a fortune back then, and much of it had to be placed with the court by 24 August 1970. An American foundation dealing with transsexuals was willing to underwrite the appeal, but this had to be dropped when it was discovered that Professor Dewhurst sat on their English committee.

Reflecting back on that time now, I regret I did not pursue the appeal with more verve, but I had little energy. I'd had the living daylights kicked out of me and we did not proceed. Yet I do have if-only moments because medical and legal opinion and comment after my case leaned towards my arguments.

A month after the decision went against me in London, a court in Grasse in the South of France ruled in the case of Helene Hauterive, a 35-year-old transsexual who had an operation identical to mine in Casablanca. Their verdict was that she was a female for legal purposes and could marry if she wished.

In New York, Dr Harry Benjamin commented on my case, 'The judge's ruling is terribly illogical. It is a very inhuman decision.'

Dr Howard Jones Jnr, of Baltimore's Johns Hopkins Medical School, America's leading institute for transsexual research, said, 'The sex an individual considers himself to be is an equally important factor. It isn't the operation that changes the sex. The operation merely reinforces a decision that has already been made. One who is familiar with this particular problem soon comes to the conclusion that you can't disregard the fact that someone believes he is a female.' What it effectively did was create a third sex for whom marriage was not possible, this third sex comprising not only all transsexuals but also certain intersex categories.

Why didn't Ormrod order the hormone tests and the Terman-Miles Test to be properly carried out? I wish he had, for if I had been proven to be an intersex I'd have received a far more sympathetic hearing. Still, that's a marginal question.

What was tragic was that just because Arthur and I made a farcical mess of things a general principle had to be extrapolated, denying transsexuals marriageable status altogether. To deny a distinct social group such a right is a very serious matter and yet Ormrod did not seem to take it seriously. He came to his conclusions irritably, as if it were only what we deserved, that we somehow had to be penalised rather than accounted for.

To my mind, the medical arguments should have been only a preamble to the central issue – how could the law have responded intelligently and usefully to the predicament of all transsexuals? If he had not taken such a narrow view, we might have made some progress – because, however you look at it, it is simply not very bright to say that one must ignore the consequences of operative intervention. If we were always and only to refer back to first causes, then civilisation could never happen at all.

These operations don't take place for the hell of it; they are not a branch of light entertainment – and yet Ormrod persisted in viewing the operation as a kind of wantonness on my part.

A lot of transsexuals living in obscurity were unmarried by my judgment and remain helpless before the law should a conflict enter the relationship. Yet I take some comfort that, as I was in Casablanca, I was one of the pioneers on the legal issues. At the time Christine Jorgensen's lawyer, Robert Sherman, was prescient if somewhat optimistic with his timing: 'The legal entity of changing sex is only now evolving. It will take 20 years before it is established.' It was to be a longer wait.

I'd finished with crying. The qualities in myself which I like least – my stubbornness, my bluntness, my egotism – were now the very ones I had to draw on to pull myself up. Not only did I intend to stick around, I intended to create a fanfare and be seen around too. It was time to put my foot back on the accelerator and go full speed ahead. No matter what, I would be a winner.

I was April Ashley.

42

REAWAKENING

*'Everything that happens happens as it should, and if you
observe carefully, you will find this to be so.'*

MEDITATIONS, MARCUS AURELIUS

Drinks with Princess Margaret appeared reasonably high
profile to me. I got there on a bottle of champagne. And
let me explain how. Our restaurant AD8 opened with a major
party. 'A' was for April, 'D' for Desmond 'Dizzy' Morgan and '8'
for 8 Egerton Gardens Mews. My partners founded a company to
run the restaurant and I had a five-year contract that took all my
earnings, including the £5,000 newspaper money, in return for
which I officially got £60 a month and free accommodation in the
studio above the restaurant.

The principal backer was Eagle Star Insurance. Kit Lambert, co-
manager of The Who, put up £2,000 and there were other investors.
Alan Kaplan, an American doctor, put money in too. He was an
addict who prescribed his own drugs.

Not very long after we opened, I was having dinner with him in
the restaurant. I listened to his morbid talk for an hour or more –
I thought it part of the job – then he staggered to his feet and had
to be helped upstairs to a taxi. A few hours later, I heard he was

dead. Alan had swallowed a bottle of pills in the restaurant but no one had seen him do it.

The extent of the drug culture back then was astonishing – I'm amazed I never got into it. I was certainly drinking for England. Everyone seemed to be out of their heads. Hardly anyone talked much sense. One evening I saw Kit hand over £1,000 – astonishing money then – for cocaine, but what to me looked like a tiny packet of sugar. I saw all sorts of people spending money like that on all sorts of drugs every night. It was awful what the drugs did; such nice people died from them, like Jimi Hendrix. It was as though they were leaping into a chemical hell.

Kit Lambert was the son of composer Constant Lambert, and terrific fun. He was assistant director on *The Guns of Navarone* and *From Russia with Love*, but abandoned film for The Who. But he could never beat drugs; he died of a cerebral haemorrhage after falling down the stairs of his mother's home in 1981. He was always a gentleman, even when he was out of his mind. One evening two policemen came to find me at the club and asked me to go to their patrol car. Kit was in it and screamed, 'April, tell them I'm a state-registered drug addict. They don't know.'

'Well,' I said, 'the whole of South Kensington does now.' I offered to look after him but the policemen would have none of that and took him off to clink. Such a shame.

Yet I still recall him on the opening night of AD8, a lively, witty host as more than 500 guests passed through what was in fact a rather small underground room. We'd got people's attention. One evening a wheelchair appeared at the top of the stairs. This was the trademark of London's most influential restaurant critic, the paraplegic Quentin Crewe who wrote for *Vogue*. Quentin's review was savage – his comment that the basis of our salmon pâté was soap was the nice bit – but it was the longest write-up of the month. I got my revenge when Henry Pembroke and Christopher Thynne bet me a bottle of champagne that I dare not accompany them to the Crewe wedding reception at the Barracuda. In fact, I felt quite confident going along between two lords. When Quentin said, 'April, I do hope you've forgiven me for the write-up,' I was ready: 'I never read my publicity, darling. I just measure it.'

It was at this reception that I met Princess Margaret. I was standing by one of the bars, flushed with introductions, and a young boy approached me. 'Is it true you're April Ashley? I'm Jeremy Sykes. You know my brother Tatton Sykes. Can I get you a drink?'

'But I've already got this big glass of champagne.'

'No, something stronger.' He plonked a tumbler of whisky into my other hand.

'Isn't that Princess Margaret behind you?' I asked.

'Yes it is. Have you met her?'

'No.'

Jeremy turned round and said, ''Ere, Maggie.' He poked her with his finger and it sank into the flesh of her shoulder. 'Maggie, come and meet April.'

With a glass in each hand, I bobbed and said, 'How do you do, Your Royal Highness.' I don't think she liked being called 'Maggie' in front of me. It must have been a great trial for her to be handed round at parties, but she wanted to mix as freely as possible in the real world.

I was fascinated by how sexy she was. Soft perfect skin, Prussian-blue eyes, thick sensual lips, an overweight voluptuous body very well held – she seemed more confident in her body than in anything else.

I was so nervous I jabbered. She was skilful at sustaining a conversation with 'Yes' and 'Really' and 'I'm sure it was'. I finished up by saying, 'Will you do me the great honour of dining at my restaurant? We'll take good care of you. There are private booths at one end where you can see everything that's going on without anyone seeing you.'

'I'll send someone along to look at it,' she said.

'Do you mean you'll have someone case the joint first?' I couldn't help myself. My big mouth again. The words came tumbling out.

She moved away. And never came.

The restaurant took over my life for the next few years. It was hard work seven nights a week and I had to be groomed for it. Nearly every penny I made went back into the business via make-up, hairdos, clothes and shoes. My work began with a cup of tea and *Crossroads* on television.

Unless I had parties, I would go into the restaurant at 8pm to check the tables and flowers. But there were always parties, sometimes four or five a night. It was good advertising. The opera likewise. So long as I appeared in public, my partners did not object. But it was always on to the restaurant afterwards, usually with a crowd, which was good for business.

Oliver Reed's sister Tracy would come in with crowds of film stuntmen. If there were problems with customers paying their bills, I was sent in to mediate. Often they'd say, 'I want to fuck you,' but I'd say, 'Now, now, pay the bill nicely and we'll talk about that over a glass of champagne.' It worked every time with even the most far gone.

AD8 was a long warm pinkish cave, small enough to be intimate, large enough to be profitable. The staff were given the choice of dressing casually or formally, but either way they all had to wear the same. They chose to dress casually. Black trousers and red shirts. Jean-Pierre, our French barman, was a true find. Customers tried to outsmart him by ordering some obscure hideous cocktail and he'd always plonk it down in front of them. I'm convinced he studied these things at night under the bedclothes with a torch.

The first couple of years were great fun. I dreamed we would become an established restaurant and go on for years. The divorce trial had given us a head start, we were booked weeks ahead, but I had a battle on my hands to overcome our original reputation for bad food. We did, though, and one of our most successful dishes was Champagne and Camembert Soup.

Gradually, I was recovering confidence, learning never to forget a name – as the Queen will tell you, this is a priceless asset in dealing with the public.

The restaurant had genuine glamour and genuine characters and was the stopping-off point for many hardcore Knightsbridge and Chelsea socialites. One of my main obstacles was that a new member of staff would cotton on fairly quickly that, when it came to the nitty-gritty, I had little say in the running of the place.

Occasionally, I'd throw a tremendous luvvie tantrum to remind them that I wasn't to be disregarded. The only improvement in my position was that the company leased a flat in Eaton Square of which I had the use. It was on the first floor and so I had the original drawing room. This room was vast and beautiful, so I would dance around barefoot in it to my Puccini and Rodgers and Hammerstein records.

Everyone came to the restaurant, from 'Angry Young Man' John Osborne to the Chinese Ambassador. Elaine Kennedy brought Ingrid Bergman; the delightful Denny Daviss brought Placido Domingo, who sang Neapolitan love songs until 1am, accompanying himself on the baby grand. Others called for 'carryout'; we used to send amazing amounts of food to Mick Jagger and my friends The Rolling Pins at some recording studio in a big house in Hampshire. It was always filet mignon. As far as I knew, they put aside all the trimmings and stuck the meat between a couple of pieces of bread; I suspect they were good at that.

I did finally meet Ava Gardner and she taught me how to drink tequila with salt and lime. She'd had plenty of training with Richard Burton and John Huston when they made *The Night of the*

Iguana on location in Puerto Vallarta in Mexico. Ava was living in semi-retirement in Knightsbridge with her little dog. She came to us about once a month, always very simply dressed, and sometimes she drank a great deal, sometimes nothing at all. She visited her old flame Howard Hughes when he was staying at the Inn on the Park. I pressed her about him but she refused to gossip. Although there was one scrap – once he infuriated her so much she hit him with a frying pan.

Kit Lambert had said he would eat his investment and he came almost every night. Often Keith Moon would join him. Francis Bacon came, bringing the young artists, always falling over and having to be helped up the stairs afterwards. He was a handful.

I'd kept in touch with Barbara Back since she tried to help kill my newspaper exposure, and she had to be helped in as well as out. Barbara was the world's worst driver. She would stop at Belisha beacons and wait for them to turn green. She took me to the première of Robin Maugham's play *Enemy*. There was a big party afterwards at The Ivy. It was torture driving there with her. Even though she went at only 15mph, I always felt in the utmost peril.

'Daddy' Pat Dolin brought Evelyn Laye and Rudolf Nureyev; Bobby Moore brought hunky footballers; Johnny Dankworth and Cleo Laine brought each other. Danny La Rue came and invited me to dinner with Liberace at his house. Even Danny's toilet paper hung out of a dolphin's mouth. Liberace, I couldn't believe. He wasn't at all amusing but extravagantly sentimental. I thought he was going to burst into tears, weeping sequins, at any moment.

Danny La Rue's house couldn't compete with Lionel Bart's, though. Lionel had a musical staircase that played selections from *Oliver!* when you walked up it. He also had a musical lavatory. It played 'Food, Glorious Food' when you flushed it by depressing a large gold crown.

Someone who never came to AD8 was Amanda Lear, which

hurt me. She'd still telephone to say how low she was. I think the
root of her unhappiness was her unease about her sex identity. I'd
say, 'You know you have a standing invitation to dine with me.'
But she wouldn't.

Ian Gibson did a two-hour *Omnibus* on Dalí in 1997 on BBC1
and interviewed Amanda. At one point, he told her that April
Ashley had said she was a transsexual and Amanda replied, 'She
doesn't always tell the truth.'

I was watching the programme with my great friend Ula
Larson and my telephone started ringing off the hook. 'She called
you a liar! Sue the bitch!'

I told everyone, 'No, no, no. She didn't call me a liar. She said
I didn't always tell the truth.'

But she has done well professionally, if not so much in her
personal life. Amanda was the voice of Edna 'E' Mode, with her
funny French accent, in the Italian dubbed version of *The
Incredibles*. She made a film with Gerard Depardieu in 2005 and I
read she had completed another for Pedro Almodóvar, whom I
adore. I was sad when she lost her husband in 2000. Philippe
Malagnac d'Argens de Villele, 51, and his young man Didier
Dieufils, 20, died in a fire at her home near Arles in Provence.
Amanda was working in Italy at the time. Half a dozen paintings
by the Great Masturbator were badly damaged or destroyed in the
fire. She was fond of Philippe. We have a mutual friend in London
and I hear how she is; it's a shame we don't see each other.

There were three Americans I always loved to see at AD8:
Johnny Gallier, Billy McCarty and Tommy Kyle. Johnny died at
the end of 2002 in New York and left me a little money, which
was nice. He was always so charming. Tommy was the most
outrageous and richest of the three. We'd first met ten years
before at a dinner party given by Joan Thring – Mrs Ting-a-Ling,
I called her – Rudolf Nureyev's manager. I liked him, he was so
mischievous, so outspoken.

Tommy was the personal assistant, manager and chief designer to Gustav Leven, Mr Perrier Water, and when in the South of France often lived at Gustav's dreamy Chateau Croix des Gardes on a hill overlooking Cannes. He took me there and it was an adventure.

Especially the mad lesbians.

43

LOVE IS ALL AROUND

'There's some are fou o' love divine,
There's some are fou o' brandy.'
'THE HOLY FAIR' (1786), ROBERT BURNS

One night, Tommy and I were dining out in St Tropez. Fluttering at us from a nearby table was a large flushed woman in middle years, accompanied by a pretty young man dressed in white. She turned out to be Madame de Juste, from Haiti. And the boy in white turned out to be a girl, one of France's top tennis stars.

When the tennis star learned of my identity, she said in that pugnacious French way, 'I don't believe you're April Ashley.'

'And I don't believe you're a woman – show me your tits.'

'Only if you show me yours.'

We unwrapped our respective bosoms in the best restaurant in town and satisfied each other's curiosity. The upshot was that they were invited up to Croix des Gardes for dinner the following day.

'I've heard so much about that house. Can I bring my husband? And my dog?' said Madame de Juste.

The next evening, corseted in beige satin, Madam de Juste arrived like a galleon being tugged into harbour, with her

299

husband, her poodle and a young male lover. As far as I could tell, they were all from Haiti, except perhaps the poodle. There was a handful of other guests, including Lil, Marquise de Valois.

Tommy had arranged for a group of gypsy musicians to come up from the town to entertain us. They went into their routine. We sat sipping brandy, half-smiles on our faces. They wailed. I've as good an ear as the next for a Romany jig, but we were drowning ourselves in brandy.

When they'd shuffled out, the brandy hit us and everything grew much friendlier. Madame de Juste said to me, 'This is an extraordinary house. I'd luff to see your bedroom.'

I took her up there. We'd hardly crossed the threshold when she ripped my zip down. It was one of those strapless black crepe shifts – once the zip is down the weight of the brooches carries it to the floor at once. I was standing there in my bra and panties and pearls. She jumped on me and threw me across the bed.

'Madame de Juste,' I said, struggling for breath, 'you have your husband downstairs and your boyfriend too and now you want to make love to me.'

'Yes, yes, that's right,' she panted.

'Obviously, you're gifted with sensuality, but where will it end?'

'I giff anyfing to make luff wiff you.'

'All right then, I'll have that on your left hand,' pointing to a conker of a diamond set in claws of platinum.

Her manner changed completely. She buttoned up her bodice, smoothed down her hair and marched out of the bedroom slamming the door behind her. We hadn't realised it but her poodle had followed her upstairs and was now trapped inside with me.

'Hello, darling,' I said, 'how are you?'

It came trotting up in its encrusted collar, wagging its tail, and it smiled at me. I was astounded: it had no teeth.

When I returned downstairs, I said to Tommy out of the side of my mouth, 'Not only has she got a husband, a lover, a tennis star and wants to jump around with me, but she's also got a toothless dog – now what do you think that's for?'

'You've got to be joking. I knew she was after you – but, no, surely not the dog?'

'Watch… Come along, my boy.' And the little oddity came wagging up, grinning from ear to ear, showing a fine set of pink gums. Tommy and I collapsed.

Madame de Juste started crying and called me a bitch and a number of other names. I asked her if the poodle were a lap-dog. At this, she hurled herself at the French windows. Luckily, these gave way and she blew out on to the terrace and disappeared. When Tommy realised where she'd gone, he went white, because after dark they let out the hounds. He managed to retrieve her before she was torn to pieces. The husband was no less strange. He didn't say a word all evening. Just smiled throughout. With a shudder, I suddenly realised that he was the dog in human form.

There must have been something in the air, because Lil, Marquise de Valois, had her turns too. She was Norwegian and wore black silk trouser suits, with her hair pulled severely back. She used to sit on the edge of sofas with her knees apart. On this occasion, I was sitting next to her after dinner.

'Phew, the weather's been so hot lately, hasn't it, Madame de Valois?'

'Do call me Lil.'

'All right, that's nice. Lil. I do like you.'

'And I like *you*.' With a tremendous lunge, she went for me. When Tommy came back into the room, Lil was chasing me round and round the circular sofa, trying to lasso me with her arms. My heels were much higher than hers, so I was jolly glad to see him.

I think it was Dame Edna Everage who said, 'Lesbianism leaves a nasty taste in my mouth.' I've nothing against it myself. Who am

I to tell people they mustn't love each other? Many lesbians have fallen for me. But I suppose the reason I've never been able to fall back is that I'm always so smitten with men.

It wasn't so much fun back in London. There was much squabbling between me and the restaurant partners, something I should have dealt with. I had moved to a new flat on the corner of Elm Park Road, where I felt safe. There were many parties. Cecil Beaton gave one at his home in Pelham Crescent. He was snooty. I think he felt I wasn't out of the right drawer. Beaton didn't have the gift of mixing. His range was narrow and he could be unpleasantly precious, with that high, thin voice running like string out of a mean, tight face. His involvement with Greta Garbo, I always thought, had the pathetic quality of a joke from which only Beaton was left out.

Noël Coward was also at this party and much more of a man, one of those magicians who fill a room with champagne bubbles by his presence alone. I met him again at Johnny Gallier's house and in the few intervening years he'd aged markedly. Despite obvious discomfort, he insisted on climbing to his feet, saying, 'I always stand for a lady.'

Julia Lockwood came to AD8 with her husband. She was in a curious mood and we didn't connect very well. Sarah Churchill came too – she was slightly easier but the old intimacy had gone. To my delight, because Sarah was a magical person, it improved again when we went to Arabella Churchill's wedding together – she was marrying a young schoolteacher called James Barton. The reception at Mary Soames's house in Cheyne Walk was full of vegetarians and squatters.

It was always good to connect with good memories from the past. One of the happiest surprises was from Goebbels's sister-in-law, Ariane. She wrote from Cleveland, Ohio, addressing the letter 'April Ashley, c/o April in Paris, London, Chelsey'. To my amazement, the Post Office delivered it to me at the restaurant — professionally speaking, it was one of the most flattering things ever to happen to me.

Ariane had quite a story to tell. This all sounds fantastic, but every word is true. While still living in Germany, she had read a story in a magazine about neurosurgeon Dr Sam Sheppard, who had been charged with the murder of his wife in America. It was a 1950s sensation and inspired numerous books, a TV series and the Harrison Ford movie *The Fugitive*. Beside the story was a photograph of him, and Ariane fell in love with it.

By this time, she was already disenchanted with Germany. Years before, when she telephoned me, there were telltale clicks on the line, which she said was phone-tapping — the authorities were worried in case she became a rallying point for neo-Nazis. She was always escaping from Dusseldorf to Paris and the South of France and had kept up her friendships with Les Lee and Everest.

She'd sold up in Germany, moved to America and made contact with Sheppard. Her love for him was confirmed, and she helped his fight for freedom. After 12 years of legal battles, including five appeals, the US Supreme Court granted a new trial and Dr Sheppard was acquitted by the second jury. Ariane had invested more than a quarter of a million dollars, most of her fortune, in the not-so-good doctor.

In 1964, they were married and moved into his all-American house in Cleveland with yellow awnings over the window, where the now 'unsolved' murder had taken place. Sheppard became a motorbike and leather fiend and degenerated into a hopeless alcoholic and drug addict. Several times, he tried to kill her. It was obvious that he was guilty of his first wife's murder. Ariane wrote to me some years after her divorce in 1968, 'He pulled a gun on me one time too many and I ran away and filed for a divorce so I could get police protection. I was hiding in a motel for three months until I had the court order to protect me. He died and the autopsy showed that two-thirds of his brain was gone. The whole thing was a nightmare. I'm slowly recovering from it all and have started dating.'

A film was made of her story, starring – another surprise – Nina van Pallandt as Ariane. I said to Ariane that Nina was beautiful and it was a compliment. She snarled back, 'She's too fucking old.'

'But she looks lovely.'

'She's too fucking old.'

Ariane was dogmatic on that. We stayed in touch over the years, but the last time we talked on the phone she was most unwell. She certainly had a most remarkable life.

Sadly, there was to be more personal tragedy for me. One evening at the restaurant, two uniformed policemen came down the stairs with dreadful news: 'Do you know Edward Maddock? There's been a car accident north of Paris.'

'How serious is it?'

'He's dead.'

'Why have you come to me?'

'Yours was the only address they found on him.'

Edward had graduated well from law school and was winning praise at the Webber-Douglas Academy of Dramatic Art. He had been driving back from St Tropez to begin his second term there. It was a wet night, a head-on collision. The driver of the oncoming car had been killed too.

Dizzy telephoned Edward's parents. Although Jack and Julia Maddock didn't approve of me, they did invite me to the funeral. I booked into the local hotel and was summoned up to the house. Jack had been crying. He put his arms round me and said, 'April, I didn't understand.' Julia took me up to Edward's bedroom, where I saw many things that I'd given him. But the room was empty. The spirit had gone out of it.

Eight months almost to the day after Edward's death, Micky

Mullen came down to the restaurant to take over on the cash-till from his sister Allison, who had a date with some famous theatrical. 'I'd love a drink,' he said, 'I haven't even had a pill today.'

At about 1am, I said to him, 'I'm off now, Micky. I've got to be up early tomorrow, I'm going into the country. Don't be too long after the last table.'

'No, it's OK, I'm going to Kit's house afterwards,' he replied.

The next thing I heard about Micky was that he was dead. Apparently, he'd got up in the middle of the night at Kit Lambert's, feeling unwell, and had taken a shower. At 9am, he was found dead in his bed. He had had some kind of apoplectic or asthmatic seizure and had choked to death. Micky had no history of seizures and his death disturbed me far more than Edward's because there was something spooky about it. Edward's death was grief. But Micky's wasn't quite explicable, and sorrow was agitated by the suggestion of something malign.

Not long after, Kit's house was gutted by fire. And then he lost The Who. With Chris Stamp, he had managed them from the beginning and success preyed on all his weaknesses. I was very fond of Kit and he was blessed with great generosity of heart and pocket. He just could not handle the success, or the drugs. I'm no one to preach, having emptied a distillery or two in my time, but drugs are the great evil.

I thought I was the showbiz part of our restaurant venture but I was now about to go into it for real. I was about to participate and witness showbusiness from top to bottom, as it were. Every which way.

Oh my.

44

ONE-EYED JACKS

'The artist must always bite the hand that feeds him...
His duty is to be a monster.'
LINDSAY ANDERSON (1963)

Joan Collins and the nice Nanette Newman were present when
we took meetings, as they say in Hollywood, for my movie.
Well, it wasn't just my movie – and, with hindsight, thank
goodness for that. There were other theatrical aspirations involved.

It all began when I was asked to play Evita at the Young Vic.
Madonna? It would never have happened if I had happened. The
wonderful Frank Dunlop was in charge of the Young Vic and a
regular at AD8. He suggested I be Eva Peron in a black comedy
about her, but just as my excitement soared it was all off. But it
gave me the acting bug once again.

And along came *Human*. This was a Mexican enterprise,
produced by George Schwarz, and directed by an assistant of
Buñuel's. It focused on a London party of which I was to be
hostess. It sounded like *La Dolce Vita* with London standing in for
Rome. And me for Anita Ekberg? I don't quite think so.

They must have been watching the films of Andy Warhol. When
we discussed it at lunches beforehand, it sounded decidedly

intellectual. As I explained, Nanette Newman and Joan Collins were also present and I was impressed. The party was to be held in a beautiful rented house in Neville Terrace.

When I turned up there on the night, there was no, no Nanette. And not even Miss Collins's fringe. I couldn't believe my eyes. They'd trawled for every freak in London and pulled most of them in. It was packed solid, a madhouse, full of drink and drugs. Everybody had been paid £1 as they went in and told to go wild. Leather queens, transvestites, trendies and weirdos, debutantes, Bertie Woosters, the Oxford lot.

I never quite understood what I was supposed to do – they'd bought me an expensive frock, loaded me with make-up, and then turned me loose among the crazies while cameras, booms and lights elbowed about.

A man in chains took a girl so violently on a green marble table that it cracked down the centre. It required seven men to carry the two pieces out of the house, an indication of their enthusiasm. I went for a pee.

Ju-Ju, who used to live with Charles Hay, was in there. She was outrageously fat. That was her gimmick. She was in there naked. In the bath. Bubbles all over the floor.

'Ju-Ju, what are all those teeth marks down your breasts?'

'That's my role. Having my tits bitten. D'ya want a bite?'

I fled. What on earth had happened to Nanette Newman and Joan Collins? They were very smart. Her people must have talked to her people, or vice versa.

A reporter asked me, 'What do you think of it all? There are two men over there kissing.'

'Good luck to them – I'm glad someone's getting something out of this.'

I found myself with a black nun on a sideboard doing a tango to David Bowie music, then somebody hit me with a chain. I was crawling up the stairs to the top of the house for a rest when I saw two studded leather legs planted in my path. In a rapid double movement, he unzipped his fly, pulled out a monstrous floppy pink piece and wagged it around in my face. That did it for me. I was off.

I saw the final cut at Shepperton Studios. There wasn't much of me left. The plot had changed. It was not particularly complex: two young people go to a party, then go to bed. It was released only in Mexico. I believe I'm considered quite avant-garde there. But I'm a bit of a prude about intrusive and extravagant behaviour in my home. When I'm not involved.

I moved to 235 King's Road, above another restaurant, and it was a comfortable habitat. A nice young actress, whom I'll call Helen – her mother is still alive but would fall off the perch if all were public – was desperate for accommodation, so I said she could stay until she'd fixed herself up. After ten days or so of being the model houseguest, she said, 'I've got a boyfriend – would it be all right if he spent the weekend here?'

It didn't make much difference to me because I had the small bedroom so that the large double bedroom would be free for guests. I went to work on the Saturday evening and didn't see who he was. I returned at about 3am, read a little and switched off the lamp.

Something disturbed me. I thought it was a dripping tap. Then I remembered: we didn't have dripping taps. I raised my head; the sounds were from the bedroom, down the hall. On and on and on it went. A regular rhythm. What could it be? Rats, mice, the plumbing? Then the penny dropped. It was a slapping sound.

Next morning I woke to the aroma of fried bacon curling under the door. Helen and her boyfriend looked like something out of a Noël Coward play in their silk dressing gowns. She and Kenneth Tynan – the great theatrical critic, producer and friend of Laurence Olivier and all sorts of grand folk – were munching down plates of eggs, bacon, mushrooms, tomatoes and fried bread.

'Good morning, April,' said Helen. 'You know Kenneth Tynan.'

'Good morning, Mr Tynan. You should always grill tomatoes with oregano, you know. It's the only way.'

'I must try that,' he said.

When he'd gone I said, 'Who slaps whose bottom?'

'Well, mostly I slap him.'

'In future give him half a dozen from me. You might have warned me, darling. I can hear everything that goes on and it's not everybody's cup of tea.'

These weekends went on for months. As did the restrained, obsessive slapping. I can hear it now. There was something so fretful, so middle class about it. I longed to shout through the walls, 'For God's sake, let yourself go, show some passion!'

Tynan wouldn't have survived five minutes with Sheherazade, with her love for sadomasochism, boots, leather and whips. The sound of that slapping symbolised for me the whole predicament of Kenneth Tynan's life: here was the man who said 'fuck' on British television for the first time, who produced supposedly naughty *Oh! Calcutta!*, yet the more loudly he revolted against the bourgeois temperament the more he revealed his entrapment within it.

Is there such a thing as dainty bondage? I don't know if they aspired to the sensual heights of Coco De Mer in WC2, which I hear is all the rage today with those seeking the sexual edge. Often I had to rush into the double bedroom before the cleaner arrived to put away the photographs that had been left on show. They decorated their love-nest with Victorian photos in silver frames of girls being spanked. Or there might be garters and various thongs hanging from the bedpost.

One day, I stupidly said to Helen, 'Why are you wearing a gym slip? Every time you bend over I can see everything you've got.' She had it all on: black stockings, suspenders, black peek-a-boo panties trimmed with blood-red satin, a school tie. It seemed eccentric for teatime, even for a gorgeous young actress.

'Ken likes it,' she said. 'He's coming round later.'

And then parcels started to arrive in plain brown wrappings. They were love-aids of a sadomasochistic character: whips, leather bras, marble eggs covered with leather, and other UFOs – Unidentified Fucking Objects. What shocked me particularly was that they were all posted from Somerset.

Helen soon had a bottom drawer full of tricks. She showed it to me. Finally, I decided to bring down the curtain on this particular Kenneth Tynan show. The reason wasn't just distaste but also that my niece, Tess's daughter, a dark and vivacious teenager who reminded me of myself, had rung up wanting to meet me. I invited her for a weekend and didn't want her to find me living in a bondage parlour. It would have confirmed all the family PR.

Also, Helen and Tynan, whose weekends often ran into midweek, were living rent free. I didn't think it unfair to ask them to pay half the utility bills, especially as Tynan had a habit of sitting on the telephone all the time. Helen was pretty penniless. Tynan said he would cover her cheques. But they bounced and bounced.

Then I went to a party given by the feminist pundit Dee Wells. Tynan was at the party too. He cut me dead, and this on top of all the bouncing cheques. I thought, 'To hell with you, Mr Tynan – this is where I go for the jugular.'

I sent a telegram to his house in Thurloe Square, demanding he pay his bill.

He wrote back, 'What a charmless thing to do.'

I cabled back, 'Where money's concerned, charm doesn't enter into it.'

He paid. I needed the money; the mood was so uncertain at AD8 that I simply couldn't afford to let him off the hook even if I had wanted to, which I didn't.

The restaurant was now in trouble, but every night I'd still have

THE FIRST LADY

to be there on show, smiling, kissing, the perfect hostess. I was expected to be wise, giving and dramatic. Sometimes the mask slipped and I had my outbursts throwing plates of food, provoked by some ineptitude from the staff.

Towards the end, there was a new member of staff virtually every month. Some of them couldn't even wait properly. I know many of the customers came in the hope of witnessing a scene. My nerves and resentment were being held in check by Valium and booze.

One night, one of the waiters came up to tell me that the kitchen was closing and would I give my order. I asked for Pacific Prawns and said to Jean-Pierre, 'I'll have another dry martini while I'm waiting.'

'Madame, do you know how many dry martinis you've had tonight?'

'Do you mean you've been counting my drinks?'

'The staff asked me to count because they couldn't believe it. If you have this one it will make 32.'

'Then let's make it 32.'

As I was walking about and chatting so much, the drink seemed to have no effect. I reckon I walked five miles every evening. I was never still, and should have been more sensible. My liver had started to play up. And Ina Barton had recently died from a combination of booze and pills. An open verdict was recorded, but that's splitting hairs – in effect, she killed herself.

Already I'd had one nasty accident at Elm Park Road. One night I had passed out in bed with a leaky hot-water bottle. Next morning I awoke with a balloon blister on my ankle. I stuck a pair of scissors into it and the water shot out. Then I bound it up and went to the doctor. 'You've given yourself a severe burn. I'm afraid you'll be scarred for life,' he told me. 'You'll have to rest that leg.'

Not a chance. With all the walking up and down the restaurant,

312

the leg wouldn't heal. Some weeks later, after work, I went off to Tramp nightclub; as I was going down the stairs, Ju-Ju's boyfriend John shouted, 'April!' The greeting was so abrupt that I swung round in my long skirt, tripped and fell. I was wearing a blouse with leg-of-mutton sleeves and could hear the poppers unpopping as I bounced down the stairs. At the bottom, the waiters rushed to help but I said, 'No, don't touch a thing, leave me for a second, I want to count my bijoux. Well, they all seem to be here. Right, I'll have a large whisky.'

My right wrist swelled up. They wrapped it in a napkin. At dawn, I found myself at St Stephen's Hospital in the Fulham Road. The wrist was broken. It was set in plaster but a few days later the hand started turning black. I understood that black fingers are the road to gangrene and the plaster had to come off. I sat in the bath for two hours to soften the plaster, keeping myself going with wine gums, then cut it off. When I returned to the hospital, I was told that the wrist had been set incorrectly. They tried to repair the damage but to this day the joint is misshapen, a claw. But breaking my wrist had one fortunate result: I had to take a week off work and this healed my leg.

My arm was in plaster for a couple of months. At the restaurant, I wore plenty of white so that the sling would glare less. Being right-handed, I was unable to prepare myself for work. But luckily my friend Oscar da Costa, the Uruguayan cartoonist and make-up artist, agreed to attend me every afternoon. The South Americans have such baroque fantasies. One day I would arrive at work as Cleopatra from Mars, the next Madame Bovary in Zululand.

Eventually, the plaster came off. They bandaged the wrist and put it into a fresh sling. That same night I was unsteadily making my bed when I tripped. Extending my left hand to break the fall, I jarred against the skirting board and smashed the other wrist.

313

Now I came into AD8 with both arms in slings. I looked outrageous.

I was swallowing Valium like Smarties. I hardly knew where I was from one moment to the next. For three weeks, I sat in the bar nodding like something in the rear window of a car as the customers filed past. The two slings gave the impression that I was wearing a straitjacket.

Soon, I was taking more than a dozen Valium a day. Eventually Dizzy said, 'Dr Atkinson tells me you've got to have a holiday.'

I went to Barbados and stayed with friends. I met Oliver Messel, who was on his last legs but sang and danced famous numbers from *Gigi* for us on his terrace. I visited Verna Hull, who often came to AD8 when she was in London. She lived next door to Claudette Colbert, with whom she'd shared a house for many years. But they'd fallen out and, despite living only feet apart, they didn't speak at all.

Upon my return, the battles with my partners started up immediately; they said they wanted me out of the restaurant, and I agreed. I didn't have the energy to fight. After all these years, I got a £3,000 pay-off – less than I had originally invested. Happily, the past was there to help again – I went to stay with Rita in California. It never rains there, does it?

45

LITERARY LADY

*'You can't find true affection in Hollywood because
everyone does the fake affection so well.'*

Hay-on-Wye lies on the Welsh side of the Welsh–English
border in the county of Powys.

You'll want the directions.

From London, you follow the M4 over the Severn Bridge to
Junction 24 (Newport). Take the A449 and then the A40 to
Abergavenny. Stay on the A40 until just after the village of
Crickhowell, then turn right on to the A479 to Talgarth. From
here take the road signposted to Three Cocks and Hay-on-Wye
(A479 end then right on to the A438), on reaching Three Cocks
stay on the same road and continue on into Hay (B4350).

I went the long way around – from California.

After the upset with AD8, I spent seven weeks on the West
Coast, but I felt lost. I couldn't settle. I was at a crossroads in my
life. I knew I could not carry on at a 32-martinis-a-night pace.
There was lots to do in America, but I was bored. Roddy
McDowall gave a dinner party for me in Hollywood; Rita and I
drove down to Mexico to watch the whales off the coast of

315

Ensenada. I felt like a tourist. It was wrong. I wanted to belong, but London frightened me. I was disenchanted. Dr Johnson indeed. I didn't know what to do. At this stage of my life, I expected at the very least to have acquired something. But I had nothing. Maybe London was a bad omen.

I decided to get right away from it, to move to the market town of Hay-on-Wye, where Viva's nephew Richard Booth rules. I've always thought of it as Camelot. In 1977, Richard proclaimed Hay an Independent Kingdom and he was crowned King and Ruler of the new state. His horse was named Prime Minister. In 1961, Richard had opened his first second-hand bookshop in Hay, shipping in hundreds of books from across the globe. He was convinced that a town full of bookstores could become an international attraction. For his efforts, King Richard was awarded an MBE in the 2004 Queen's New Year's Honours.

He conferred on me the title of First Lady, Duchess of Hay and Offa's Dyke. Mind you, there is no denying that he is a man of some dottiness, given to falling off horses and inadvertently backing his car into other people's sitting rooms. When his castle burned down, he said that what woke him was the sound of applause. He got out of bed to see why his subjects should be demanding his presence at the ceremonial window in the early hours of the morning. Only then did he realise that it wasn't applause at all, but the sound of crackling beams. Typically, it was during the firemen's strike. On April Fool's Day 2000, Richard held an investiture of the Hay House of Lords and created 21 new hereditary peers for the Kingdom of Hay in the State Room of Hay Castle.

It was at the castle he suggested I open a restaurant. I had first visited Hay with Viva in the early 1960s, before it became famous as the world's first 'book town', and then for the annual literary festival, which brings in around 70,000 visitors and £3 million. And attracts big names like Bill Clinton, who called Hay 'my kind of town' and likened the festival to a 'Woodstock of the mind'.

Richard's had lots of star names at the festival – Beryl Bainbridge, Louis de Bernières, Margaret Atwood, Germaine Greer, Bill Bryson and Ian McEwan among them. And, oh my, my would-be lover Paul McCartney performed there too. You read about it in everything from *The London Review of Books* to *Vogue*. It's an event now.

Richard was always inviting me to Hay. He was rather keen on me and would take me to lots of hunt balls and that sort of thing. One evening I was in some fabulous silk and a young man came up and said, 'I've got an erection just looking at you.'

I said, 'Oh, don't worry about that – let's go right into dinner.'

I certainly seemed to be having an effect. Once, and only once, Richard asked me to marry him. He said, 'This is an official marriage proposal but I must tell you I've only got a little cock.'

I thought it better to simply ignore both subjects. Nevertheless, we always go along so well.

When I first arrived in Hay, the locals didn't like it because I would always turn up in an enormous Rolls-Royce belonging to Richard; I would always give them the royal wave. It was silly – it's not a good idea to play the big celebrity with people when you live among them. They do not like it all and it took a long time to win them over, but I did. It was lovely to hear them say I mustn't leave and that they were all fond of me. It was incredibly touching.

They are tough people with a vigorous sense of humour, sometimes melancholy, occasionally violent, and inclined towards eccentricity. I couldn't hide behind London sophistication there, because the Hay locals have their own variety, which penetrates it. Hay appreciates the individual, not the type. Gradually, people started to talk to me. I knew and spoke to everybody in the whole town.

Without altering Hay's fundamental nature, the book business has nonetheless given it something of an international atmosphere. When I got there, the town was congested with millions of books – in the castle, in the old cinema, in the converted workhouse. Richard told me, 'When I started the most prosperous feature of the Hay economy was probably the fruit machine at the British Legion Club – it was making £400 profit per week.' As the book trade prospered, the town drew more and more eccentrics into its sphere – specialising, for some reason, in unfrocked priests.

I did the very first interview for Richard for *The New York Times* and lots of other public relations for him. When I did those jobs, I didn't have to pay my rent, which was seven pounds a month.

With the help of Rita, I moved into a flat above one of Richard's shops. My new address was terrific, not one to fall down on: No. 1, The Pavement. I loved its pitched ceilings and small gable windows, which looked out to the Radnor Hills. The view was lovely but I was feeling rotten. I was vomiting. I blamed something I'd eaten or my squiffy liver. After Rita departed for the Home Counties, I took to my bed and stayed there with a bucket beside it.

A friend called Val was coming for the weekend, so I pulled myself together and got out of bed. On the Saturday evening, we went to the Baskerville Arms in Clyro, where the hound-loving Baskerville family built Clyro Court in the 19th century. After staying there, Sir Arthur Conan Doyle was inspired to write his macabre story – although, in consideration of his hosts, changed the location to Devon.

At dinner with Val, I felt better than I had in ages. It must have shown, because people I hardly yet knew came up to tell me that I was glowing. But on the way home, I began to feel breathless and decided to walk in the air. I had a blackout and came to, feeling terribly shaky, in the doorway of Golesworthy's Outfitters opposite my flat.

Val helped me up to my bedroom and as I was recovering on

the bed a sharp pain shot under my ribs. Val held my hand for a moment or two, then I said, 'It's OK now, go to bed; I'll see you in the morning.' Just as she was about to switch out my light, a much more severe pain hit me in the centre of the chest. It was like being kicked by a horse. My neck was thrown back and my shoulders forward.

Dr Harvey arrived at midnight and said, 'I think you've had a heart attack.'

'But, Dr Harvey, I don't smoke, I'm underweight.' I didn't mention the martinis.

'You do drink and you've been under a lot of stress lately. I'm almost sure that's what it is.'

I was taken to the Nuffield Clinic in Hereford. When they traced a cardiograph, they found my heartbeat all over the place. The first 24 hours is the critical time. If you survive that, you're likely to survive the heart attack. Every hour or so, they woke me up to trace another cardiograph. I'd lost much of the feeling in my arms. Between the shoulder and the elbow they were dark and puffy.

I was inside for just over two weeks. They wanted me there for a month because Dr Wood said my heart was still very scratchy, but I was terrified of having another attack worrying about the bills. I didn't know how much I was insured for. As it turned out, it was up to £10,000. They instructed me to avoid cholesterol, dark meat, chocolate, sweets, salt, white sugar, not to overdo the stairs and to acquire a potty, no sex for the time being – I behaved myself for ten minutes, then thought, 'What the hell, if I'm going, I might as well go with the few comforts I can muster.'

Out came the bowls of sugar, the boxes of sea salt – and there are worse things in life than dying in the arms of a big Welshman. After a few more weeks, I felt fit and went to London to see Viva. She was on good form, and was lining herself up for imminent celebrity, because her memoirs were due out. I was sitting on a sofa in the drawing room when suddenly I felt most peculiar. It was as if the floor had given way. My face drained of blood and expression and no longer felt part of me. 'Viva, something's happened.' But I didn't know what.

The doctor suspected that I'd had another heart attack — a minor one, a hiccup as they say, which is really quite common even for healthy people, but coming after the major one it frightened me very much. I returned to Hay and took to my bed for five months' solitary confinement.

I had little money. I did a careful budget and calculated that if I cut out all alcohol and most food I could afford to rent a television set, which, with sea salt, was my only luxury, but it did prevent me from going gaga. I lived on cabbage and baked beans with occasionally a wine gum for pud. I would sleep all through the morning if possible, to make the days shorter. And I hardly went out — you don't when you can't afford to buy someone a drink. I stayed in bed to avoid losing weight.

I struck up conversations with Heaven, with beautiful Edward Maddock. I'd shake my fist at the ceiling and say, 'Hey, Edward, what's going on up there? You're supposed to be looking after me, so put that angel down and pull your finger out.'

I started dreaming of Holland, definitely a danger sign, so I went to London and met up with Tommy Kyle. I was whisked off to the South of France. Tommy took his yacht, the *Casa Nina*, out and we bumped along the coast for a few days with Mrs Ting-a-Ling and Lulu.

In St Tropez, we tied up opposite a coffee bar. I was on deck in my curlers and spotted Amanda Lear among the coffee drinkers. I said to Tommy's friend, Brian, 'Do go and ask her on board for a drink. I can't cross the road like this.'

I saw Brian talking to her. I threw her a tiny wave, and she hopped on to her bicycle and pedalled off as if pursued by devils. I've not seen her since.

Harold Robbins, that grand man of naughty letters, and his wife Grace were tied up nearby and invited us across for dinner. Linda Christian was with them; she floated through it all like a cork. Nothing sank her. What about me? Here I was in St Tropez, all sun and sizzle and glamour, but not forever. I was a have-not, not a have-yacht.

I had to return to Wales. And the dole.

46

BARE ESSENTIALS

'Go on, get stuck in!'
JAMIE OLIVER, THE NAKED CHEF (1999)

My Liverpool background dictates that you don't take state handouts. Years ago, the gentry doled out the cash to the peasants and it's still that way to me; whatever you call it, for many of my generation it's demeaning, shameful. Yet, I could not exist on cabbage.

I went to the social services offices in Brecon. I told the woman who interviewed me that I hadn't worked because of my heart attack. She gave me £14.50 on the spot and I went bright red. Their doctors decided I was to be registered as a disabled person because I wasn't supposed to stand for more than four hours a day or stretch my arms above my head.

Mr Evans of Wrexham made contact with me, a charming careers officer who suggested I go on a rehabilitation course learning to put tops on bottles.

'Mr Evans, it's very kind of you but I haven't come all this way to start putting tops on bottles.'

He suggested that the platinum-blonde Forties movie star Veronica Lake worked in a factory in her troubled times.

'Did she? How heartbreaking. It's probably what killed her. What else have you got?'

'There's a short cookery course…'

Well, Gordon Ramsay-it, why was he messing around with bottle tops? This was more like it, three months at Radbrook College in Shrewsbury. Richard let me keep on the flat in Hay and I went to Shrewsbury to look for temporary digs, tramping round boarding houses all day, one Edwardian door after another – with no luck.

Finally, I came to the last on my list, Mrs Williams of Park House. She opened the door and said, 'I only take men.' My face hit the doorstep and she must have softened at this because she said, 'You do look tired. Come in for a cup of tea and we'll talk about it.'

She took me on a week's trial. She was a delight and for the rest of it Terry Wogan kept me sane. I really believe he kept me from going crazy. His show bolstered me up in Shrewsbury. It helped me deal with all the absurdities, all the bureaucracy, for I hated doing that course. But it was either that or milk bottles in Essex.

Terry Wogan should be available to all, prescribed on the National Health. Like Guinness, Wogan is good for you.

For the first two days at Radbrook, I was anonymous. On the third day, it was out. I went into the dining hall and 200 pairs of eyes turned and stared to a chorus of murmuring.

For hygiene, I was wearing a hairnet, one of those that make you look as though you were carrying a load of rolled veal on your head. I'd cut it and tried to make it look more like a turban, but that hadn't helped. Before, I had always relied on my glamorous shell to protect me in moments such as this. Now I had to face them looking like Ena Sharples, which, oh my, is definitely not me.

I was groping wildly for a champagne cocktail but there was only canteen coffee. I sailed towards a table on sheer willpower and felt much better after I'd occupied a plastic chair and joined a discussion on student power and the Fight For Peace movement.

One of the women in my class said I was a rich bitch who was exploiting the taxpayers' money for a lark, but Mrs Williams knew better. 'My, you have made it cosy in here. I hope you will stay, April. You never go out, you never eat. I don't want to speak out of turn but I suspect you're going through a rough time. So I'm dropping the rent a bit and I've got a television for your room.'

The class was of all ages, some young kids of 17, the majority in the middle years, and a widower of 65 who decided it was time he learned to boil his own eggs. Much of it wasn't new to me and, although I wasn't the best in the class, I was the fastest, especially with the boning knife. All that bacon in my past.

I was the only short-course student to be invited to the end-of-term college ball. I was in my cockfeathers and a low-cut black dress, and the principal asked me to join his table for a drink. I downed a massive vodka and set off. Halfway across the hall my heel snapped, I lurched, and my breasts tumbled out. The whole place went up in a storm of laughter and I decided it was my bedtime.

On my last day, I was packing up to leave when Mrs Williams came up to say there were eight women and one man to see me. They were from the class, including the woman who had called me a rich bitch. They hadn't wanted to leave without telling me how much fun it had been having me in their class.

The main purpose of the course, from my point of view, was to push me back into life rather than provide a marketable skill. I went on a one-year business course at the Coleg Howell Harris in Brecon.

I need my solitude, but I also need company. In Hay, I found my good cause: Charles Simpson, who was 82. He'd been a nervous wreck since the age of 40, when he retired into leisure from his garage business, but he was fighting fit. He'd buried two wives and lived alone in a substantial house that had belonged to the second of them, the highest house in Hay after the Castle. I mowed his lawn, cooked for him, gave him the town gossip, steered him away from the bottle and tried to make sure he didn't muddle up his boxes of pills.

I was at Coleg Howell Harris when I was told of Viva's death. It wasn't unexpected and the loss took time to make itself felt. During the last few years, I had tried to visit her as often as possible, and always on New Year's Eve. After such a life, it was awful to see her all alone in her bed, reading the *Evening Standard* on the last night of the year.

'Come on, there's a party down the road.'

'No, I can't, I couldn't, I mean I shouldn't, no.' But she'd already be climbing out of bed and making for the black velvet skirt.

Her autobiography had not been received as she'd hoped. The book was her final gesture to life and, after it flopped, she took to her bed. Viva's last time out was when I took her to lunch round the corner at the George and Dragon. I bullied her into it – she liked to be bullied; the second we arrived I set her up with a large gin and tonic. Afterwards, she walked back to the house content and erect, having forgotten all about her stick.

She didn't go out again. Although terribly lonely, she refused to see anyone except me. The maid and nurses kept everyone away. I smuggled Rita in one evening, to Viva's fury and Rita's consternation. Although Rita had become a visitor at the Stoke Mandeville Hospital for the Disabled, and saw many unfortunate things every day, she wasn't prepared for the change in Viva.

But Viva's mind was still wonderfully complete; towards the end she wrote to me in Hay, 'I am like Oscar Wilde, dying beyond my means, the china has all gone, but if it doesn't keep the night nurse I shall have to start on the pictures – I detest doing it, but I am too frightened a coward to end it all which would be the best way.'

In her will, she left me all her pictures. On my last visit she said, 'Take Santiago de Compostella with you.' It was a carving that she knew I loved. 'Take him, the pictures are going so fast, you'll have nothing.' But I couldn't take him. When she died, there were still a few pictures left; she left me a little capital too and so finally I was able to come off social security.

One drawing Viva left me was by Augustus John, for whom she had worked all those years earlier. It was titled 'Young Viva King Naked and Masturbating'.

Oh my, indeed.

I sold it to Bunny Dexter, who liked things about sex. She offered me £2,000 and I accepted. She had it in her flat in London but after she died I'm not sure who got it. I'd like to see it again. There was another work, a painting by McDuff of two little boys with nothing looking in a shop window at Christmas time. Christopher Wood, who operates in St James's in London and is now regarded as England's leading expert on Victorian paintings, offered me £500 for it. Christopher – who's often on the BBC's *Antiques Road Show* – looked a little aghast when I said I was sending it to Sotheby's for valuation. I knew it was worth something. And, oh my, he ended up paying me £5,000 for it. It must be worth so much more now.

I would love to have held on to those treasures from Viva, but I had to live and that's what she gave them to me for – living.

I asked Richard if he were going to his aunt's funeral and if so to give me a lift. But he said he wasn't mad about death and wouldn't be going, so I didn't go either. She wouldn't have minded. I still miss her very much, more now than at the time of her death, and looking back I wish I had attended the funeral, because a funeral has nothing to do with the dead or with creating the right impression with the other mourners – it is to fix something in oneself.

There was more death. Charlie Simpson died and left me his house. I had no idea he had come to rely on me so much. One day I had told him I was thinking of returning to London and he said that, if I did, he would die. He was such a sweetheart and I felt responsible for him.

I moved in to take care of him but if I had known what was going to happen I would have run off. He never slept the last year of his life, he was so ill. He was always falling out of bed, once into the electric fire. It was very demanding. I don't know about Charlie but it almost killed me. Anyhow, I managed to stick it out till his end.

He wanted to leave me his money too. It wasn't an awful lot – about £10,000 – I said, 'No, you must leave that to your daughter.' The house was not their house. The house belonged to Charles's second wife and I felt that was OK.

Viva and Charlie. It's strange. I knew no love at all as a child and I always felt a stiffening of the back if someone touched me. I longed for a proper mother and father, yet Charlie and Viva weren't father and mother to me – I was mother to them.

Now I needed to get the house in order, which meant painting it inside and out. When I suggested it to Charlie, he said, 'But it's only just been done.' That, it turned out, was in 1952.

I was a woman of a certain age with a property of a certain age. I was settled, it seemed. But unsettled too. Flora Bella, a coral-coloured whippet bitch, moved in with me and I got on with living a quiet life. She did fart a lot, but I got used to it.

Guests were a little horrified, but Flora always gave them a rather nice ladylike look. There were friends to visit and I'd slip back into my old ways for a couple of weeks here and there, but I did try quite hard to stay on the straight and narrow.

I was a tourist attraction in Hay. I helped Richard with the bookshops, with marketing. It brought in a little money – which was needed, for being a homeowner, of course, meant bills and more bills. You pay some, you get some more. A bit like life, really.

47

SEX MYSTERIES

'Elementary, my dear Watson.'

SHERLOCK HOLMES (CLIVE BROOK),
THE RETURN OF SHERLOCK HOLMES (1929)

We're all very complex individuals and the idea that what you see is what you get is rarely accurate.

In London, I'd always have great fun at the actors-only Pickwick Club, just off Leicester Square. I made many good friends there, including the delightful Denholm Elliott who for me was one of the very great character actors of his generations. He and his wife Susie had a home on Ibiza and I'd see them there.

Their children Mark and Jennifer were around, and we'd have lunches and dinners with others there for the summer. Jeremy Brett, before he took on the life role of Sherlock Holmes, was a regular on the island. He'd been Freddie Eynsford-Hill in *My Fair Lady* with Audrey Hepburn and used to drive me mad singing 'On the Street Where You Live'.

'I have often walked down the street before
But the pavement always stayed beneath my feet before
All at once am I several storeys high...'

Hum it. It's one of those songs that stick inside your head. He'd been dubbed in the film, but he didn't have a bad singing voice; it was the constant sound of the same lyrics that were quite maddening. He had his dark moods, but mostly he was fun.

Denholm Elliott had gone off to mainland Spain to play Will Scarlett with Sean Connery and Audrey Hepburn as Robin and Marian. Susie always wanted to meet Audrey Hepburn and asked me to babysit the children while she went off to the film set near Pamplona. I told her not to sing 'Viva Espana!' as she'd be in Basque country and they'd lynch her for that.

I was happy to babysit but I couldn't drive, so how was I going to get them to the beach? Jeremy said, 'Don't worry, I'll be the chauffeur,' and he was for two weeks. It was really quite grand and the children were not too much trouble, although Mark used to push the limits.

Jeremy was a great help and enjoyed himself. He had a great passion for hunky German tourists and would take off with these men from time to time, but he never let us down on his driving duties. It's funny the contradiction of reality and perception. Who could imagine the man who over ten years became the definitive Holmes getting all excited over a strapping blond German lad?

Denholm, who died on Ibiza in 1992 from complications from AIDS, was also a contradiction. He'd been married to Virginia 'Born Free' McKenna before Susie but was adamant to me about his sexuality. They came to stay with me in Hay and I prepared the guest room for the two of them. But Denholm insisted to me, 'I'm gay and I need my own room.' Yet he and Susie were very much a couple and loving parents. It was a lifestyle that worked for them.

People marry for so many different reasons, and the more they've seen of life, the more ad hoc their reasons become. Yet nearly always the reasons centre on the fight against loneliness, the fact that life acquires meaning only in its relationships, however awkward, transient or intolerable these may be.

In my romantic theory, marriage seemed a desirable state because it fixed you in the fellowship of the world. In the past, in my time, it was also one of the accoutrements of womanhood. But marriage is no shortcut to fellowship of the world. You acquire such fellowship the day you are born, no matter how often the world appears to drive you into a corner where you ache and weep alone. I've endured more than my share of ostracism and ridicule, more than the usual inducement to imagine that God has singled me out for the special horrors.

Each time an obstacle presents itself, you must steel yourself, harden, toughen, in order to endure it. But endurance is a passive virtue, though not a meagre one. And obstacles have to be overcome, not merely endured. And in order to overcome, you must extend yourself. It is necessary to cultivate a certain ruthlessness, a certain rigour with regard to yourself as well as to others.

This process of toughening, extending, softening is inner growth. It may not enlarge your wisdom, but it does enlarge capacity – and capacity is a kind of wisdom. The softening is vital. If you do not soften, you will come to find the world a cold and malevolent place, with yourself the coldest thing in it. And experience will turn you into a coward or a bully. Cowards and bullies have an identical view of life – as an arena filled with threat. Always to be on your guard against attack does not make for a lovely existence.

Long before he became a colourful public figure, Grayson Perry certainly had a difficult time growing up. He was my toy-boy lover for a time. He's an Essex boy, born in Chelmsford, and I met him at the James Birch Art Gallery in World's End when he began spending time in London. He was 20-something then. His transvestite alter ego Claire had been 'born' in 1975, when he was 15 years old.

By the time Grayson won the Turner Prize in 2003, his Claire was a well-known figure in the art world, a lover of dolly dresses, big hair, cartoon bows and a blonde wig. He's now married with a teenaged daughter and has clearly dealt with any ill feelings he may have had about his identity in the early days. I certainly found him fun; there was no angst in our relationship. We used to go to galleries and have drinks and dinner; it was a very normal male–female relationship as far as I was concerned.

It was in Hay that it all ended. One evening we were leaving the house to go to dinner at the pub. Nothing special. On the doorstep, he said, 'Oh, I can't go out. I don't want to.'

I asked him what was wrong but he just looked confused. I said I'd arranged to meet friends and was going with or without him. I tried to persuade him not to be silly, but he'd got something in his head and was stubborn. I left him to it and went off for the evening. The next day we said our goodbyes and that was the end of the affair.

It had been a sweet and gentle relationship. I was a little upset that it finished abruptly like that, but he was so young and only just really finding himself. As Claire, he would go to the Beaumont Club and I think they must have helped him. I know they have been wonderful for many people; they're Britain's biggest support network for transgender, transvestite, transsexual and cross-dressing people.

I think he has done brilliant work in ceramics, especially with the autobiographical images of himself and Claire, and his family. He must be proud of what he's achieved.

After we parted, I was back in showbusiness. I played myself – who else could do it? – in *Ligmalion, A Musical for the 80s.* Ligmalion means 'leg-up' and I think it's something to do with the casting couch. The idea was that this young lad played by Jason Carter is being educated on how to rise in society. It was all ad-libbed – there was no script. I had to lecture him on the merits of fashion with lines like, 'I am the Duchess of Hay, clothes do not make the man.'

The director, Nigel Finch, filmed me at Clyro Court. The great diarist Kilvert mentions both the house and its occupants. An entry for 1870 tells of a great storm that destroyed the gable in which the housekeeper slept. She and her bed passed through two floors before coming to rest in the shambles of a morning room. On examination, she was found to be still asleep, smelling strongly of brandy.

Which is probably what everyone needed after the reception for *Ligmalion*; it was a television film and didn't do that well, even though people like Tim Curry and Alexei Sayle were in it. So was Sting, but I was about to meet an altogether different rock star.

And he wasn't interested in tantric sex. Oh my, not by a long, long shot.

48

DOWN UNDER

'Nothing succeeds like sexcess.'
Sir Larry Lamb (1974)

I jetted off to Australia to appear on *The Michael Parkinson Show*. Parky was splitting his life between Britain and Australia in those days, and might still be doing that; his show was huge Down Under. I stayed at the Sebel Town House on Elizabeth Bay and it was five-star luxury. I hadn't been there long when one of Elton John's people rang me up and said, 'Elt wants to take you out to dinner.'

I said fine.

Then she rang back and said, 'Elt can't do dinner. He wants to take you to tea.'

I said fine.

She rang back. 'Elt can't do tea. He wants to take you to lunch.'

Well, this game went on for days. I'd known Elton for years, since he used to come to AD8. I said, 'Tell him I can only do dinner.' That put an end to the daily phone call and we finally did have dinner.

Later, I left the hotel and went to stay with my friend Geoffrey. But I'd fallen in love with the bar at the Sebel Town House. I would, wouldn't I? So, most nights after dinner, we'd pop in a cab and go and have a nightcap at the bar there.

One night I was sitting at the bar and talking to the barman, who by then was one of my best friends in Australia. Geoffrey and I had had quite a bit to drink and were in a good mood. Suddenly, this huge crowd of young men arrived.

One of them stood out because he was incredibly handsome and had this mane of hair. He kept looking at me and smiling and I kept looking back and smiling. And then one by one all his friends disappeared until finally I was alone at the bar with him and Geoff.

I went to the loo and when I came back Geoff was standing over in the corner. This young man, Michael Hutchence, said to me, 'Come to my room for a bottle of champagne.'

I couldn't resist him.

I said, 'That would be very nice. What about my friend Geoff?'

'Oh, he'll wait for you.'

He was staring into my eyes intently. And shaking. I went over to Geoff and said, 'Am just going to go off and have a bottle of champagne with this lovely man, is that all right?'

He said, 'Yes, darling, I'll wait for you. I want to hear about this one.'

I didn't have a clue who Michael Hutchence was. We went upstairs and had champagne and suddenly I was naked.

And he was naked. He had the most incredibly beautiful body. And he had the most enormous whanger. He wanted to do it every which way. He was certainly desperate for sex. There was no conversation as such – just sex.

It would be very rare if I didn't tell someone my history, but not in this case. As with all one-night stands, there is little point in telling. These men don't find anything different about me because there isn't anything different. They always thought they'd hit the jackpot.

I didn't know about Michael's reputation as a sexual adventurer. He certainly didn't display any foreign sex toys to me. He had enough of his own – more than enough. He was wonderful – a man who wouldn't have disappointed any woman. I could hardly handle him at all. I am really very shy, but I love a man with a sense of humour, who is very sure of himself sexually. It was hugely enjoyable, pleasure for pleasure and no ulterior motives.

Michael was an absolutely beautiful man and I was flattered – who wouldn't be? We relaxed afterwards, had a couple of more glasses of champagne and he was very pleasant. And then we kissed goodbye and he closed the hotel-room door. I was in such a good, high mood I wandered back to the bar swinging my knickers around my finger.

Geoff was waiting. 'Do you know who you've been to bed with?' I didn't and he explained it all to me. Michael had come in with band members and some of his road show, the entourage, and they'd taken off one by one so he could be alone with me. When I was in the loo, he'd asked Geoff politely if he'd get lost and Geoff had said no but he'd stand out of the way while he tried his luck.

He got lucky. But I had no idea of his identity. As I explained, we'd been endlessly at each other, not talking.

Geoff said, 'He's the lead singer of INXS – they're one of the world's most successful rock groups.'

Of course, I followed his career and life after our night together; and he had such interesting lovers, among them Helena Christensen and Kylie Minogue. The whole Paula Yates saga was so tragic. As was his death – so sad, alone in a hotel room. When he died so young – he was only 37 – his sexual antics got more attention than his music. Why such a man would kill himself is impossible to answer. He was God's gift to everybody.

I can only repeat that we are all complex people. I'm certainly no exception. When I returned to Hay, I should have been settled, but there was something... I don't know what. Money had much to do with it. By the mid-1980s, the bank owned more of the house than I did. I was trying to improve the place and had it looking glamorous. I wanted to put in two bedrooms, a little sitting room and a bathroom on the top floor, but it was going to take the whole of what the house was worth to do.

I spoke to Mr Hughes, my bank manager, and he said the only way to solve it was by doing bed and breakfast. There are some moments in your life when you can do something and there are other moments when you can't. I decided it wasn't my time to be a B&B landlady.

It was such a small amount in those days, just a couple of pounds a night, and I thought, 'Do I want all these people roaming around the house?' I wasn't ready for that. It wasn't the work that frightened me; it was the idea of facing all these bloody strangers knocking on your door, coming in, sleeping in your beds and then having to get up and do the breakfasts. It didn't seem like a solution to my feeling of, I suppose, a sort of claustrophobia with Hay and the house.

What decided it was my own stupidity. I was asked to appear on a couple of talk shows. I did one in London for ITV with Larry Hagman, who was big on *Dallas* at the time, and the wonderful American character actor George Kennedy. The other I did in Birmingham with Engelbert Humperdinck.

When the car brought me back from Birmingham, it was around my 50th birthday and I thought to myself, 'They just wanted to see what you looked like at 50. You stupid bitch, why did you do all of that?' I should have refused them all. They paid you nothing anyhow.

That evening I settled down with my dog and my beer, which I always had in the evenings when I wasn't going out. I put the television on and I couldn't see anything. The first thing I did the next morning was to shoot around to the doctor's. I thought I was a diabetic.

Dr Wilson told me, 'No, April, you're fine. More than likely go and have your eyes tested.'

I'd never needed glasses and suddenly I needed glasses. I'd always worn shaded glasses, but that was just because I liked everything to look soft.

So there I was at 50. I had this huge Victorian house and vast gardens that I used to do myself. And I was sitting there thinking, 'I'm going bloody blind.'

It wasn't joined-up thinking.

If I was lucky, I would come out with about £30,000 if I sold, because I wasn't going to win a race for the house with the bank. That wasn't a contest. I wanted a new beginning.

I'd always wanted to live in America.

I decided I was going to sell everything. Flora would be looked after by friends. I had a garage sale but I wasn't much good at bargaining. In short, I gave the whole bloody lot away and made £100 out of a whole house.

I packed up all my personal bits. And got on a jet plane. I didn't know if I'd be back again.

49

CIVIL SERVICE

*'As soon as I stepped out of my mother's womb... I realised
that I had made a mistake — that I shouldn't have come,
but the trouble with children is they are not returnable.'*
<small>THE NAKED CIVIL SERVANT (1968), QUENTIN CRISP</small>

I flew to New York and into Hell's Kitchen. The address turned
out to be more appropriate than I would have liked.

I went with a friend, who turned out to be a terrible drug
addict. He used to disappear all the time. It was Christmas and he
was nowhere to be found.

My answer to this was to have a party. I had the nice apartment
we'd been given to myself and invited a crowd of people I knew
in Manhattan. On the off-chance, although convinced he would
be busy, I contacted Quentin Crisp, who'd become so famous
after the screening of *The Naked Civil Servant* on television a
decade or so before.

I said, 'Quentin, can I give you a small party?'

He was delightful. 'Oh, April, darling, that would be lovely.'

'But being Christmas time would that be OK?'

'It's a strange thing. Everybody thinks celebrities are visiting
come Christmas, and you always end up spending Christmas alone.'

He had nowhere to go. It was astonishing. He arrived, this most charming man with his bouffant and lavender; he had just the most exquisite mannerisms and everybody loved him. It turned out not to be too Scrooge a Christmas for any of us.

Then, at about quarter to twelve, he said to me, 'Oh, April, I have to go. I have to catch the Tube.' He didn't say the 'Metro'.

I said, 'Would anybody here like to drive Mr Crisp home tonight?' Every hand shot up.

We met and talked a lot while I was in New York – which wasn't too long, as it turned out. By New Year's Eve, I was gone – to California. This mad girlfriend of mine, the daughter of a long-time friend who I knew in Rome, turned up and she asked me to go with her.

We moved into a bungalow where Marlon Brando used to take all his women, on Sunset Boulevard just down from the Chateau Marmont. It was charming, but every day I had to walk down and carry a gallon of wine back for this crazy friend. She wanted cheap wine and it came to about three dollars the half-gallon.

It got so tiring walking back and forward for that drink. I had never driven a car in my life, but the few times my friend had taken me out I watched carefully.

I got up one morning and she said, 'Are you going to go for the wine?'

I said, 'Yes. This time I'm going to drive, so I want the keys to your car.'

'But you can't drive. No keys.'

'That's OK then, no wine. I'm going back to bed.'

She threw the keys at me. I got behind the wheel of the car and I couldn't get it going.

Our neighbour Jeff West saw me and said, 'Oh, April, you have to put it into "park" if you want to start the car.'

I drove beautifully to the shops. I drove back perfectly and parked it perfectly. The only thing is I didn't put it back into 'park' and, when I was getting out, the car starting rolling forward. Happily, there were bollards. I took four lessons and got my Californian driver's licence.

And I got married again. I became friends with Jeff, who ran a nightclub called The Pink in Santa Monica. It attracted quite a crowd and had a reputation of being a New York-style club. People like David Bowie and his wife Iman and all sorts of actors and actresses like Bud Cort and Susan Tyrell would show up for his birthday party.

It was Jeff, a gorgeous, big Texas man with jet-black hair and green eyes, who explained the complex problems of my friend – who wasn't just on the wine but also severely involved in drugs. I was always so naive in this area – it was something I never got into or wanted to have anything to do with. In those days, they were snorting cocaine off the counters of hamburger bars. Ketchup, my favourite, was so passé.

My friend got more and more unwell. I went over to Jeff's and told him, 'Jeff, she won't get out of bed. She's drinking a gallon of wine every day.'

He told me, 'You are so stupid. You don't know why those men come in the door?'

I said, 'They're friends of hers.'

'They are all drug dealers, she's a drug addict. Some of them fuck her for a line of coke. That's what she's doing.'

'Oh my God.' This little girl that I knew from all these years before, her mother that I adored? Suddenly it all fell into place. As did my life.

A friend telephoned. 'Would you like to borrow my house in Palm Springs?' He was going to Colorado.

By this time, I had bought a little Honda and I said that it would be marvellous, so nice to get away for a little while, to just be quiet. I got to Palm Springs. I was on the terrace and I rang Jeff.

'I was just ringing to see if you would like to come and spend the week with me in Palm Springs.'

He said, 'Oh, God. It's a miracle.'

I asked him when he was leaving and he said, 'Right now!'

We laughed a lot and got on very well. We had a glorious week together. In the evenings, we'd cook marvellous meals and have such a romantic time. In due course, I went off to live with Jeff. The only thing I got from my friend was the ability to drive. Astonishingly, all these years later she is still in the same bungalow and still, I'm told, getting through a gallon a day. These days, that's about my petrol consumption in the car.

I don't know how Jeff and I decided to get married. It was really on impulse, one of those romantic moments. We both loved sailing and we were talking about the great ships and the ocean liners. Wouldn't it be marvellous to get married on the *Queen Mary*?

Well, we did. John Gregory, the 34th captain of the *Queen Mary* – the wartime troop ship-turned-tourist attraction dry-docked in Long Beach, California – agreed to marry us in his private quarters on 13 July 1986. Captain Gregory was well aware who I was and was more than happy to marry us. He did a lovely thing in the ceremony by saying: 'Do you, the beautiful April, take...' He made it special.

Jeff wrote out and read this poem, which I still have:

There is a field...
a field of flowers and feelings
long ignored by the bypassers
along this way.
There is a field...
with mountains and memories
on the horizon that few can see
But along this way

some of us dare
Dare to wander without hesitation
Dare to dream the impossible
and Dare to be ourselves.
April,
I hand you these flowers
as words
as you stand in the field
with grace,
Love, Jeff

John Gregory was so special to us back then. 'What's important is to be happy,' he said to me in his 1950s BBC announcer's voice. And I was. Terribly so.

When news of the wedding got out, the *Daily Mail* in London contacted Arthur, who was still on the Costa del Sol. He told Nigel Dempster, 'I don't suppose she'd be allowed to do it in Britain, but American law must be different. I've retired from being a barman and I'm certainly not getting married again.'

Jeff and I lived together for quite a long time, but I wanted to find work and needed to get a Green Card. We had to have all these interviews, so that the authorities could be sure we were genuinely cohabiting. These were frightening beyond words. They didn't ask me if I was in love with him. You're being asked the same questions at the same time in two separate offices and it's nerve-racking because you can see one another while you're doing it.

One of the enquiries was: 'Do you have a real Christmas tree or a fake Christmas tree?' In our politically correct world, I don't suppose they're allowed to ask such invasive questions today.

Then an official appeared and said, 'Mr and Mrs East and West...'

'Jeff,' I said, 'I've got it. He wouldn't dare joke.'

I had the Green Card allowing me to work in America rather than relying solely on Jeff's income. The first job I went for was a hostess in a restaurant; to be a hostess in an American restaurant, you have to be a dogsbody. I worked at a couple of restaurants in San Pedro, which I'd visited as a teenager. Then I moved to the Marriot Hotel in Long Beach. I was 50-something at the time, but still very glamorous. I was very slender and I moved like a rocket. I would leave the young girls standing.

But the restaurants opened and closed rapidly and the work was transient. It was not easy finding a job. I think many of them wouldn't employ me because I was over 19. There were lots and lots of jobs I went for. I went for boutiques. I went for shops. I went for all kinds of different things. I seemed to be running around like a headless chicken.

Then, Jeff told me he wanted to live alone. Things had changed with his life (we were to have a peaceful divorce a few years later), and I moved to San Diego and decided to work for Greenpeace. I'd supported them for more than 20 years. The assistant manager was this young lad – they were all so very young – and he just thought I was the most glamorous thing in the world. He told me, 'Oh yes, we'll give you a job right away. When can you start? Do you want to start tonight?'

I said, 'It's at night?'

'Oh yes, we go out about four o'clock. We get a bite to eat and then we go canvassing.'

I went out with him. I was so shocked. Going out and knocking on people's doors. I didn't do it alone, of course, not for the first week. You'd say, 'Good evening. My name's April and I'm with Greenpeace and we're here fundraising.'

I couldn't get over it. People started writing cheques out for me. You had to make a quota, which was $110 a night, otherwise you didn't keep the job. I was on my very first night and I made my quota. I came back and everyone was so shocked I'd done it.

Subsequently, however, I went through a period where I couldn't get a penny out of anybody. Then I did a bit of research. I discovered I'm not really an environmentalist; I'm a conservationist. I found that, when I started talking about the whales, the sharks and saving the dolphins and keeping the oceans clean, people would become fascinated. Sometimes they'd be so fascinated that they would let me talk for hours and then they wouldn't give me a penny!

I did have some different luck too, though. I did Armand Hammer's house. The butler opened the door and said Dr Hammer was ill, but added, 'What I would do if I were you is I'd drop a note to Dr Hammer.'

Next day, I wrote to Dr Hammer and two days later back came a letter with a £1,000 cheque.

Some of the cities were marvellous to do and others were horrendous. We had one black guy canvassing in a very rich, right-wing area. The police were called instantly and told him, 'Whatever you do, go and hide yourself because you'll be killed.' We had two boys from Sri Lanka. One woman hosed one of them down and told him, 'Get off my doorstep.'

Gradually, I became one of the better earners. I was gaining my confidence, and doing more and more research, and it got to a point where people would really listen to me and what I had to say. Even if they didn't give me a lot of money, they would still give me money.

But it was dangerous. I went to one door in Santa Monica and the man who opened the door was blind drunk. He reached behind the door – and brought out a spear gun. Those things would go right through you at that range. I said, 'Oh it's all right. I get the message.' I walked down the stairs and I looked back up and he still had the gun pointed at me. It could have gone off. I was so badly shaken I couldn't work that night. I had to go and sit for four hours and wait to be picked up.

One evening in Palos Verdes, one of the richest places in America, I was waiting to be collected by the Greenpeace van. The houses are so far apart there because they're effectively great palaces. It was pitch black and not a star in the sky and suddenly these headlights went on and this car was driving at me at 100mph. At the very last minute – I couldn't have jumped out of the way – it switched direction and all I could hear were kids screaming from the car as it roared off.

Another time, a girlfriend had dropped me off and just as I was waving to her these kids came out of nowhere – they had knives and they tried to rip my stomach open. I screamed and screamed and they ran off. Oh my, there were some pretty hairy moments.

But I'd found something I believed in. I was making a modest living. I wasn't some Save the Planet zealot, but I was happy that I was trying to make a little difference. I was settled but still wanted adventure.

Sailing across the Pacific with a mad Nazi provided that.

50

ALIVE-ALIVE-OH!

*'I'll take my chance against the law. You'll take yours
against the sea.'*

MR CHRISTIAN (CLARK GABLE) TO CAPTAIN BLIGH (CHARLES LAUGHTON),
MUTINY ON THE BOUNTY (1935)

Peter Finch's daughter Anita and Shirley Ann Field both tried
to stop me. But I was determined to sail across the Pacific;
it had been my dream for years. So what if my partner in this
enterprise was a little strange? What could possibly happen to me?
I was strong, tough and nearly 60 years old.

My friends Manfred and Ginny had introduced me to Ronald,
who was planning to make this wonderful Pacific trip. He had a
limp, a hair transplant that he kept smoothing down, was short
and box shaped, and older than me. We talked over dinner and
from the first moment I began to have my doubts.

Had I ever eaten human steak? Had I ever killed anyone? Did I
think I could commit murder? He went on and on in his heavy
German accent. But the fact was that I really wanted to sail the
ocean. I thought I could cope with Ronald and his rather odd
behaviour and attitude to life. You'd think smiling cost him money.

We had several lunches and dinners and he invited me to sail

351

with him as far as Cabo San Lucas at the tip of Baja California. I was a little disappointed, but said that was fine. Next, it was all off. Ronald had met the woman of his dreams and not only was she going to sail with him but she was also going to have sex with him. That was fine too. Nothing to do with me. I told him, 'Ronald, I'm so pleased for you. Have a good voyage.'

Two days later, he called me in a panic. His dream woman had gone. She was mad. She was crazy. Would I sail with him, first stop the Marquesas in the South Pacific?

'No Cabo San Lucas?'

'I'm going straight for Nuka Hiva.'

French Polynesia. In 48 hours. My job was no problem. I was working in a hotel gift shop and bored. But my cat? Lily Ashley-Buttufco-John Wayne Bobbit-Harding-Gulluly was the problem. Ronald paid two months' rent in advance, my wages as it were, and I offered my apartment rent free to David, a friend from Greenpeace – all he had to do was keep Lily safe.

I had to look after myself. Anita and her husband Val and Shirley Ann Field drove down from Los Angeles to see me off. They were concerned about the fact that I was going off across a giant ocean on a 42-foot yacht with a man I barely knew. Ginny was also worried and kept telling me it was not too late to change my mind.

But I was following my dream. I took our sailing papers to the harbour master and when I told him our first port of call was Nuka Hiva he said, 'How incredibly exotic.'

For a moment, I thought he was talking about me.

Manfred was there and let the mooring ropes go and we slipped into the main channel of San Diego Bay. It was a Sunday and the channel was crowded but it wasn't long before we were on our own; a little under 3,000 miles to go.

On our first day out, Ronald pulled out a photograph of himself in the Hitler Youth. There he was, as bold as brass, with a Swastika on his arm. He was very proud of it. Too proud. I suddenly became very uneasy. Human steak? Was that going to be me?

He knew I had grown up in England during the war and there he was flaunting this photograph, boasting about it. I told him to put it away and not to speak about it again. I was furious, thinking of Liverpool being bombed every night, of all the horrors of the war.

I knew it was not going to be a comfortable voyage, either mentally or physically. Now, believe me, I am not a spiritual person in the sense of second sight or mediums, of all things mystical. I can't predict what I'm going to have for tea. Yet at sea out in the Pacific I had the most extreme experience. I had just got out of my bunk and I had this overwhelming feeling of someone standing behind me. I thought it was Ronald. I spun around and there was nothing there. But there was a smell, something so very familiar. It was Tim Willoughby.

I felt his presence. He'd always said he'd sail to Tahiti from the Mediterranean. He wasn't there all the time, but there was this feeling of goodness around me – and it wasn't anything to do with Nazi Ronald. It felt so comforting, for Ronald kept falling asleep at the wheel and I was up and down every 20 minutes making sure we were on course and not about to hit the *Titanic* or something just as large.

He'd go on and on about sex and clearly wanted me to get in his bunk with him. One night he tried to get in with me but I shouted him away. Another time he was much more aggressive and tried to rape me. But I was much faster, for his bad leg slowed him up. It was agonising to be with him, for his mood changed quicker than the weather.

We'd sailed past the Marquesas, Nuka Hiva, Tuamotu, Manahi and were on our way to Rangaroa, the second largest atoll in the world. It's all smack in the middle of totally shark-infested waters. When we got there the water was rough, but Ronald insisted he would take me to dinner at the yacht club for my 60th birthday. I protested that the dinghy would capsize.

But we went on. The owner of the restaurant presented me with a birthday bottle of champagne. So we had that, we had wine and then cocktails at the bar. Then, it was time to get back to the yacht. The owner said the water was even worse now and we shouldn't attempt it. They had a room. But you couldn't tell Ronald anything.

As we were approaching the yacht in these enormous waves, he suddenly announced, 'I've lost my wallet with my passport and credit cards.'

'Ronald!' I screamed. 'Why would you take a passport and credit cards to an atoll in the middle of the Pacific Ocean?'

With that, he whammed me in the face with his fist. He did it six times. It caused some kind of concussion and I couldn't see out of my left eye. Ronald scrambled on to the yacht. It's hard enough getting on to a yacht at the best of times but in these enormous seas and half-blind I missed the line.

I fell into the water. I clambered back into the dinghy but in a moment it turned over and I was in the water again. The yacht then bumped me and knocked me almost to the bottom of the sea. It was so clear – and I could see sharks. We'd watched them feeding at the entrance to the lagoon the day before.

It's not true that you go down three times and then drown. I went down six times, tumbling in the water and almost drowned. It was like being in a washing machine. Ronald was watching all this. He looked quite mad. Finally – he knew lots of people were aware I was on his boat – he let down the ladder. Somehow, I pulled myself up.

I thought my ribs were broken, but they were only badly bruised. And that was pain enough.

Ronald said, 'You're so silly...'

I stopped him and warned him that if he touched me again I

would find some way to get ashore and have him arrested. I couldn't get out of my bunk for three days. Every movement was agony.

I was injured. In the middle of the Pacific. I had little option but to be on my guard and sail on. When the weather got better, we took off for Tahiti. I was very wary of Ronald but I felt the comforting presence of Tim again. He was there every day. I could smell him. When we got to Tahiti, however, his presence completely disappeared. I know it makes me sound like some mad old bat, but I can only say that is what I felt.

We were on Tahiti for two weeks waiting for Ronald's credit cards to arrive and I bought the most beautiful lei. I attached a card from Tim's sister Jane and from myself to it. One sunset I pushed the flowered garland into the surf and watched it float away.

Finally, the credit cards arrived, and as part of our business arrangement he bought my plane ticket back to Los Angeles. Manfred and Ginny were marvellous, but it took a few weeks to get over my voyage across the Pacific. I'd always wanted to do it – and I'd done it – but, oh my, it was an ordeal at times. Ronald, as far as we all know, vanished off the face of the earth.

I was content living an anonymous life in San Diego. I'd get up at about 7am and go out and feed the stray cats who appeared from nowhere overnight. I attended to my plants. I had a huge orchid tree just outside the door. Inside, my apartment looked like a rainforest.

I did some television advertising for a racetrack – which Bing Crosby, of all people, had originally opened; I worked in a jewellery shop, in art galleries, for charities and as a tourist guide; and to everybody I was just April. I had many friends, but I was concerned about money. My British pension, which I couldn't get until I was 65, was set at around £21 a week. What's that?

If I'd stayed in Britain – and, as a heart-attack victim, had lived on the dole and been a parasite – I would have had a full pension, housing and benefits. That's not the Liverpool way.

Times have changed dramatically since I had my sex-change – and, by the way, that's now called a gender reassignment – in Morocco. Most of my life I have lived with the Catch-22 of it, although as time went on the British National Health Service recognised transsexualism as a medical disorder and offered hormone and surgical intervention to bring the body into line with the mind. But people like me had no rights in their new gender.

I thought it was time I sorted out my life. I wrote to Tony Blair, explaining that for 40 years I'd held a passport in the name of Miss April Ashley and I would like a new birth certificate to go with it. I'd been in the body I always wanted for four decades – wasn't it about time? Life had moved on so much. The awful Justice Ormrod was dead. And so was Arthur – of a stroke on 24 June 1993. I was in San Diego when I heard he was ill and I flew to Spain to see him. When he saw me, he burst out crying. He still had all my photographs and he said that I was the only one he had ever loved. I had to wonder what he cared about. He abandoned his wife and four children for his sexual urges. He didn't care about me.

He admitted he had cheated me. He knew he did wrong. He said so on his deathbed. He'd defrauded me and harmed me. He asked me to forgive him. I didn't but I did, if you understand. For all their leads in life, things had not worked out too well for Arthur's family. Johnny, who never took to me, sold Rowallan Castle and its 7,000 acres in 1988 to pay death duties. He was married three times; maybe he's happier now.

Going to see Arthur replayed the horrors of the divorce for me, I remembered – at the height of the divorce proceedings – being in Sloane Square one day and seeing this woman coming my way. She was very well dressed and I thought, 'Oh my God, I can't remember her name.' She was coming directly towards me. Instead of saying anything, she swiped me across the face, didn't say a word and carried on walking. That happened at least three times. People just whacked me across the face. I was in a pub once, dressed in Chanel, looking extremely elegant, and all these young lads told me, 'We're going to wait for you and beat you up!'

But all these years earlier, the world was a different place. Wasn't it? Hadn't things changed?

Well, not legally, for me. The rules were still spelled out by the Births and Deaths Regulations Act, 1953, which regarded birth certificates as records of fact at the time of birth. People like me were like ghosts – did we really exist? Ormrod's ruling meant that transsexuals still could not marry, had difficulties with employment law and if they broke the law could find themselves in the wrong prison.

The regulations were more enlightened since Casablanca – of course they were – but not in certain very important areas. Britain is the most civilised country on earth, but so backward about sex. I still love my country, but for so long the government condemned me to being a freak who lived in exile.

I never heard a word from Tony Blair. So I thought I'd try the Deputy Prime Minister of the UK instead. At least I knew John Prescott personally.

51

FAMILY VALUES

'There is nothing bad in undergoing change.'
MEDITATIONS, MARCUS AURELIUS

I've felt like an orphan for most of my life. In fact, I had officially
been one since 1974, though I didn't find that out until ten
years later.

My bloody mother! She never wanted children. She pitted one
against the other and she was wicked to everybody. She died in
Swansea. Marjorie who called her 'That Woman!' had apparently
tried to contact me, though I never heard anything.

In 1984, the telephone had rung and this voice said, 'Hello,
Auntie April?'

'First of all, don't call me Auntie,' I replied. 'And who are you?'

'I'm Maddie.'

'Hello. I remember you; you came to London to stay with me.
You're Marjorie's daughter.'

'How are you?' I asked her, friendlier now. 'How's your
grandmother?'

'Oh, she died in 1974.'

'What did she die from?' I asked.

'Cancer,' came the reply. That didn't come as a surprise after her factory work during the war. I didn't know how to feel. I still don't. This woman scarred all of our lives, the whole family.

There were more family shocks in 2000. I opened a friend's website in London and I got an e-mail from my great-nephew; I e-mailed him back but it didn't work and I got terribly upset about it. I said, 'Oh, God, this family vendetta is going to go on into a third generation, how stupid.'

My great friend Peter Maddock listened to my concerns about not being able to contact the boy and said, 'Oh, don't be silly, darling, I'll put an advert in the *Liverpool Echo*.'

They all lived around Liverpool and Manchester. Apparently, all his friends rushed into the pub and said, 'Is this you, Scott?'

Back in San Diego a couple of weeks later, I couldn't sleep one night and was dozing on the couch at four o'clock in the morning when the phone rang. A voice said, 'Are you April Ashley? Why are you trying to get hold of my son?'

I said, 'Just a moment, who are you?'

'Well, I'm your nephew.'

'Oh. Who's your father?'

'John.'

'Freddie?' We called him John. 'Oh my goodness. It's four o'clock in the morning here. Could I have your phone number and I'll ring you back a little later?'

'OK.'

Because my eldest sister always had problems, I said, 'By the way, how's Theresa?'

He said, 'Oh, she's dead.'

'What did she die of?'

'I don't know, she died years ago.'

Four hours later, the phone rang again and somebody I didn't recognise said, with real cruelty in their voice, 'Oh by the way, Roddy, Ivor and Marjorie are also dead.'

I said, 'Holy mackerel. How did they all die?'

'I don't know, except for Ivor, who died of emphysema.' That didn't surprise me, because Ivor smoked about 50 packets of cigarettes a day.

I got on the phone to Peter, crying my eyes out. 'It's like a holocaust,' I told him. 'My whole family's gone. I don't know how they've gone. I don't know how they died...'

He said, 'What are you whingeing for?'

'Wouldn't you?' I asked him.

'When was the last time you spoke to those people?'

'Well, it's more than 40 years ago.'

'Well, what are you whingeing for?' he asked me again. 'I'm your family, shut up.'

He was right, and so practical.

Then, out of the blue, I got an e-mail: 'By the way, Roddy is not dead.' It was from Roddy's daughter.

I wrote back and said, 'Where do you live?'

Back came an e-mail saying, 'I've had a talk with my husband and we don't think this conversation should continue, we don't think we should have anything to do with you any more.'

They're grown-ups. They've got children of their own. They can make up their own minds. But to write an e-mail just to say they don't want anything to do with me...

I would ring John and I had the courtesy to call him John. He didn't use his second name until he was about 30, when suddenly he decided that he hated the fact that he had the same name as my father, Freddie.

'Hello, John, how are you?' I would ask him.

'Fine,' he would reply.

'How's your family?'

'Fine.'

'How's life?'

361

'OK.' He would never, ever call me by my name and never get into a conversation.

'How's Roddy?' I'd ask him. Roddy and Freddie had been quite good friends when they were younger.

'Oh I don't know; I never talk to him.'

'But you two were quite close when you were young.'

'No we weren't.'

'Yes you were. You used to go everywhere together. I was always jealous because you wouldn't let me in.'

'I don't remember that. There's a lot of things I don't remember. I don't even know where he lives.'

I stopped calling. There was no point when somebody didn't want to know you.

Then, late in 2005, I got an e-mail from Marjorie's son, Rod McKee. He told me, 'I don't understand my family. I think it's wonderful that you, the weakest of them all, should have turned out to be the strongest of them all.'

Rod has moved to France with his wife and lives quite a long drive from Tourette-sur-Loup, but they have been to visit me. So I don't feel totally abandoned by my family – although it's strange that so many strangers have accepted me, loved me, while my main family did not.

In January 2006, documents from the UK National Archives were released. I suppose I'm a bit of an archive myself now, but such things do bring back memories. Among other things, they revealed that Graham Sutherland had grave doubts about his 80th-birthday portrait of Sir Winston Churchill. 'I'm sickeningly worried about the shortage of time,' wrote Sutherland. He did complete the painting in time but Churchill's wife Clemmie hated it. She burned it a few years later.

It brought memories flooding back for me of the rogue Gerald Hamilton, on whom Christopher Isherwood based the title character of his 1935 novel *Mr Norris Changes Trains*. I met him with Barbara Back. She loathed him. He fascinated me. His opening remark was: 'You know I'm Mr Norris from the Isherwood books, don't you?' I did.

He had a hideous, heavy face with mottled skin that hung in drapes as if drained of a lifetime's excess, a lower lip drooping down towards his chin like a giblet, bloodshot bloodhound eyes and bristling eyebrows, which he trained upwards. He'd been born in Shanghai, the son of a British merchant, and, wherever the raffish were to be found, so was he – Berlin before the war, Tangier after it, the King's Road in the 1960s, conning his way from one extravaganza to another. He threw names around like confetti. 'My darling friend, Nicholas of Romania, he never touches water – he brushes his teeth with a light Hock.'

Gerald exuded criminality, vice, corruption in high places – but this, like his snobbery, was so unbridled, so theatrical, that I never felt threatened by it, only enthralled. He seemed to be the repository of secret knowledge, like a jovial version of the sinister Devil-devotee Aleister Crowley.

I know at one time he carried two cyanide capsules under his wig in the event of finding himself in an impossibly tight corner. And during the Second World War he was arrested attempting to escape across the Irish Sea to Dublin disguised as a nun.

Churchill interned Gerald twice for his supposedly pro-German sympathies. There was a feud between them. Now, when Graham Sutherland was commissioned by the House of Commons to do the official portrait of Churchill, Sir Winston could give him only a few sittings. Sutherland approached Hamilton to model the body because their measurements were similar. This was one of the reasons why Churchill so took against the picture. Another, said Gerald, was that Sutherland had caught the tragic emptiness of Churchill's eyes.

I like Churchill's verdict on the portrait to Somerset Maugham: 'I look as if I were having a difficult stool.'

A year after the Sutherland sittings, Hamilton again modelled Churchill, this time for Oscar Nemon's enormous bronze. These modellings he called his 'revenge'.

I used to call on Gerald for a chat at his tiny flat above the Good Earth Chinese Restaurant in the King's Road, where a willowy Oriental youth, who was devoted to him, supplied his various requirements.

'You naughty baggage,' he'd say to me, 'I see you've been in the papers again. I can't offer you much, the whisky's gone I'm afraid...'

Oh my. To be a 'naughty baggage' again. I hate getting old. I used to be like a gazelle. Now, everything has gone south. When I take my bra off, it's: 'My gosh, the floor is cold.'

52

THE TEACUPS OF THE CURIOUS

'Kind hearts are more than coronets
And simple faith than Norman blood.'
'LADY CLARA VERE DE VERE' (1833),
ALFRED LORD TENNYSON

I used to enjoy a cocktail at the Beverly Hilton but, watching the Golden Globe Awards on television in January 2006, I hardly recognised the place. They've really given it an overhaul. It looked magnificent, as did all the stars. It's just that they seem to have so many hangers-on these days. I was pleased that *Walk The Line*, the movie about Johnny and June Carter Cash, did well. The gay Western *Brokeback Mountain* got four Globes. I still think I'm more of a Robert Mitchum fan, but Heath Ledger and Jake Gyllenhaal, who played the lovers, looked like nice boys.

The ceremony, the nominations, reflected such a change in attitude. It was encouraging to see Felicity Huffman get a Best Actress award for *Transamerica*. Naturally, she got even more of the spotlight for being a 'Desperate Housewife'. I'd never heard of a transsexual movie heroine before. Her character Bree, formerly Stanley, is in the pre-operative stage. She's at the gender crossroads and I read that, to try to understand her part, she had worn a male prosthetic. I hoped it might turn into an Oscar for her. Of course, altogether different from my 'Oscar'.

It is a much more progressive world since Casablanca and Dr Burou. Sex-change operations in 1960 were associated in the public imagination with Dr Frankenstein. The first report of one was made by a German, FZ Abraham, in 1931, but there were no details about it. The first popular account was in 1933 in Niels Hoyer's book *Man Into Woman*. It is the story of a male Danish painter who became Lili Elbe after a series of operations only vaguely described.

The term 'transsexualism' was invented in 1949 by Dr DO Cauldwell, who used it to describe a girl who obsessively wanted to become a boy. The word was taken up by Dr Harry Benjamin, whose researches led in 1966 to the first systematic study, *The Transsexual Phenomenon*.

In 2004, Nadia Almada, a transsexual, won the *Big Brother* television show in the UK. I was also intrigued early in 2006 to read about Colin Bone who at age 60 had decided to have a sex-change. A gynaecologist, he will return to his post as a consultant and medical director at an NHS hospital, the Queen Elizabeth Hospital in King's Lynn, Norfolk, as Celia MacLeod. In today's world, it was his position rather than his sex-change that made the story newsworthy. He'd been a guest of the Royal Family at Sandringham and had met the Queen, although he'd never treated any of the Royal Family as a doctor.

What intrigued me, of course, was the life he must have led for all these years even with a supportive wife. He said he had been aware of 'ambiguities and confusion' since he was a schoolboy: 'When I was nine I acted the part of a princess in a school play and I was extraordinarily reluctant to take my costume off afterwards; it just felt right.'

The lesson, I feel, is that it is never too late to become the person you want and need to be. To find that happiness.

I am pleased he can have so much help. He was to have hair removal, reconstructive surgery to his face and voice training to give him a more feminine air. After a year of living as Miss MacLeod, he will then be eligible to undergo full gender-reassignment surgery, as they now call it. How different from my experience – but how marvellous too.

In 2006, these operations were available throughout the world. And those who change their gender have full legal rights following a long-awaited ruling by the European Court of Human Rights. With the UK's Gender Recognition Act of 2004, a birth certificate can be amended to show that a transsexual who was born a man was born a woman. And that people marrying or beginning a new relationship will be unable to discover whether their partner is a transsexual if they choose not to tell them. One of the people involved in the ruling was Christine Goodwin – and she complained she'd not been allowed to claim her pension at 60. She'd had to wait till she was 65.

I went to the pension people in Newcastle and enquired if I could get my pension backdated. It caused quite a telephone tussle until they found a nice supervisor. I felt like James Bond, certainly some sort of spy, as my files are all coded and top secret.

Much of the credit for the change in the law in Britain rests with Stephen Whittle OBE. He changed sex after being born a woman, and married his partner in 2005. Then, they'd been together for 26 years and have four children conceived by sperm donor.

I, and all other transsexuals, have lived in a legal limbo until these past couple of years. Stephen Whittle and his colleagues at 'Press for Change' (see Appendix 2: Help and Advice Contacts) have helped introduce equality. It's taken such a time for people to realise that transsexuality is not a psychiatric condition. Just as the Earth is not flat. But it can be heartbreaking.

When I was younger, people would really shy away from me. I

had gone to Royal Ascot with Clive Raphael on one occasion; at one point, he suddenly came up to me, ashen faced, and said, 'Come on, we're leaving here now.'

I said, 'Oh no. It's so lovely, I can see the Queen... and you can see the horses so well from here, Clive...'

He said, 'April, come along.'

He took me outside and then just burst out crying. I asked him what was wrong and an official came up to him and said, 'Is that April Ashley?' and he said it was. He said, 'Get her out of here.' Simple as that.

Some sex-changes try to overcome it by turning themselves into parodies of femininity – which, of course, makes their predicament worse. I was always just myself and tried to bear in mind that men and women have far more in common with each other than otherwise. When a television company came to my house in Hay-on-Wye to film me for a documentary on one occasion, they told me, 'Just go about your normal business and we'll film you.'

'Well, I'm going to mow the lawn now.'

'Oh. Can't you do something more feminine, like wash the pots?'

'But I don't wash the pots. I hate washing pots. I get someone else to wash the pots. I'm going to mow the lawn.'

'Like that?'

'Like what?'

'In jeans? Couldn't you wear a dress or something?'

'But I don't wear a dress to mow the lawn. It's a crazy idea. I wear jeans and Wellington boots to do that.'

Although they were supposed to be researching a documentary, they had all these preconceived ideas that they wanted me to exemplify. Sex-changes, like everyone else, have to be human beings first and their label-group second.

When I was in Hay, the kids were the worst – the eight-to

twelve-year-olds. Sometimes they were comic. 'She's a lesbian, you know,' I overheard one puppy say to his friend. Oh my, how some of the more squeamish parents must have toiled when trying to explain me to their offspring. The thought of simply telling them the facts of life would have sent some of them into gibberish. I'm sure their children would have asked at all the wrong moments – in front of Aunt Maude, during *Match of the Day*, when the whisky bottle was empty...

I'm not so fanciful as to imagine that my history should arouse no comment. And I readily admit that what may have been tough for me nevertheless has many comic aspects. In fact, laughter is usually my own first reaction when I think about my past, because a sex-change has one thing in common with every other man and woman – the comedy of being human in a superhuman universe.

One of the problems of my newspaper exposure all those years ago was that thereafter I became always a sex-change first and anything else second. I don't blame the newspaper. It had to happen and I always wanted to escape a furtive life. But it also meant that to survive I had to be brazen. Afterwards, I was notorious and it was left to me only to exploit my personality. I was forced to become an artist of life. Most people play a variety of roles, whether they realise it or not. To have only one is a great loss and prevented me from doing many things.

The operation gave me my chance for happiness, but that state of mind is no less elusive for me than it is for everyone else. Today I know my limitations, but I often ignore them. The distinction between man and nature is man's fearlessness in pursuit of the impossible. Relaxation, acceptance, happiness belong to old age, one's very last moments. The greater the exertion, the greater the relaxation.

Because I will never admit I am remotely close to the time for relaxation, I am still insecure in many ways. For example, I tend to grab at people if I like them. This is not due to my upbringing. My childhood was the worst time but it geared me up for the rest of my life.

Which is beginning again.

POSTSCRIPT
RAINBOW'S END

*'I've always thought that just over the horizon there is
something marvellous waiting for me...'*
APRIL ASHLEY (2006)

Don't tell, but I'm on the second bottle of champagne at
Colombe d'Or.

All these years, and my birth certificate inside that large brown
envelope says I was born female.

It has brought so much flooding back. It says my father was a
tram conductor and he probably was when I was born, but I only
remember him being at sea. John Prescott, bless him, helped me
with the procedures and the bureaucracy involved. He made sure
I had all the right documents and knew what to do. I always get a
Christmas card from John and his wife. He's been so loyal and
kind to me.

Dr Neville Rosedale was also so wonderful. He was 82 in 2006
and had been my gynaecologist since 1960. He and his wife Pat
have been good friends to me, but I'd lost touch when I was in
America. To get my new birth certificate, I needed to prove I'd
had the operation – I needed paperwork. I had an old London
number for Neville, but tried it anyway with the new code. And

there was his voice on an answering machine sounding as calm and reassuring as he had 45 years earlier. I left a message. He called me back: 'Records? I've got them all going back to when we first met.'

He sent them off to the Gender Recognition Panel and I believe that's why I got my birth certificate so quickly; he had all the details of my examinations over the years. Most people would have cleared such stuff out, but Neville is a noble man; he stills hold two free clinics a week for poorer patients.

As always, Peter Maddock held my hand throughout. We went to one of those lovely Nash houses behind Oxford Street in London to swear an affidavit that all my information in applying for my new birth certificate was true. There was a very lovely Indian gentleman behind the counter and he read and reread my information. He was fascinated by it.

Peter, who likes to get on with things, said, 'I'm Miss Ashley's solicitor and I can sign that for you.'

'Oh, no,' replied the official. 'It would give me great pleasure to sign the document.'

And he did, with a smile. It was one of those lovely moments.

On 11 August 2005, the UK's General Register Office let me know that they had received a copy of my full Gender Recognition Certificate – and could make a new record of my birth. Which they did.

And 45 years and four months after I became the woman I wanted to be, I had a piece of paper to prove I really am April Ashley.

I feel free at last.

APPENDIX 1

The Gender Recognition Act 2004 is on the Internet. A print version is also available and is published by The Stationery Office Limited as the Gender Recognition Act 2004, ISBN 0 10 540704 6. Braille copies of this Act can also be purchased at the same price as the print edition by contacting TSO Customer Services on 0870 600 5522 or e-mail customer.service@tso.co.uk.

APPENDIX 2
HELP AND ADVICE CONTACTS

The Beaumont Society
27 Old Gloucester Street
London WC1N 3XX
Info line (24 hr): 01582 412220
E-mail: enquiries@beaumontsociety.org.uk

Women of the Beaumont Society is an organisation that offers help to wives and partners who find their husband's behaviour difficult to understand.
www.beaumontsociety.org.uk/wobs/index.html

The Beaumont Trust is a charitable educational resource for medical, voluntary and lay people who wish to increase their knowledge on the subjects of transsexualism and transvestitism.
http://members.aol.com/Bmonttrust/

FTM Network is a national self-help group, open to all female-to-male transgender and transsexual people, or those exploring this aspect of their gender.
www.ftm.org.uk

Gender Identity Research and Education Society (GIRES) is a registered charity providing education, based on research into

gender identity and intersex issues, which helps all those able to improve the lives of people directly affected by these issues.
www.gires.org.uk/

The Gender Trust is the only registered charity in the United Kingdom that specifically helps adults who are transsexual, gender dysphoric or trangender, i.e. those who seek to adjust their lives to live as women or men, or to come to terms with their situation despite their genetic background.
www.gendertrust.org.uk/

Gendys Network is an organisation that aims to help all those who have encountered gender-identity problems personally, transsexuals, transgendered people and gender dysphoric people of either sex, and for those who provide care, both professional and lay.
www.gender.org.uk/gendys/

Mermaids (UK) is a support group for gender-variant children, teenagers, their parents, families, carers and others.
www.mermaids.freeuk.com

Press for Change is a political lobbying and educational organisation that campaigns to achieve equal civil rights and liberties for all transgender people in the United Kingdom, through legislation and social change.
www.pfc.org.uk/

The Samaritans are available 24 hours a day to provide confidential emotional support for people who are experiencing feelings of distress or despair, including those that may lead to suicide. Free phone 08457 90 90 90 (UK)
www.samaritans.org.uk

APPENDIX 2

UK Trans Alliance is a grouping of trans-support organisations from throughout the UK. These organisations represent the full spectrum of trans identity and include in their membership individuals who may describe themselves as transvestite, transsexual, transgender or any other personal gender identity. www.uktransalliance.org.uk

INDEX